THE LANGUAGE OF DIALECTICS
AND THE DIALECTICS OF LANGUAGE

The Language of Dialectics and the Dialectics of Language

by

JOACHIM ISRAEL

MUNKSGAARD

HUMANITIES PRESS, USA
HARVESTER PRESS, ENGLAND

The Language of Dialectics and the Dialectics of
Language, 1st edition, 1st printing, 1979

Copyright©1979 Munksgaard, Copenhagen

Cover: The work of art by William Fredericia, design by
Martin Bassett

Printed in England by Billing & Sons Limited
Guildford, London and Worcester.

Danish edition ISBN: 87 16 0242 6

Published in North and South America by Humanities
Press
Library of Congress Cataloging in Publication Data:
Israel, Joachim.
The Language of Dialectics and the Dialectics of
Language
Bibliography: p.
Includes index.
1. Dialectic. 2. Materialism. 3. Knowledge, Theory of.
4. Marx, Karl, 1818–1883—Knowledge, Theory of. 5.
Language-Philosophy.
6. Social sciences—Methodology. I. Title.
B809.7.182 1979   146'.3   79–4305
American edition ISBN: 0 391 01000 X

Published simultaneously in Great Britain by Harvester
Press

To Samuel, who at the age of two taught me what it means to have a language.

Without life, there would be no death; without death there would be no life. Without above, there would be no below; without below there would be no above. Without misfortune, there would be no good fortune; without good fortune, there would be no misfortune. Without facility there would be no difficulty; without difficulty, there would be no facility. Without landlords there would be no tenant — peasants; without tenant-peasants, there would be no landlords. Without the bourgeoisie, there would be no proletariat; without proletariat, there would be no bourgeoisie.

Mao Tse-tung

Contents

Foreword

This book is conceived as a contribution to the ongoing debate concerning the methodology of the social sciences. Over the past years, attacks have been directed against a "positivistic social science", though the term "positivistic" has not always been used in a clear manner. Sometimes that label was, and still is, used to indicate one's opposition to, or dislike for, certain theories or methodological approaches. Having been trained originally in a "positivist" tradition, I have tried, in earlier works, to discuss some of the epistemological and methodological problems which seemed to me to be pressing. (see e.g. J. Israel 1972).

My original intention was to write a book about the possibility of a Marxist social psychology (partly because my publisher offered me the opportunity to write a text on social psychology). However, this endeavour turned out to be rather difficult. What does a Marxist social psychology imply? One reasonable explanation is that it should be a social psychology based upon Marxist epistemological and methodological principles. In other words, it should be based upon a Marxist philosophy of science. There does not, however, exist unanimous agreement about the basic principles for such a Marxist epistemology and methodology. To the contrary there exists a great variety of interpretations as to the content and meaning of such a Marxist epistemology and methodology. Some of these interpretations present even contradictory claims.

One traditional way of looking at Marxism is to consider it as "materialistic" and "dialectical". But both terms are highly ambiguous and in need of clarification. This I set for myself, as a first task, answering the question: what are we talking about when we use words like "materialistic" and "dialectical".

The word "materialistic" is used in at least three different, though related, contexts: (1) contexts concerned with problems of *ontology*, (2) contexts concerned with *epistemological* problems, and (3) contexts concerned with the analysis of *methodological* problems, for us those specific for the social sciences. These three contexts are intimately related to each other, but the distinction introduced between them should allow for an analysis that attempts to solve some of the complicated problems we will have to deal with.

In the *first chapter* of this book, we will try to analyze some of the meanings of the terms "materialism" and "idealism" in these three contexts. One of the results of our analysis is that when this distinction is used in an ontological context, it is based upon a dualistic notion, that is logically contradictory to any type of dialectical reasoning. Hence one cannot accept a distinction between "materialism" and "idealism" within an *ontological* context of discourse, and at the same time, claim to accept the basic presuppositions of dialectical reasoning. A Marxist, for instance, cannot claim to be a "materialist" in ontological matters, and at the same time, to be reasoning dialectically. He has to choose between them.

In an epistemological context, the opposite to an "idealistic" position is not a "materialistic" one, but one that is "realistic". This implies, broadly speaking, that one accepts a world existing independently of the knowledge-producing subject. I argue for a realistic position. One, however, which is not phenomenalistic, i.e., that takes perception and sensory experience as the *basis* for knowledge, but rather for a realism in which language is the *basis* for epistemological analysis. I argue that in order for our experiences to acquire meaning, we must be able to speak about them, to express them in words. Therefore, a central problem becomes: what does it mean to possess language. This question, but not the different genetic question concerning the ways we acquire language, is discussed extensively and so are its implications for the foundation of a social science. I argue for the thesis that the sharp dualistic distinction between knowledge of language, and knowledge of reality, has to be abandoned. Knowledge of language *is* knowledge of reality. Language itself is part of reality. So far we have stated that the term "materialistic", in an ontological and epistemological context, is not useful, and ought not be applied even, or rather especially not, in a Marxist approach. The concept remains for the methodological context. Here we think it meaningful to talk about a "materialistic" position, e.g., one which emphasizes the central role of the "material" process of production in the analysis of society. But in this context, the term, which is analyzed in more detail in the first chapter, is used in a restricted way, and does not necessarily have ontological connotations. Chapter one ends with a series of theses concerning methodological problems of the social sciences.

In *chapter 2*, together with the third, the central chapters of this book, we try to undertake an analysis of what we mean when we talk about dialectics. I try to indicate that dialectical reasoning presupposes at least four conceptual categories, namely, the category of totality, of intrinsic relations, of process, and of relatedness. Each of these categories, the presuppositions on which they are based, and the consequence of their use, is analyzed and discussed in detail. When trying to specify the basic categories of dialectical reasoning we face a dilemma. By *talking* about dialectics we may *understand* what dialectical reasoning is. But we not only want to talk about dialectics, we also want to use dialectical reasoning in our account in order to *grasp* it. Hence, in order to *grasp* dialectics, we must *understand* what we mean when we talk about it. But in order to *understand* what we mean, we must *grasp* it by using it. It is therefore obvious, that the concept of "praxis" has a central role to play in this presentation.

When we analyze what we mean by a "dialectical relation", we face the problem that elements in a dialectical relation are described as different and identical. Philosophers have maintained that such a claim is contradictory. Those defending dialectical reasoning have sometimes accepted this criticism, replying that traditional logic, for instance the law of contradiction, has to be abandoned.

I try to show that this is not a solution, rather a semantical analysis of the word "identical" indicates that we use it in two different ways. Furthermore, I assert, that we can. use these to different meanings of "identical" only in relation to each other, not separately, in our common-sense language. Thus we arrive at a central thesis of this book: That characterizing a dialectical relation can also be formulated as one of the basic rules of the broad logic of common-sense language.

For this reason we embark upon a discussion of the dialectics of everyday language. This is done in *chapter three*. There we start with a discussion of such dualistic notions as "mind" and "body". Since dualism is logically contradictory to the presuppositions of dialectical reasoning, and that its substitution by monism does not solve the problem, we try to transcend both through a "unitary" approach, which is seen as characteristic of dialectics. We have chosen linguistic analysis in order to illuminate this transcendence, using P.F. Strawson's analysis of the concept "person". We also relate it to P. Zinkernagel's analysis of "conditions for description". The rest of the chapter is dedicated to the problem whether there exists a basic logic in language about society and social systems.

In *chapter four* we return once again to epistemological problems. We discuss the notion of "knowledge" and try to indicate that it comprises four related concepts. Furthermore, I maintain that a central concept of dialectics "negation of negation", is basic to epistemology. I attempt to clarify it through a concrete example.

In this chapter a specific Marxist interpretation of knowledge, as a mirror of reality in consciousness, is discarded. It is shown that it is untenable from an epistemological and psychological point of view, as well as logically contradictory to central theses of Marxist theory.

Alternatively, I try to understand the process of acquiring knowledge as a process of production. This is exemplified through a discussion of Piaget's genetic epistemology.

I am afraid that some of the arguments in this book will give rise to opposition from two different and opposed circles. People trained in the tradition of analytical philosophy—as well as some of those calling themselves Marxists—may have difficulties with the analysis presented here. If this is the case—and if the reason is not errors of a logical kind in my presentation—I have to seek comfort in the conviction that one of the most important skills to be learned is how to sit comfortably between two chairs. During this project I have had the opportunity to discuss my thoughts with a great number of persons, including graduate students at European and American universities, who patiently listened to and critically appraised my presentation, forcing me to rethink and rewrite.

Some of them I want to mention and to express my gratitude to them: Professor Johan Asplund; Mr. Lukas Böök, who read an earlier draft very carefully and critically; Mr. Ron Eyerman who, in addition, corrected my English; Professor David Harvey; Professor Ingvar Johansson; Mr. Walt Sheatsby.

Mag. art. Mrs. Nini Prætorius and Dr. Peter Zinkernagel deserve special mention. Their work concerning a general logic of language has profoundly influenced my thinking. Dr. Zinkernagel through a continuous discussion has provided me with many insights, so that many of my ideas are really his, though the errors are mine. I also would like to thank Professor Mihailo Marković, whose friendship and interest during a number of years has been very important to me. I have received much stimulation by reading Karel Kosik's book *Die Dialektik des Konkreten*. Though I have never met him, his book is the one I want to single out when speaking of intellectual debts of gratitude. It is a shame that a regime which claims to be "socialist" has treated him in a most disgraceful way and prevented him from working and publishing his profound and original Marxist thoughts.

Last, but not least, I want to thank Ulla for her cooperation, criticism and all kinds of stimulation.

Lund, Sweden, September 1978
Joachim Israel

1: A review of Ontological, Epistemological and Methodological Problems

Small-scale irrationality is of little importance compared to the global irrationality created by dominant "scientific" world views fostered by "genuine" science.

Arne Næss

1.1 SUMMARY

We will start each chapter with a short summary of its content in order to inform the reader about what is to come.

In this first chapter we try to show, in a very short and sketchy way, some of the problems connected with the distinction between materialism and idealism in three different contexts: the ontological, the epistemological, and the methodological.

First, we want to discuss what we think it means to talk about materialism vs idealism in these three contexts. We will do this in order to show that the distinction is useless, in an epistemological context, and directly opposed to dialectical thinking, in an ontological context. Only in a methodological context does such a distinction make sense.

In section 1.2 we discuss what ontological problems in general are about. Then we try to show that there is one solution to these problems which is obsolete, namely, the assertion that the world consists of material. This concerns a metaphysical problem, which we do not need to deal with here. Saying this does not mean, however, that social scientists concerned with dialectics should reject metaphysical problems in this ontological sense. In an ontological context they must deal with, (1) the presuppositions upon which dialectics is based and, (2) questions concerning the "nature" of man and society.

Thereafter, we expand the discussion of materialism vs idealism into the problem of dualistic thinking in general relating dualism to dialetics and its claim to being an holistic approach. This latter approach transcends a dualistic position as well as its traditional alternative, monism.

In an attempt to clarify these problems, we then give a short account of their historical background. We indicate that Aristotelian ideas fostered a holism, but at the same time also presupposed a teleological approach: goals and purposes were imputed to all things in nature and to their movements. Therefore, these ideas could not resist the breakthrough of modern physics as accomplished by, e.g., Galilei. A great change was introduced by Descartes through his *dualism* of matter and mind: a dualism which was built upon and developed partly as a consequence of these new trends in physics, and especially, mechanics. This dualism has to a large extent survived, and strongly influences the metaphysics of social science, especially of psychology. This is one reason why dialectical reasoning has met such great resistance in these fields.

The section ends with a short discussion about three interpretations of materialism in an ontological context: (1) the identity thesis, (2) the idea of genetic materialism, and finally (3) the analysis of "material" things and their role in our everyday life, by representatives of linguistic philosophy.

Section 1.3 outlines epistemological problems. It is pointed out that on the epistemological level idealism is opposed to realism (not to materialism). Realism asserts the existence of a world independent of the subject, whereas, idealism maintains that the world consists of our ideas, sensations, and so on.

One basic epistemological issue concerns the relation between the subject, who has or produces knowledge, and the object of knowledge. Three positions are outlined: one, assuming a passive subject exposed to the world of objects; another an active subject producing ideas; and finally, an active producing subject who is at the same time, a product of the world existing independently of him. It is this last position which will be assumed throughout this book. Therefore a notion of praxis has a central place in our theorizing.

Two problems concerning a realistic epistemological position are discussed thereafter. One deals with the question whether all knowledge is mediated through perception. I argue that this is not the case. In fact, what may appear to be perceptionally correct, may from a theoretical point of view be false. Therefore, a distinction between "appearance" and "essence" is introduced on the level of scientific analysis where the latter terms refers to explanations within a theoretical context.

The second question deals with the problem of whether only empirical knowledge, i.e., knowledge gained through perception and controlled observations, can serve the foundation of science. This thesis is also rejected.

We then discuss a problem connected with epistemological idealism. K. Popper has argued that the central tenet of idealism can be formulated thus: "the world is just my dream". Popper maintains that such an idealism cannot be refuted. It can only be argued against. Arguments can be brought forward that such is not the case. For example in order to be able to make a distinction between a dream and the real, I have to know what "the real" is. In fact, this distinction is already made before I can express doubts about it.

This problem carries over to the relation between language and knowledge. Traditionally the foundation of epistemology has been perception. Since perceptual experience in the end, is private, a consequence of this position has been to maintain that the truth of our knowledge is uncertain and, therefore, hypothetical. Such a position has the same weakness all relativistic standpoints have. Once can ask whether the very statement, that the truth of all our knowledge is uncertain, is a statement which is true or not.

One way of solving the dilemma is to accept that there are statements which are correct in a way that we can be certain because their denial would be an absurdity. To maintain, e.g., that there could exist a living human organism without a body indicates the type of absurd statement we are referring to. One consequence of this position is that we accept the solution that knowledge of language logically implies an ability to produce (some) correct statements about the world.

This again implies that a notion of "correctness" is presupposed in the knowledge of language, since all attempts to explain what correct is, presupposes the knowledge of this concept. The consequence of this for theories of truth is then touched upon.

Finally, it is argued that the common-sense language, through which people interact in their daily activities, is the basis of epistemological analysis. I argue against the objection that, accepting this implies an epistemological idealism. Language is as real as objects, e.g., means of production. More important than this, is the argument that nothing could be said which is correct or false, if such statements did not presuppose a world about which they can be made.

The section on epistemology is closed with a discussion of knowledge as a relation. Knowledge can be thought of in two ways, as something which one has, or it can be thought of as a relation between the producer and the produced: a relation between subject and object.

It is argued here that we can relate ourselves in various and innumerable ways to a world existing independently of ourselves. What does such a relation imply? Traditionally, the position of realism views the relation between subject and object such that the object is independent, as well as extrinsic of the subject. We hold, that the world of objects is independent and outside the subject's body, but not extrinsic to him. The subject relates himself intrinsically, i.e., he confers meaning upon a world that is independent of him. This relation of cognitizing, i.e., intrinsically relating, is a human predicament. At the same time, by stressing this instrinsic relation, a sharp separation of the subject and object is rejected. Instead, subject and object are seen as a unity, though one that is separable and differentiated, this again is basic to dialectical reasoning.

In section 1.4, methodological problems are analyzed. These are concerned with the ways society is studied. There is not one set of descriptions of society and the social world. The social world is what we make of it, in the daily life-process, and through the cognitive structures we impose on it.

In section 1.4.1, methodological idealism is described as the attempt to understand the social world as a manifestation of universal and unchangeable prerequisites. Methodological materialism, on the other hand, is defined as a view of the social world that is historically limited, and as being in a continuous process of transformation. That which constitutes the social, i.e., *praxis*, is understood as the changing, transforming, and transcending activities of man in his daily life-process. Praxis is objectified in social institutions, ones that can be transcended through changing those activities which make up such praxis.

Praxis must be distinguished from the means or the ways it manifests itself. The means of praxis are work, in the sense of the process of production; language, and morals as manifested in politics and power relations, indicating man's dependence on nature, on other man and on common goals, respectively.

In section 1.4.2, there are nine thesis spelled out in which methodological problems are summarized. The first thesis states that the life-process is the starting point for social scientific analysis. This comprises the basic process of production, the process of the production of knowledge, and of institutions. The second thesis stresses the interrelationship between work, language and morals. In the third thesis language is analyzed and a dualistic distinction between language and reality rejected. Language is constitutive of social reality, as well as being a part of social reality. The interrelation between language and the process of production is stressed again.

In thesis four it is asserted that the use of language presupposes an intersubjectivity of meaning. This intersubjectivity is not something carried into the social world from outside. It is presupposed, and by that it is a central aspect in defining what constitutes the social world. Here various explanations of intersubjectivity are touched upon.

Thesis five maintains that man is always in society and, therefore, the social sciences are a part of that which they study. Social scientists cannot uphold a detached position, and if they claim to, it is probably an expression of a lack of self-reflexion on their part.

Thesis six complements the previous one by claiming that the social sciences do not reflect the social world, but contribute to its constitution. In this sense, they can either fortify the given or become instruments of change. Thesis seven claims that man is not only an object but is also a subject, and that a social science which does not recognize this fact does not recognize its possibilities and, as well, is easily transformed into a manipulative technology. As a consequence of the seventh thesis, the eighth argues that social science is always a moral or "political" science, and, therefore, that social values cannot be expunged from it.

Finally, the ninth thesis is connected to the conception of man as a cognitizing subject. It is, however, stressed that this does not lead to the conclusion that, therefore, epistemological problems can only be analyzed subjectively. The cognitizing subject is always in an historical and social world, and, as a cognitizing subject is already a social subject. Therefore, epistemological problems are not only to be viewed from the point of the subject, but also must be anchored in the social world. This is facilitated when language, instead of perception, is taken as the point of departure for epistemological analysis. The chapter as a whole is intended to give a preview of the problems discussed in the book. They all will be taken up again within different contexts. The reader who may be annoyed by the frequent references to subsequent chapters and pages is asked to be indulgent. We hope that this chapter will provide a frame and conceptually prepare the reader for the analyses in the coming chapters.

1.2 ONTOLOGICAL PROBLEMS

Ontological issues are concerned with "what there is", as it has been stated, and in more detail, they are concerned with the "nature of things", the "nature of the universe", or, with the "structure of reality". Ontological systems usually comprise categorizations (e.g. the bifurcation of reality in matter and mind), principles of such categorization, ideas about basic processes, and so on.

Idealistic ontological conceptions, assert that the nature of reality is cognitive, in the sense that reality exists as ideas, thoughts, or as the content of consciousness. Some of these idealistic conceptions deny the existence of a material world; others, like Hegel's, do not. For him reality is Spirit (Geist). But the Spirit has necessarily to be embodied. Therefore the material world is a necessary precondition for the activity and self-realization of the Spirit (see Ch. Taylor 1975, p. 109).

Materialistic ontological conceptions are, roughly said, based upon assumptions that reality consists of material, matter or stuff. More specifically, traditional ontological materialism tried to form a cosmology by presupposing (1) the existence of an irreducible brute matter or material, spread throughout space in a flux of configurations: (2) that material in-itself is senseless, purposeless, i.e., it does what it does, following a fixed routine imposed on it externally, which means that its motions do not arise from the internal nature of its being (see A.N. Whitehead, 1948 p. 18 ff.).

These various ways of posing the problem are today obsolete. One would be surprised if someone seriously maintained that the true nature of reality is Spirit.

We readily accept the existence of a "material" world. What this world is made of, what the building stones are, has been and still is discussed within the framework of the cosmology of modern physics. Social scientists need not worry about *these* problems, and cannot participate in discussions about them insofar as they are not well versed in the theory and metatheory of modern physics.[1]

There are, however, ontological problems which have not lost their actuality. They concern the relationship between "nature" and "mind", between "mind" and "body", in general, and more specifically, "being" and "thinking". Problems concerning the accomplishment of change in the social world may also be of this nature. What are the "forces" of change and transformation, i.e., do ideas, or "material" conditions, change the world. Furthermore, what is the relation between "ideas" and "material" conditions. Finally, in common-sense language we clearly distinguish between "things", "thoughts", and "feelings". Such distinctions refer to underlaying ontological assumptions. These we shall try to bring into the open. Before we set to work, we want, however, to mention another aspect of the problem.

1.2.1 A short note on metaphysics

The ontological problems which we are going to discuss can, if one wishes, be characterized as metaphysical problems. Should not scientific discourse reject metaphysical problems? No, we do not rule out the discussion of metaphysical problems in general. We do not accept the arguments used by logical empiricists, for example, the assertion that propositions about the "nature" of something are meaningless. We think they are not. Whether they are meaningless or not, depends on how one uses the term "meaning" and on the criteria to assess it.[2]

In fact, we think that one cannot dispense with metaphysical assumptions prior to, or implicit in, scientific theories. Furthermore, we agree with a position that maintains that metaphysical ideas may have an antidogmatic function, since they "play a decisive role in the criticism and in the development of our knowledge" and that "a science that is free from *metaphysics* is on the best way to become a *dogmatic* metaphysical system" (P.K. Feyerabend 1968, p. 15).

Social scientists must always take a stand on certain ontological issues, though sometimes they may be unaware of it. At other times these standpoints may be defended as part of scientific method, forgetting that it has its own metaphysical basis.

Take for example a rigorous behaviourism, which rejects a language that uses "mentalistic" terms, on the ground that such terms are unscientific. In asserting that, one has already taken a position not only concerning what constitutes "science" but in addition the very attempt to translate mentalistic terms into the language of stimulus, response and reinforcement, implies taking a definite stance on such issues as the "nature of man", the relationship between physical and physiological conditions, on the one hand, and mental on the other. Social scientists must take a position on at least *two* basic types of ontological problems. *First* of all, if they wish to develop a dialectical social science, they have to analyze the issue of a dialectical vs non-dialectical, e.g., a traditional "positivist" social science. Here, four basic issues are at stake; they can be labelled as follows:

(1) A *holistic* versus a *dualistic* approach:

(2) An approach which looks at relations between things, phenomena, and ideas, as *intrinsic*, as opposed to *extrinsic* relations;

(3) A *process* approach versus an *ordering* and *categorizing* approach;

(4) A *relational* versus a *substance*, or a *thing-approach*.

The implications of these four labels will be discussed in detail in the beginning of chapter 2 (see p. 60). So far we only want to state that these four labels refer to the four necessary presuppositions for a dialectical social science, and that they imply a choice regarding ontological issues.

The *other* basic issues on which social scientists must take a stand, concerns the "nature of man", the "nature of society" and the "nature of the relation between man and society". All these issues can correctly be labelled ontological.

Furthermore, social scientists do not only have to take a stand. One can show that they always do, even if they deny it. Logical-semantic analyses of social scientific theories, e.g., psychological, sociological or economic theories, will reveal the implicit extra-theoretical positions, taken with regard to the three questions mentioned above. Notions concerning the nature of men and society form presuppositions for these theories. We have argued elsewhere that these presuppositions are of a normative, stipulative kind (J. Israel 1972a and b).

An example could be the stipulations concerning the "rational behaviour" of economic man that served as presuppositions in neo-classical economics. Another is the point of view that society has to be looked upon as a system of continuously ongoing (revolutionary) changes, i.e., based on struggle and conflict. This, in our opinion, is the central and decisive assumption which makes Chinese political theory and daily praxis so different, not only from the capitalistic societies in the West, but also from the so-called socialist societies of the Soviet type (U. Israel, 1977).

1.2.2 Dualism and its alternatives

When we speak about human beings, we use two types of descriptions. *First* of all, we talk about their size, their weight, their physical characteristics in general. We talk about them in the same way as we talk about inanimate objects. In other words, we use descriptions in terms of the language of physics and physiology (e.g., when we talk about brain-processes). Secondly, we use words like "feeling", "desires", "wishes", "goals", which means we use teleological descriptions: we describe human behaviour in terms of intentions and purposes. In fact, when we are puzzled about the behaviour of another person, we try and explain it to ourselves by using such teleological descriptions. We usually are satisfied when we have been able to "explain" what puzzles us in terms of purposes, goals, desires, inclinations, etc.

There is another feature to our common-sense descriptions. We talk about people's perceptions, about their thoughts, and about what they *intend* to say, when they describe their perceptions and thoughts. We ascribe meaning to their talk, and their descriptions as being intentional. Intentional and teleological descriptions, then, are a second way of talking about human beings.

We use physical as well as psychological language for descriptions. But does this mean that man possesses two types of characteristics which basically are different? One, which can be described in the language of physics, the other in the language of psychology?

If this were so, we could talk about the dual nature of man, his body and his mind. Furthermore, in our daily common-sense language we not only use bifurcations as, e.g., mind and body. We talk also about matter and mind, and about nature and spirit (though this distinction may be somewhat obsolete).

In epistemological contexts we talk about subject and object, about the inner-world of experiences and the outer-world of objects. We oppose language to reality.

In psychological contexts, in addition to the mind-body bifurcation, we differentiate between natural desires and rational will (a distinction of great importance, e.g., to Kant). In sociology, one can set the individual against society.

In summary then, our daily common-sense language has plenty of dualist distinctions. Our common-sense view of the world seems to rest on a series of bifurcations, which in turn seem to be manifestations of ontological issues. In general, we can summarize these issues into three positions: (1) a dualistic position, which explicitly or implicitly, accepts that our world is divided in two basically different substances, qualities, or general characteristics: physical and psychological, which not only are separated, but are of a really different nature though are in some way related to each other; (2) a monistic position, which maintains that although we presently use different languages, the progress of science will eliminate psychological descriptions altogether.

These claims have been worded differently at different times. One extreme position holds that all sciences—including psychology and the social sciences—can be reduced to physics by translating their descriptions into propositions couched in the language of physics. This "translation" view, "though at one time not uncommon as a defence of the unity of science, has been almost universally abandoned" (D.M. Rosenthal 1971, p. 2).

Another position characterized by its proponents as "materialism", is still accepted. Its claims are somewhat more modest. It concedes that psychological and physiological descriptions are different. In spite of that, it is maintained by those who hold this view, that everything which is described in the language of psychology can also be expressed, in a different way, in the language of physiology. The more physiology and the study of the brain progresses, the more will that be possible. The basis for this assumption is the so-called "identity thesis", which maintains that every mental state is identical to a physiological state. For example, an after-image of a yellow spot corresponds to a given state in the brain.[3]

We will soon present some arguments against this thesis. So far, we conclude that the second position can be called "*materialist monism*", since it tries to reduce psychological explanations to physiological ones. But even such a monistic position usually presupposes at least implicitly, a dualistic notion of body and mind.

(3) The position which rejects dualism and at the same time is critical of the identity thesis. This position accepts the fact that we use two different kinds of language. It refuses, however, on the one hand, to accept that these two languages reflect different worlds, e.g. one world of *material substances*, and one of *psychological* substance (instead of the somewhat obsolete term "substance" one could use other words as "characteristics", etc).

On the other hand, though it does not deny a correspondence, in particular cases, between mental and physiological events, it doubts that more complex situations can be described in physiological terms.

Take, for example, a person who has to make a choice concerning his future career, who considers different alternatives with regard to the length and costs of education, future career possibilities, family traditions, and, etc. It is difficult to see how an explanation of such a situation in terms of the language of physiology would be more precise and more fruitful, than one in the language of psychology. Furthermore, such a physiological description could probably only be put forward with no relation to our common-sense language or, at best, a rather curious one, "in such a way as to make nonsense of all our current vocabulary" (Ch. Taylor 1972, p. 453). This is a strong argument, since it can reasonably be maintained that our common-sense language, not only is the basis for day-to-day communication, but also for the more precise languages of science.

To formulate it in a very broad and general way, the third position, while rejecting any dualism, assumes that we deal with different aspects, i.e., relations, of one totality, and that these different ways of describing are all necessary to a comprehensive picture of our world.

In summary then, we find three positions: (1) A *dualistic* position, dividing the world into matter and mind, and/or using other types of bifurcation. (2) A monistic position of translation and reduction, i.e., the explanation of mental events by means of a language of another type. Such a position usually is based upon, at least implicitly, a body-mind dualism which it tries to reject. (3) A position which takes as given that all mental events are embodied. It starts with a holistic notion, where the others do not and logically cannot. It is this position that we will develop and defend, on the grounds that it is a presupposition for any dialectical approach.

1.2.3   *The historical background*

We may better understand the issues at stake by sketching an historical background, even if this can only be done very briefly and superficially. The Aristotelian world view, being concerned with the idea of a meaningful order, dominated thinking into medieval times. Man was seen as a part of the cosmic order. To understand this order and to make it meaningful, human purposes and ideas were projected into it. Thus, the behaviour of inanimate objects was explained in terms of human purposes and final causes. This Aristotelian idea of the unity of nature and man was abandoned in an epistemological revolution, as it has been called (Ch. Taylor, op. cit., p. 4).

Advances in physics—especially by Galilei—made it possible to explain the motion of inanimate objects without using a psychological language. Descartes, whose influence with regard to a dualistic conception of the world can still be felt, was greatly impressed by the new science of mechanics. He considered its principles as sufficient for description and explanation of the behaviour of inanimate objects, and their relations to one another.

It seemed plausible to Descartes that the human body could also be viewed as a mechanism, functioning as a clockwork, and thus being subject to these same laws of mechanics.

But this conviction brought him into conflict with his religious beliefs concerning an immortal soul. Whereas the body was mortal, the soul resting in the body was immortal. Thus he concluded body and soul must be different; the one being "material", the other being "spiritual". Hence, he could conclude that the soul, in opposition to the body, did not function in a mechanistic way.

But he had to find an explanation for this difference in kind and in function. He postulated the existence of two different substances each being independent of the other. The first substance, called *res extensa*, was characterized by its extension in space. Living and inanimate bodies were made up by this substance. The other substance, *res cogitans*, had a different quality: it was characterized as possessing the quality of thinking or cognition. An entity which was characterized by *res cogitans* could not possess extension in space. The only entity which fulfilled this demand was the soul. Therefore, man as distinguished from other animals and inanimate bodies, is according to Descartes characterized by possessing both substances: a body extended in space and being mortal, a well as an immortal soul, characterized by cognition.

The solution to the conflict which Descartes experienced between his scientific and religious convictions has pervaded scientific thinking to our day. Much of modern psychology, having accepted the dualistic notion of body and mind, though naturally not the Cartesian version and motivation for it, still struggles on grounds which could be abandoned through a reformulation of basic ontological assumptions.

The opposition between a dualistic and other, especially holistic, ontologies has continued until today. Various notions of dualism were, e.g., accepted by English empiricism. Various notions of holism were accepted by philosophers of German Romanticism, by Hegel, and by Marx, at least as I will try to interpret him.

1.2.4   *About materialism*

It is our thesis that the dualism between idealism and materialism is opposed to the ontological presuppositions of dialectical thought. We will have ample opportunity to defend this thesis later on (see, e.g., p. 61). Here, however, we want to analyze very briefly three notions of "materialism" and their consequences.

Since the concept is vague, there are many ways to talk about materialism in an ontological context. One way of using it, is the previously mentioned "materialism" that defends the identity thesis. The negation of this thesis may be formulated as the following: mental events are not only different from physiological events, they, for that reason, have to be described in a specific language. They may also be causally related to physiological events. It seems, however, difficult to see how a mental event (e.g., an after-image), could be the cause of a physiological event (e.g., a state of the brain), as well as the other way round. It seems much more reasonable to view both events as different aspects of a total process: Different events occur contemporaneously and have in common that they are all necessary to establishing the unitary process. These different aspects can, and probably must, be described in different ways. For that, it seems reasonable that some events or some aspects can more profitably be described in one language, whereas others are more fruitfully described in another. Still, both events could be looked upon as various aspects of very complicated processes. Some of these are so complicated, that it is difficult to see how they could be described in the language of physiology without being supplemented with concepts which, e.g., allow for the description of purpose and intention.

Perhaps one problem with this analysis consists in the fact that we speak about different types of description. But we never ask what it means to give a description: to be able to express oneself through language. If we consider this, we can immediately demonstrate that language comprises physiological events-sounds as well as mental events, i.e., meaning. It is not possible to say that sounds and meaning are identical and that the one can be reduced to the other. Nor can we say that they are causally related to each other. They are both necessary aspects of a total process. As we will point out later (see p. 84), a totality, in the dialectical sense, implies that the elements which make up a whole are different, though interrelated, and that they have identical characteristics when taken as a whole. The analysis of what this means exactly has to be deferred until we can in more detail analyze dialectical relations and totalities.

So much for the first use of "materialism". The second example is taken from dialectical materialism, as analyzed by F. Engels (though not by K. Marx). In Engel's writings one finds a version of what could be called genetic materialism (see, e.g., his book *Anti-Dühring*, 1959). An assumption is made there that matter is primary to mind. Furthermore, genetic materialism maintains that mind originates out of matter, and that it is its highest and most elaborated stage.

Genetic materialism, as very briefly described here, presupposes the dualism of mind and matter, even if it declares mind to be a stage or product of matter (whatever that means).

Furthermore, what does it mean to say that matter is primary to mind? One explanation could be given in historical terms: a world of inanimate objects existed before human beings appeared. But such a statement does not seem immediately interesting from an ontological point of view. A second interpretation could be made in terms of the identity thesis discussed above.

A third interpretation could be that "material conditions" affect our ideas. But in this case, an analysis of the word "material", in the Marxian sense of "material conditions", would have to be made. As we will see, it does not have the same meaning here, as it does in ontological contexts (see p. 41). This also indicates that we are no longer discussing ontological problems, but a specific sociological hypothesis, concerning the relation between social existence or being, and ideas or ideology. These are quite different problems.

There is a third way of talking about materialism. In daily, common-sense language much of our discourse is about "material" objects. Our daily life-world consists of what has been called "particulars" (P.F. Strawson, 1964). These comprise chairs, books, shoes, etc., i.e., "material" objects, but also occurrences and events, short episodes, specific persons, etc.

Two questions arise: 1. What does the word "material" mean in this context? 2. Do we not introduce a dualism when we talk about different types of particulars?

When we talk here about "material objects" we use this expression in *a specific and restricted sense:* we refer to "solid, three-dimensional things with a certain endurance over time", as distinct, for example, from gas or a smell. We do not, however, make any implicit or explicit assumptions of an ontological kind regarding the nature of these "material objects" for example, that they consist of "material", of molecules, etc.

Thus we distinguish between "material" objects and other particulars. But this does not necessarily imply that we accept a dualistic matter-mind ontology. We only say that some particulars are three-dimensional, solid, etc., and others are not.

But Strawson makes another important point. When we try to identify particulars for ourselves and for others, we use individuating facts as identifying references. For example, I may say to my son: "Could you please get me the book over there". He answers: "Which one?" I can then use identifying references: The book on the table, the book with the green cover, the book which I had when yesterday I read a story for you, etc.

Strawson underlines that identification of things is facilitated when it rests on a spatial-temporal framework because, "the system of spacio-temporal relations has a peculiar comprehensiveness and pervasiveness, which qualify it uniquely to serve as framework within which we can organize our individuating thoughts about particulars" (Strawson, op.cit., p. 25).

This framework can not, however, be separated from the particular objects, since these objects constitute the framework itself. But now take another example. If I say "it was not my thought but his", and somebody asks me whom I refer to, I have to identify a specific *person*. In this case, I try to identify a "psychological" particular, a thought, by reference to a "material" particular, a person. The problem, however, is more complicated. As we will see later on (p. 160), the concept of "person" cannot be used unrelated to the concept of "body" (a "material" way of speaking), *and* to the concept "state of consciousness"—a psychological way of speaking.

We will discuss the meaning of "to identify" in a very detailed manner since it is of great importance (see p. 101). We will also discuss what to "identify a person", as distinguished from the identification of a person's "individuality" or "personality" (see p. 103), means.

Since three-dimensional, solid things, with an endurance over time, seem to constitute our framework for identification, Strawson argues that they are *basic particulars*. They can be identified with no reference to "non-material" particulars, whereas the last mentioned, at least as a rule, have to be identified by reference to "material" particulars.

One special category of particulars is always dependent on another category for identification. "The dependent type is the class of what might be called 'private particulars'—comprising the perhaps overlapping group of sensations, mental events and, in one common acceptance of this term, sense-data. The type on which it is dependent is the class of persons" (Strawson, op. cit., p. 41).

This assumption is opposed to empiricist ontological assumptions, which make sense-data into the basic categories of knowledge. It may, on the other hand, save one idea of genetic materialism, namely, that "material objects" are basic and, in this sense, primary. But in the way the assumption is now phrased it only states that the identification of "non-material" particulars is dependent on the identification of "material" particulars, whereas the reverse is not correct.

Thus, we have her another interpretation of primacy in addition to the ones previously presented. This interpretation, however, is concerned with *epistemological* problems, much more than with ontological ones. It does not imply, therefore, that we have saved one of the basic theses of genetic materialism. Certainly we have divided our world of particulars into "material" and "non-material". But in doing so, we use only criteria for talking about them, and do not make any assumption about their nature, i.e., assumptions of an ontological kind. With this we will stop the discussion of some of the problems of ontological materialism.

As a short introduction it will serve my purpose if I have been able to indicate how complicated the problems are, when we deal in matters of ontology. The vagueness of the concept "materialism" in this context should also have been indicated.

Furthermore, it should have been made clear that social scientists (even Marxists social scientists) need not be concerned with the ontological problem of what it means to speak about the "materiality" of the world. Where they must take a stand concerning the problem is dualism and, in consequence on the ontological presuppositions of dialectics. For that reason, these two related problems will be treated in more detail in consecutive chapters.

1.3   EPISTEMOLOGICAL PROBLEMS

As for the other sections of this chapter, this will serve only as a short introduction, since problems of epistemology will be treated in several chapters, as they are central to this book.[4]

On the epistemological level, philosophical *idealism* is not opposed to materialism but to *realism*. Realism, briefly, assumes the existence of a world independent of consciousness (though it does not necessarily make any assumptions concerning the nature of this world, or what it is made of). Idealism assumes, on the other hand, that the world *is* consciousness.

One central issue in epistemology is the subject-object relation, i.e., the role of a subject who possesses or produces knowledge and that which the knowledge is about, its object.

Somewhat schematically, three positions can be distinguished. *One* asserts that the subject is more or less a passive receiver of sense experiences or of stimuli, which either impinge on his sense organs, or act as mirror images, which are reflected in his consciousness. Common to these various notions is an attempt to minimize the active contribution of the subject-knower in achieving or producing knowledge.

There are, however, important differences between a behaviouristic stimulus-response theory, as it may be called, and a theory in which knowledge is a reflection or mirror image of the world (as, e.g., in some interpretations of Marxist epistemology).

Behaviourism as understood here, essentially maintains that all behaviour is a response to stimuli. It therefore excludes from consideration intentional and purposive action. Thus the distinction here rests on behaviour as opposed to action.

The reflection or mirror image theoreticians, on the other hand, do not sufficiently take into consideration the active contribution made by the subject in the production of knowledge. As Marx pointed out, this activity of the subject was understood by idealistic philosophy, though there, this activity was understood as cognitive activity alone (K. Marx in his "first thesis about Feuerbach", 1932).

The *second* position, that held by idealistic philosophy, maintains that knowledge is a product of the human mind. Some of these philosophers, Berkeley for example, went a step beyond and denied the existence of a reality independent of our thoughts and cognitions. Hegel, on the other hand, asserted that all which exists is a manifestation of Spirit, including the existence of a "material" world, being a necessity for the self-affirmation of the Absolute Spirit.

The *third* position assumes that knowledge is a relation between a subject and an object in which the subject produces cognitive objects. However, these cognitive products are closely related to a world of objects which exists independently of the producing subject. This world of objects can be said to be "material" in one definite and restricted sense. When we talk about "material objects" we refer, as mentioned before to "solid, three-dimensional things with a certain endurance over time".

The relation between the knowledge producing subject and the world of objects, being independent of him, is mutual. The subject is not only producing knowledge. He also produces a world of objects, and the social world concretely. Thus he is, at the same time, a product of pre-existing social and physical conditions, as well as of the objects of his own creation. Therefore this production of knowledge is not dispensed in the air. It is closely related to his daily, *practical* activity. This practical activity is a social activity in the double sense of being shared by others, and of having a meaning that it shared with others.

Therefore, the concept of praxis has a central position in the epistemological position we will develop (see p. 233).

In the past, social science has too often neglected epistemological problems. With regard to scientific knowledge it often has taken for granted that scientific knowledge as such is unproblematic. Therefore, the argument goes, one ought to concentrate on the *methods* by which *reliable* scientific knowledge is obtained. Too often uncritically and without an awareness of its theoretical consequences, the first of the three indicated positions is adopted. We want to show here, however, not only that the role of the subject and its conceptualization in the process of production of knowledge is central, but also that this indicates a division line with far reaching consequences. This division line is concerned with the notion of man as an agent of social processes and of social change, as well as being the object of such processes. This, in turn, places concepts like "action", "agent", "mediation", "process", and as mentioned, "praxis" into the centre of our discussion.

1.3.1 Some problems connected with a realist position

A realism which maintains the existence of a world independently of the subject is sometimes coupled with another thesis. This states that knowledge about this independent world is directly obtained through perception. To this thesis another is often added. It states that only empirical knowledge, i.e., knowledge through perception obtained by controlled observations, is the basis for all scientific endeavour.

The first thesis, that we obtain all our knowledge directly through perception, seems difficult to uphold. Let us present a simple example. We *perceive* every day that the sun sets below the horizon, though we *know* that such is not the case. We know that the earth, through its movement, makes it appear as if the sun were setting. Thus as one solution, we may introduce a distinction between "appearance" i.e., that which is accessible to our sense organs, and "essence", i.e., the knowledge we may obtain through a theoretical analysis in which perceptual observations are placed in a consistent theoretical-explanatory context.

This distinction is of great importance for a Marxist social scientific enterprise; we will return often to its consequences (see p. 66).

One question follows from this: why don't we, in daily language, always differentiate between perception and theoretical knowledge? One answer is that we learn to use "natural interpretations" (P.K. Feyerabend 1975, p. 73). This means that there exist configurations of a perceptual nature *and* a linguistic expression: "describing a familiar situation, is for the speaker, an event in which statement and phenomenon are firmly glued together" (op. cit., p. 72). This again, in turn, is a consequence of learning processes, especially the learning to use language, which start early in childhood when a child learns to connect words and actions.

Feyerabend says that the teaching procedures are such that we, "from our early days learn to react to situations with the appropriate responses, linguistic or otherwise. The teaching procedures *both* shape the 'appearance' or the 'phenomenon' and establish a firm connection with words, so that finally the phenomena seem to speak for themselves without outside help or extraneous knowledge" (ibid, p. 72).[5]

Feyerabend adds that the language used is, in turn, influenced by beliefs and the language of earlier generations, but to us, seems to emerge from the thing themselves.

The belief we used to illustrate the thesis of natural interpretation, namely, that it is the sun which is setting, can hardly in itself be called what Feyerabend labels "an appropriate response". In fact, if judged by what we know, it is *not* appropriate. Does this mean that common-sense language is less exact, and therefore truth-worthy, than a scientific or technical language? It may be less exact than, e.g., a formalized scientific language. But formalization would not be possible without access to a common-sense language, serving as the basis for formalization. The main question, however, is concerned with the truth-worthiness of common-sense language. It seems that the statement, "the sun is setting", is a good example of the lack of precision of common-sense language and, therefore, one could argue, it should not be trusted.

We will argue later on that there exist basic rules for common-sense language which cannot be violated without making our use of language meaningless. One example would be the attribution of psychological characteristics to inanimate objects (e.g., "this stone just had a perception of red and hot"). These rules seem to be related to basic ontological conditions.

On the other hand, it seems to be undeniable that expressions of our common sense do not always follow advances in physics. There seems to exist a lag between certain common-sense expressions and the results of modern physics (see also Whitehead's assertion in note 1). The second thesis mentioned above, that only controlled observations form the basis of scientific knowledge, is also doubtful if expressed in this categorical formulation. In the most extreme case it would amount to the assertion that there exist "pure" observations, which are independent of any conceptualization that precedes or accompanies observation.

In addition, as Feyerabend points out, "questionable views on cognition, such as the view that our senses, in normal circumstances, give reliable information about the world, may invade the observation language itself, constituting the observational terms and the distinction between veridical and illusory appearances" (op. cit., p. 66).

1.3.2   Some problems connected with an idealistic position

K. Popper (1972) pointed out that the simplest form of idealism may be caught in the formulation that "the world (which includes my present audience) is just my dream" (1972, p. 38). Such an assertion, he maintains, cannot be refuted, since all attempts to show that there are real things can be met by the argument that these, too, are a dream. Popper maintains that one can argue against such a position, and be convinced that it is false, but still, he maintains, it cannot be refuted in the way an empirically testable theory can.

This can be seriously questioned. But it seems clear that such an assumption can be refuted by arguments which are logically conclusive. In order to say that the "world is only a dream", I must be able to make a distinction between a dream and that which is not a dream. In order to make such a distinction I must *know* what it means to use the words "dream", "real", "object", and so on.

In other words, in order to defend the idealistic contention that the world is a dream, I have already to accept a distinction between "the imaginary" and the "real", which means a world which is not a dream. As M. Merleau-Ponty points out: "For if I am able to talk about 'dreams' and 'reality', to bother my head about the distinction between imagery and real, to cast doubt upon the 'real', it is because this distinction is already made by me before any analysis; because I have an experience of the real as of the imaginary" (1970, p. XVI).[7]

In addition, could a person *talk* about a dream without having learned to use language? "People who on waking tell us certain incidents (that they have been in such and such places, etc.) Then we teach them the expression 'I dreamt', which precedes the narrative. Afterwards I sometimes ask them 'did you dream anything last night?' and am answered yes or no, sometimes with an account of a dream, sometimes not. *That is the language game*" (L. Wittgenstein 1958, p. 184, my italics).

Since we obviously cannot talk about dreams without having learned to use language and, therefore, to have learned *knowing* a language, we can ask: Can we, in any meaningful way, say that we know a language or, we know how to use language, and, at the *same time*, assert that this language has nothing whatsoever to do with a reality existing independently of the language user? And is not language (viewed as a system and not as speech acts), a part of reality itself? Furthermore, how can I say that I have *knowledge of language*, but no *knowledge of reality?* Is there knowledge of language which is not also *knowledge of reality?* Can we say that we *know* how to use language, but we do not know how to use it when we talk about reality? Do we know how to use language only if we use it about language? This idea seems absurd. Therefore, we must conclude that *knowledge* of language also is *knowledge* of reality (see also p. 33).

This discussion brings us to one of the central problems of epistemology, that of the relation between knowing and language.

1.3.3   About knowing and language

Traditionally questions in epistemology have been formulated as following: (1) How do we get knowledge; (2) What does it mean to have knowledge about something; (3) Can we be certain that our knowledge is true? The first question concerns essentially genetic problems (as how we did learn to use a language), and problems concerning the production of knowledge. The second is a semantical question concerning the meaning of the expression "to have knowledge". The third question concerns the problem of justification of the knowledge we think we have. Let us start with the third question.

In the introduction of the "Phenomenology" Hegel treats a classical problem of epistemology: "It is natural to assume that before philosophy enters on its subject properly, namely actual knowledge of reality—it must first come to an understanding of knowledge itself" (1967, p. 131).

In order to understand what true knowledge is, it was traditionally argued, that we must first have a criterion against which we can test the truth of a proposition. But such claims lead to difficulties. As Hegel points out in his "Logic", any examination of knowledge can be only carried out by an act of knowledge itself. Therefore if we try to formulate a criterion according to which we can decide whether a proposition is true, we may ask what are the reasons for exactly using this criterion. In other words, we have to justify the use of the very criterion. This can be done in two ways which both lead to unsolvable difficulties. There has also sometimes been suggested a third alternative, which, as can be shown, leads to contradictory claims.

First, one may maintain that in order to justify the criterion chosen we must find another, "a meta-criterion" to justify the original. In this case our reasoning leads us to an infinite regress.

Second, when spelling out the criterion and trying to justify it, we may appeal to the very criterion we have chosen. In this case we reason in a circular way. Assume, for example, as traditional empiricism does, that we maintain that propositions are true when they can be verified through empirical observations. Then we must ask how this very principle can be verified. Our answer cannot be: by an *empirical* study of how we proceed when we make empirical observations, because in this case we presuppose the very existence of the principle which we want to justify.

A *third* solution, sometimes suggested, is to say that there is no knowledge which is absolutely true. All knowledge is then only true relative to some conditions to be specified. But this principle of relativity is logically contradictory. Is this very principle that all knowledge is only relatively true, true in an absolute way? If yes, then there is at least one proposition which is not relatively true and the principle is false. If the principle is only relatively true, i.e., relative to certain conditions, then under other conditions it may be false.

In discussing traditional empiricism we asked what status does the proposition have, which asserts that a proposition is true when it can be verified empirically. The principle itself, as formulated, cannot be a synthetic proposition, and hence be empirically verified. If it were so we would reason in a circular way, as indicated above. It cannot be analytically true either, since it is not a definition of truth. Hence in addition to synthetic and analytic propositions, there seems to exist a third category of propositions. Perhaps analyzing this problem can give us a hint at a solution.

Let me put forward the following proposition P_1: "Human beings as users of language can put forward propositions". Let us now negate this proposition P_1. We thus have P_2: "Human beings as users of language cannot put forward propositions". But in order to put forward P_1 and in order to negate P_1 through P_2 we have already done what we negate in P_2. We have put forward propositions, namely P_1 and P_2. Hence we can put forward a third proposition P_3: "From a logical point of view, it is correct to say that human beings can put forward propositions since negating this is logically contradictory". We thus have established the fact, that we can put forward at least one proposition which is correct or true. Furthermore we do not need to justify the truth of this position by any other criterion than the use of language itself. In other words, when we use language we must do it in such a way that our speech makes sense.

This example points at the fact that it seems logically sound to take as a point of departure that we can have some knowledge being such that we can be certain it is true.

If one says with G.E. Moore, that one *knows* the hands which one holds up in front of oneself are one's own hands, and is asked, how can one *know* such, the answer must be: "*I have learned to use language*". The point is, as Wittgenstein underlines, not to prove that one knows there is a hand, but the fact that we could not *understand a person* saying that he possibly could be mistaken. What kind of mistake would that be, and what kind of language is he using? (1970, §32).

The rejection of the sceptical position has several consequences. One of them is the following. If I can argue that I know that the hands in front of me are my own, since I have learned to use language, then "to have a language", seems to imply that one is able to make certain statements which are true, such that their denial would make our speech contradictory or meaningless. We will have ample opportunities to return to this problem.

A second consequence of the rejection of the sceptical position is this: If we possess some knowledge which is true then it will not only be unnecessary but also impossible to justify that such is the case.

We have previously argued that trying to justify the truth of a criterion of truth leads to an infinite regress.

If we cannot justify the truth of *all* our propositions, there may be some which are true without being in need of justification. We have presented one such proposition and shown that if we deny its truth our use of language would become meaningless and self-contradictory.

How can we find other such propositions not being in need of justification? Let us start the investigation of this problem from a different angle, then much traditional epistemology. In this tradition, the basis of investigation has been perception and sense experience. This has at least two consequences. First of all, if theories of knowledge are based upon perception, they usually, though not always are anchored in psychology, because the scientific study of perception is an area of psychology. But this implies that new knowledge with regard to psychological theories of perception must lead to changes in epistemological theories. This is exactly what has happened.

Though this cannot be used as an objection against employing perception and sense-data as the basis for epistemology, it can be used as an argument for the notion of the historical limits of an epistemology and of any meta-theory. New knowledge may thus change our ideas concerning the way we obtain or produce knowledge, as well as the rules for producing knowledge, e.g., scientific knowledge.

There is a another, and more important, problem, if epistemology is anchored in perception and in psychology, from where then does psychology take its epistemological principles? On what principles can psychological research be based, and how is psychological knowledge obtained?

The *second* consequence is the following. Perception and sense-data are, as such, always subjective and private. This not only means that I cannot share my toothache with others. It also means that I cannot be sure that *my experience* of something being red is, for example, shared by others.[8] Another person may *say* that he has the experience of red and that it may be the same experience, but I cannot be certain that his is exactly the same experience (I think that the notion of the uncertainty of the truth of our knowledge is directly related to the tradition in epistemology basing knowledge on perception and sense-data).

In the final analysis, I cannot know, but only hope, that my sensory experience is the same as another's sensory experience. I am locked up in my private universe. Hence all phenomenalistic epistemology seems to end up in solipsism.

If we object to using perception and sense-data as the basis for an epistemology, what alternative do we have? In the previous discussion we have already given a clue as to where to switch our starting point. We maintained that "another person may *say* that he has an experience of red and that it may be the same experience ..." If another person *says* that he sees a red thing and we doubt it, we do not necessarily need to investigate his perception. *We can analyze his language and his use of language.* This is a vantage point because language in general, and the concepts used in language in particular, are not private. A man alone cannot use language since he alone cannot follow a rule as Wittgenstein has pointed out, and as we will discuss later.

Language is always public and intersubjective. Concepts are social in the sense that they are institutionalized. A concept can be said to state rules about how to speak, and the use of it, at the same time, follows such rules.

What does it mean to say that language is public and

intersubjective, and that concepts are social? It means that they are used by several persons and therefore shared. Regarding concepts it means that their meaning is understood by many in an identical way. That a concept is social can also mean that it forces itself on us (L. Wittgenstein 1958, p. 204).

It would, however, be ridiculous to maintain that *all* concepts confer the same meaning on many. Such an assertion would imply that there do not exist vague concepts. The point is rather that there exist concepts which are such that their use is generally valid because they are related to other concepts in such a way that their meaning cannot be understood except in terms of these interrelations.

Take, for example, the concept "person". It implies, in everyday or *common-sense* language, the concept of "body". To say that "yesterday I met a person on the street, but he did not possess a body" does not make sense. The very notion of "common sense" implies that there exists a *sense common* for those using language.

Another example of concepts to be used only in relation to each other are "facts" and "truth". We will have ample opportunity to discuss this matter and we will maintain that there exists a broad logic of common-sense language forming intersubjectivity and making it possible.

Our proposal, then, aims at a vindication of the thesis that language instead of perception ought to form the *basis* for epistemology.

Somebody may object that there is a close interrelation between language and perception. We do not deny that. The problem we are discussing is: What is *basic* to having or producing knowledge? Is language to be based on perceptual phenomena, or is all our human experience based upon that which we can talk about, i.e., language. In the first case we have to study perception and perceptual phenomena when we want to know how we produce or obtain knowledge. In the second case we have to analyze language and the use of language, in order to understand how sensory experience may be used in obtaining or producing knowledge. Thus if we accept that language is basic to perception we accept (1) that our perceptual experience can only be expressed through the use of language; (2) that our perceptual experience becomes *meaningful* experience only through the mediation of language. This is so because meaning belongs to signs, to words, to concepts. "Meaning is the expression of a semiotic relationship" (V.N. Volosinov 1973, p. 28).

The consequences of postulating language as basic to perception in the production of knowledge are the following:

(1) the anchoring of epistemology in psychology is avoided.

(2) the anchoring of knowledge in basically private experience is avoided and by that solipsism is avoided,

(3) the analysis of knowledge becomes a semiotic or linguistic problem in the first hand

(4) since language is social, intersubjectivity is to be presupposed not to be explained *a posteriori*

(5) intersubjectivity is based upon a general logic of language which provides our common-sense language with common sense,

(6) all specialized languages, e.g., scientific language, as well as the formalized languages of logic and mathematics, presupposes the use of a natural common-sense language that is based upon a set of rules. These rules in turn form a general logic of language. When we say that language is intersubjective then we refer to this network of rules forming a general logic,

(7) these general rules are such that they cannot be further explained because all explanations presuppose the very existence of these rules. The way we can judge the validity of these rules is by violating them. In this case what we say becomes without meaning, or self-contradictory. Using language meaningfully then implies following these basic rules of the logic of language.

1.3.4   *Language and knowledge: Some further deliberations*

Previously (see p. 27) we have maintained that the basic logic of language consists of rules stating the interdependence of certain concepts. As one example we mentioned that the concept of "person" and the concept of "body" cannot be used independently of each other. The same can be said of the concepts "person" and "intention".

When we say that two concepts cannot be used independently of each other we mean that the use of one concept *implies* the other concept.[9]

One may object to this reasoning by maintaining that we have argued in a tautological way. "To be a person" by definition means "to have a body".

Let me reply to this accusation in the following way. Would it be possible to talk about having and using a language without reference to a person? Could we understand a statement that a person says something without his being at a certain place? Or would it make sense to say that a person finds himself at a certain place without his body being there, etc.[10]

Our conclusion is that such statements, far from being tautological, indicate that there exist *interrelations between certain concepts, which are irreducible.* These interrelations are of a logical kind, such that if we disregard them, our statements become nonsensical or self-contradictory. We cannot speak about having a language and not having a body, or being a person and not finding onself at a certain place, etc.

Our use of language here seems not only be dictated by *logical* reasons. But these reasons seem to be anchored in *ontological* conditions. We might—if we wish—talk about dealing with "onto-logical" conditions. Though we should emphasize that we *cannot explain* the logic of our language by means of reference to ontological conditions because all these explanations can only be made by following exactly those rules which we try to explain (see also chapter 3, p. 205).

When we point out the relation between having a language and having a body we also imply, at least indirectly, a relation between language and action. To use language is to act (we speak of "speech-acts"); being able to act presupposes a body, as well as intentions, i.e., states of consciousness.

There is a second and still more important argument for the relationship between language and action. We have maintained that there exist strong and irreducible relations between certain concepts, interrelations which cannot be violated without making language nonsensical. To say this amounts to saying that there exist basic "onto-logical" rules, which we follow when we speak. We will discuss these rules in detail later on (see p. 169).

Here we will restrict ourselves to indicating that we follow these rules without necessarily being aware of them. This means that we do not interpret them and then decide that we will follow them. Instead, we *act* out these rules in the context of our practical activities. Our daily praxis, in other words shapes our language and our language influences our praxis such that we at least know what we *cannot* do.

The interrelation between irreducible concepts can also be expressed such that certain things cannot be said. It may be difficult to state what a certain concept, e.g., the concept of "person" comprises. It is less difficult to state what it does not comprise. I think that this principle (we can call it the "principle of negativity" has a central role in epistemology (see p. 224).

Some statements are true since their negation would make the use of our language meaningless. It is true beyond all doubt that if I am a person in the sense of a living human organism that I have a body. Furthermore, what can be said about myself can also be said about others. (In fact it has been argued that the knowledge which I have, namely that I am a person presupposes the knowledge that there are others who are also identified as "persons" (P.F. Strawson 1964, p. 160).)

But if it is correct that there are other persons than myself, I also have to accept that there exists a world independently of me. If I were to deny that, it would amount to saying that I know that I am a person and that I have a body, but I do not know whether there exist others about which the same can be said.

We can in this way indicate that our argument is directed also against such an idealistic epistemological position that not only emphasizes perception and sense-data as the *basis* for our knowledge but, in addition, asserts that perception and the ideas it may give rise to are the only objects about which we can have knowledge at all. Hence it denies the dependence of perception upon a reality independent of the perceiving subject.

In the previous section we discussed some of the consequences of shifting from perception to language as the *basis* of our knowledge. An additional consequence will now be discussed.

The fact that I know how to use language means that I act in accordance with certain rules, not in some abstract way, but in *concrete, social situations.* It means not only that I know how to act, but how to act in a linguistically correct manner. Hence to have a language, or to use a language, means that I can at least make *some statements* whose correctness or truth cannot be questioned. If *their* truth were questioned it would be an indication that one does now know how to use language. Thus the knowledge of language logically implies the ability to produce some correct statements about the world (P. Zinkernagel 1976). In fact one needs to have a language in order to formulate the very question of correctness. Furthermore, it implies that this is a statement about which we can invoke our principle of negativity: a statement which cannot be negated without depriving ourselves of the 'possibility' of differentiating between correct and false.

A denial of the statement amounts to saying this: It is not the case that knowledge of language implies that we can make some correct statements about the world. Assume we could accept this statement as true. We must then give reasons why such is the case. Two assertions seem to be possible:

1. We can never be sure that our statements are correct. In this case we end up with the same dilemma, which we discussed at the beginning of the previous section.

2. The distinction between correct and false must *always* be proved empirically. Take again the following statement: It is correct that the hands I hold up in front of me are a part of my body. How can I prove this statement empirically? And even if I could, would it be necessary? Would it make sense to say: My hands are not a part of my body?

If we accept that we can make some correct statements, then we must also accept that we know what "correct" means. That this, in turn, implies that we can differentiate between correct and false, i.e. that we also know what "false" means.

This reasoning leads to another important consequence. It implies that we cannot explain what "correct" means. All explanations of what "correct" means presuppose that we know the very word "correctness" and that we can use it, i.e., that we can make correct statements.[11]

This does not mean that everything we say must be correct or that we cannot make false statements. Neither does it mean that we cannot prove the truth or falsity of statements. It implies only that, in order to formulate decision procedures for testing the truth and falseness of statements, and, further in order to carry out such tests, we must have the notion of correctness. This means, again, that we can make some correct statements such that their denial would be absurd, though they are not in themselves tautologous.

In fact, when we make statements about which we are not sure of their truth, we have developed decision procedures according to which they can be judged. These procedures also presuppose knowledge of the concept "correctness".

In the sense in which we have discussed it can be said that

language is the basis of our knowledge. It could now be argued in criticism, that such a thesis implies epistemological idealism. To such an accusation we reply, first of all, that language is as *real* as human bodies or means of production, etc.[12]

But there is a stronger argument against such an accusation. We cannot talk at all about anything being correct or false, without implying that there exists a world independent of ourselves. Only about such a world can statements be made, statements which are either correct or false.

Our predicament as persons means that we *act* upon the world and *use* language. Acting in general and using language cannot be separated from each other. Thus the fact that to be a person means to act and to use language presupposes the existence of a world upon which we can act. We also can use language *about* our actions and *about* our language-using. If we would not presuppose the existence of a world, then we have to conclude that when we speak about our actions and about our use of language, we end up in complete confusion. Let me give one example. If I tell a friend of mine that yesterday I wrote 10 pages on my typewriter, how could he prove the truth of my statement, if there were no world in which there were typewriters.

Thus, if we deny the existence of a world independent of ourselves, we either deny that a person can act, or we use the word "action" in such a way as to be completely incomprehensible in our daily common-sense language. But it is *this* language which is a precondition for *acting* towards and together with others, and which develops as a consequence of this interaction.

In other words, we would deny the possibility of interaction, i.e., a necessary precondition of society, thus the possibility of society itself.

In summary, if there would not exist a world independently of ourselves, what would form the basis for our actions and for the ways we talk about them?

We are stating here certain conditions which are common to all who use language. Thus if we know we can act, we also know we can act upon a world independent, but not unrelated, to ourselves. To deny this would be as contradictory as to deny that the hands in front of us are ours. How do we know all this? Because we have learned to use language. Furthermore, to learn to use language presupposes a society and in turn learning language makes society possible.

Our reasoning also implies the rejection of a traditional distinction between *knowledge* about language and *knowledge* about reality. Language, the world of objects, and the social world (which cannot be separated from language) together make up reality.

Therefore, *knowledge* about reality includes *knowledge* about language. *Knowledge* about language is *knowledge* about reality and especially about social reality.

We will return to and discuss this problem in great detail later on (p. 93).

To use language as the basis of epistemology also means that we attribute special importance to common-sense language, i.e., the language that people use in their daily praxis and interaction. Since producing and reproducing of life is the basic human activity—*the* life activity—and, since these activities can only be carried out through language mediated interaction with others, it would be a curious proposition to maintain that we could not make correct statements in this common-sense language. It would imply that non-verbal actions and verbal actions are not only separate, but also unrelated. In fact, it seems to be the other way round: action and language make up a unity. This holds as a *genetic* explanation, i.e., for the explanation of how the knowledge of language has developed, as well as for *operational* explanations, i.e., how language works, what it means to have a language.

1.3.5   A short excursion into the problem of linguistic relativity

We have argued for using common-sense language and its inherent logic as the basis for epistemology. It can now be argued that common-sense language is dependent on a special ontological or metaphysical basis. Furthermore, it can be argued that this basis can vary and, therefore, "the world picture" on which a specific language is based will influence our way of thinking about the world. People with different languages thus may experience the world in *completely* different ways.

The thesis of linguistic relativity is sometimes called the "Sapir-Whorf" hypothesis, because it has been defended by the anthropologist Edward Sapir and his student Benjamin L. Whorf (for a review see H. Gipper 1972).

Whorf, who among other things, carefully studied the Hopei-language and its peculiarities, maintains that the specific grammatics and syntax of a language affect our experience such that we organize the world according to our specific language. He rejects the notion of a general logic, i.e., a system of rules which form a minimum basis for all human language. His principle of linguistic relativity thus makes the world view, including our view concerning the use of language, dependent on the specific language we have learned. Since people have learned different languages, they differ as observers because the world views they acquire with their language differ (1956).

It is not certain whether Whorf defended what may be called an extreme relativistic position, but if he did, arguments against such a position can be proposed:

(1) as with all relativistic theses, a thesis of linguistic relativity is self-contradictory: if all world views are different and dependent on a specific language, in which language can *this* view be expressed? And further is the thesis itself a relativistic or an absolute thesis?

(2) If all languages are specific and dependent on their typical grammatics and syntax, how is it possible to translate one language into another? How, for example, is it possible for Whorf to translate the peculiarities of Hopei-language into English in a way that allows an English-speaking person to understand how Hopei-Indians speak and think.

(3) Is it possible to say that observers using different languages are not equivalent, i.e., are different such that they have nothing in common? Is it possible to speak about something being different without saying what it has in *common* with other things? Later on (p. 101), we will argue for the thesis that words like "different" and "same" are complementary, and that concepts referring to them cannot be used independently of each other.

(4) Could Hopei-Indians talk to each other, make themselves understood, cooperate with one another, *and* at the same time avoid following the rules we have codified in terms of the law of contradiction? And if their communication is non-selfcon-tradictory, is it then not reasonable to assume that speaking in a non-selfcontradictory way is something common to all languages?

(5) If there had not been some common grounds, how would it have been possible for Whorf to act together with Hopei-Indians at all, not to mention how it was even possible for him to *interact with* them?

(6) Theories of relativity can only function if there is at least one factor which is constant. Einstein's theory of relativity, e.g., uses speed of light as a constant factor. The same claim can be made for theories of linguistic relativity (this argument is just another version of our third argument concerning the interdependence of "common" and "specific", "same" and "different").

In rejecting the extreme relativity thesis we do not deny that, given a basic common logic of language, there develop language peculiarities such that a specific language may affect the way the world is interpreted. When viewed as a social system, a language stores the historical experiences of a given social praxis and mediates the experiences to the next generation that learns it. (See about that A. Schaff 1964). Since social praxis varies in cultures and societies, language does also. (The eskimos for example, have a number of different words for "snow" which reflects conditions under which they live and which affect their social praxis.)

A final argument for a less extreme linguistic relativity is the following. If we assume that a basic logic of language is a precondition for using language at all, do we not then assume that this precondition is independent of historical processes and cannot be transcended? The theory of relativity could be changed only *if* we discovered another factor as being constant instead of the speed of light. This is, of course, a possibility. Can we, however, assume that human nature could change such that we could speak of persons without bodies? Such seems less probable than a theory which postulates that we can move faster than light.

Still, one may argue, that our knowledge could change such that the theories concerning a general logic of language will become obsolete. This may be possible, but in what language could this alternative theory be formulated?

Finally, does not change and transcendence presuppose continuity in some respect?

1.3.6   *Knowledge as a relation*

So far we have discussed knowledge as something which we can

possess. We have also mentioned the notion of producing knowledge. A process of producing knowledge always involves a *relation*
between the producer and the produced. The process of production
of knowledge, therefore, can be viewed as a relation between a
subject and an object. The subject relates himself in various and,
probably, unlimited ways to objects or configurations of objects.
This implies that we cannot present a total description of the world
of objects or of reality in general. We can illustrate this with a
simple example. In saying this highway is dangerous, we can refer
to many things. We can mean that it has many curves, or that its
surface is slippery, or that there are risky crossings, that it is
narrow, or that there are steep precipices at its sides, or that rocks
may fall down, or that vision is rendered difficult or that driving is
monotonous, or.... Thus giving a total description seems to be
impossible. What we can do, however, is to place these partial
descriptions within the framework of a totality. Which means we
take the notion of totality as a starting point and try to place our
descriptions and the knowledge we may have into the context of a
functioning and structured whole. The partial descriptions, then,
ought to express various and interrelated aspects of this totality.
(The notion of totality will be discussed on p. 62.)

Our point of view not only holds for common-sense description
and knowledge, but also for scientific reconstructions. At any time
and in any science there will exist competing theories which are
practically or wholly incompatible. They present different and,
often, alternative descriptions of reality. Take as a simple example,
theories of stratification as opposed to class-theories in sociology.

The same holds for metascience, the methodology or philosophy
of science, as well as for the pre-theoretical assumptions or
presuppositions on which scientific theories are based (see J. Israel
1972a, where some of the presuppositions of the social sciences are
analyzed).[13]

To summarize: we relate ourselves in various and innumerable
ways to the world existing independently of us. This holds for daily
activities, when we are interpreting events, objects or experiences
(the highway is dangerous, for example), as well as for scientific
interpretations. These interpretations are not arbitrary in the sense
of being independent of the world, or being totally subjective. This
much can be inferred from our notion of knowing as *relation*

between a subject and an object, where both contribute to the outcome.

It is, however, imperative to be more precise with regard to the relations we speak about. The version of epistemological realism which we will pursue here, can be called "*relational realism*". Two assumptions are usually made in realism: (1) the world is *independent* of the subject and (2) It is external to the subject.[14]

Later on (in chapter 4) we will argue for the first assumption and against the second. Thus we will speak about a world being *independent* of a subject who relates himself intrinsically to it. The discussion concerning external versus internal relations is of central importance for the methodology of dialectics and will be treated in detail when we analyze dialectics (p. 78).

Here we can say in preliminary fashion, that the expression "the subject relates himself intrinsically to the world existing independently of him", implies that the subject confers meaning on the world of objects. They signify something to him. This can also be expressed such that the world, existing independently, is nevertheless a human world. As such is cognitized and interpreted. The world may exist and not be recognized, but in this case it does not exist *for* the subject. The activity of cognitizing and interpretation is a human predicament. It is part of the definition of what a human being is.

If we take the two attributes, *independence* and *extrinsicality*, there are then four epistemological positions possible: (1) the world is *not independent* of and *not extrinsic* to the subject. This can be characterized as the position of traditional epistemological idealism; (2) the world is *not independent* but *extrinsic*. Hegel's position that the Spirit embodies itself in the material world could possibly fall into this category;[15] (3) the world is *independent* and *extrinsic* to the subject: this being the usual position of epistemological realism; (4) finally, the world is *independent* of the subject, but not *extrinsic*; to him. This latter, the position of epistemological realism, is both dialectical and relational and will be one of the central themes of this book.

One final remark should be made here. A relational realism, which implies that the subject can relate himself to the world in various and innumerable ways, does not lead to a radical relativism and hence will not be faced with the dilemma discussed previously. In order to avoid such a relativism our approach must be anchored in a set of rules referring to conditions which cannot be done without.[16]

These conditions have to do with the predicament of being human, as previously argued, and with basic rules for language and society. These will be discussed in due time.

1.4 METHODOLOGICAL PROBLEMS

For the last problem in this introductory chapter we will discuss briefly the third area of relevance to an idealism–materialism dichotomy: the methodological. Since we deal only with the social sciences, methodological considerations will be restricted to them. Methodological questions are concerned with the ways the social world is different from the physical world, i.e., how society is to be studied.

Looking at the social sciences we find that there is not one set of descriptions of the social world. Rather, there are several sets of descriptions, organized into theories, which are different and alternative.

The social world is what we make of it. This can be understood in two senses: in the daily life-processes where, through our work we transcend and transform that which is given, and in the conceptual structure we impose on what we do. Thus our theories about the social world do not reflect it. They contribute to its construction. This means either of two things. Our theories can fortify and legitimate the existing or alternatively, they can contribute to its criticism and change.

There is another reason why we find different sets of descriptions of the social world. We postulated earlier that it is not possible to give total or exhaustive descriptions since we can relate ourselves to the world in innumerable ways. This holds not only for simple objects such as chairs, but to an even greater degree, for the description of such complicated and complex phenomena as a society or social system. Therefore we must make selections depending on the purpose of our theorizing.

Finally, society must be approached from two different thought complementary angles: As a network of relations and as a system of institutions.

1.4.1   *Methodological idealism vs materialism*

What is society and the social? One answer is to view the social world and its processes and structures as manifestations of universal and unchanging (functional) prerequisites. These prerequisites are postulated as such because human nature—being unaffected by social processes—is viewed as requiring a certain structure that guarantees order and harmonious development. All human beings are, according to this view, born with certain capacities. They are supposedly used in order to maximize utility. The individual owes nothing to society and society therefore should not restrict his actions. These individual actions, especially choices to maximize utility, when taken together, make up social processes. The latter thus are defined as the aggregate of individual actions. Society is then the results of the will of its individual members, who are guided by norms and values held in common. Conflicts arise when individuals deviate from these norms. Therefore they have to be punished. This, with different variations, is the theme of an idealistic methodology.

In contrast to this position, we deny the assertion that social processes and structures are manifestation or consequences of universal and unchangeable prerequisites. Instead, we emphasize the historically limited nature of such processes and structures, underlining the necessity of studying their genesis in order to comprehend their actual functioning. Thus we take our point of departure in change, transformation and transcendence, viewing order and structure as characteristics of this process.

This historical relativism, however, carries within itself the danger of being transformed into a self-contradictory relativism, where nothing is given, everything is seen as historically limited. Therefore we must find something which *constitutes the social* but at the same time allows for continuity in change which accomplishes and is the product of change.

The social world is an open world. It is a world with an open horizon, to use one of Husserl's metaphors. It is thus a world of possibilities, of change and of transcendence. But how is this to be accomplished? In answering this question we can also state what *the social* is. Not being unchangeable or necessarily presupposed, but that which *accomplishes* change and at the same time is the product of change and therefore is changed in the very process of transforming. *Praxis* fulfils all these requirements.

Society, the social world, is "history on its way". As such it is manifested in the daily life-process of man: the process through which man produces his world, transforms the given and is himself produced and transformed as the result of his own activities. These activities of transformation and of transcendence are *praxis*. Praxis is that by which change is accomplished. At the same time it becomes institutionalized. This means that praxis becomes objectified, i.e., transformed into institutions, which then form the frame of the ongoing process of transformation. Hence praxis is the activity of transformation and, at the same time, the congealed, *temporarily* inert product. Furthermore, to complicate the picture, when social institutions are changed and transcended, the content and form of praxis has to be changed in order to accomplish new transcendence.

We face the social as a complicated dialectic, where the *producer* of change, transforms the *product* and where this process, in turn, transforms the form in which such transformation occur. Independent of how we choose to do it, we must produce our lives. This means that we must produce the objects necessary for sustaining our lives, and the objects—e.g., tools and instruments—necessary to transcend the given. Furthermore, since we can only produce our life in interaction with others, we must produce the social institutions within which it is formed. These institutions include a family- and kinship-structure, an economic and political structure, and a linguistic structure (i.e., concepts which are socially institutionalized).

These institutions are at the same time objectified praxis, i.e., social actions transformed into objectively existing structures; this means that societal institutions exist before any specific individual. We are born into a given family structure, determined by specific institutions. We are born in a language structure and into an economic and social system with its structure. These structures exist independently of any given individual, but are not unrelated to him. Social institutions are created by man, obtain an independent status, but are changed through human actions.

This is the basic tenet of *methodological materialism*. The characterization "materialist" is a consequence of the fact that the point of departure is the daily life-process, is human praxis. An important aspect of this praxis is work, at least in those societies, which we know with their present level of (technical) development. The term "material" refers here to the concrete activities of our daily life as opposed to abstract speculations that remain aloof from the tangible actions in which praxis is manifested. It is in this sense that Marx used the term, i.e., to indicate his opposition to the philosophers of his epoch who believed their speculations to be sufficient activities. "The philosophers have only *interpreted* the world in various ways; the point is to *change* it." Marx here summarizes his opposition and suggests an alternative.

In this context "material" does not carry connotations of an ontological kind. Thus, as a social scientist, one can be a methodological materialist without being an ontological materialist.[17] (See further p. 43.)

1.4.2   The meaning of the expression "process of material production"

How does Marx use the world "material" in the context of, e.g., "material production"? Does his use of this expression imply ontological assumptions?

Let us start with a well-known quotation from the German Ideology in which he says: "Man can be distinguished from animals by consciousness, by religion or by anything one likes. They themselves begin to distinguish themselves from animals as soon as they begin to *produce* their means of substance, a step which is determined by their physical constitution. In producing their means of subsistence men indirectly produce their actual material life" (Mega 1/5, p. 11).

The quotation contains two assertions: (1) that man is distinguished from animals when he produces his means of subsistence and (2) through this production man *indirectly* produces his actual *material* life.

What does the expression "actual material life" mean? It refers to basic, fundamental conditions of human existence, namely those societal relations through which man produces and reproduces himself biologically and socially.

This is easily understood when one looks at Marx's conception of man. Man is a social being who can only exist in and through society, and who "can develop into an individual only in society" (1972, p. 228).

A social being is in one sense an "interacting" and "co-operating being". For survival man must instigate "a co-operation of several individuals, no matter under what conditions, in what manner, and to what ends" (Mega 1/5, p. 19).

The most important and central process of cooperation is the process of *material* production, which Marx also called the "life process". In this social process human labour transforms nature, i.e., *material* extracted from nature, into products for the satisfaction of human needs.

This process of production is social because, apart from accidental exceptions, "production by isolated individuals outside society ... is as great an absurdity as the idea of development of language without individuals living together and talking to each other" (1972, p. 228).

Marx here juxtaposes material production and language. Furthermore, within the economical sphere production is not an isolated process. It is intimately related to the processes of exchange, distribution and consumption, e.g., of raw materials and of labour power, and consumption can be viewed as production, e.g., of labour power (1953, p. 11).

Furthermore, man not only produces objects for need satisfaction, but also the social institutions which function as the framework for this production process. It is therefore as Marx says, that production "indirectly" produces man's actual *material* life. This can be interpreted such that when Marx talks about "material life" we understand the expression to include the production of "material" objects and social institutions as well as these very processes themselves.

What does the term "material" signify in the expression "actual *material* life"? I think his selection of terms and expressions must be understood as part of a polemic within German philosophy concerning the interpretation of history. Traditionally history often was conceived as the "actions of princes and states, as religious and all sorts of theoretical struggle" (Mega 1/5, p. 28). As a consequence, "the *real* production of life appears as ahistorical, while what is historical appears as separated from ordinary life" (ibid). The conception of history which Marx envisaged as opposed to this, took its point of departure in the "real process of production, starting out from the simple *material* production of life, and on the comprehension of the form of intercourse connected with and created by this mode of production" (ibid., p. 27).

The word "material" is then used by Marx to characterize that which he emphasized as the *real* life process; the daily struggle of people to produce the conditions of their life. The word "material" refers to concrete *social* processes and *social* relations, to the actions of men.

Marx's *methodological materialism* is based upon a definite conception of the nature of society and the nature of man. This conception gives rise to a number of methodological rules for the study and the analysis of society: *one ought to concentrate in social scientific and historical analyses on the process of material production, including the production of objects, relations and institutions in order to understand its specific historical form.*

Hence we interpret methodological materialism as rules for the study of society. This position gives rise to at least two questions:

(1) Does Marx's materialism have any connection with those ontological problems which we discussed in part 1.2.4. (2) If there are no such connections, are there no other ontological presuppositions implied in methodological materialism?

1.4.3 Are there ontological assumptions implied when we speak about "methodological materialism"?

Let us analyze some contexts, stemming from different periods, in which Marx uses the word "material".

Marx ascribes to man powers, faculties, or potential abilities. (For a discussion of Marx's conception of man see, e.g., E. Fromm, 1963; J. Israel, 1971; M. Marković, 1974; B. Ollman 1971.) One such power is the ability to transform nature into objects of human need. This transformation takes place in the labour process. There is, however, a division in this labour process which Marx says, became "a real division from the moment when the distinction between *material* and *mental* labour appears". (Mega 1/5, p. 21, our italics.)

In this quotation a traditional dualistic position seems to be implied between the mental and the material, where the latter is synonymous with "corporeal" or "physical". As a consequence Marx distinguishes between "intellectual" and "material production" (e.g., in the "Manifesto", Mega 1/6, p. 526 or in "Theorien über den Mehrwert", Vol. I, 1974, p. 256).

The ontological implications of using the word "material" in such contexts as those mentioned cannot be tied to a traditional body-mind dualism, but is in Marx's writing only an expression of a traditional common-sense way of speaking. It does not represent support for an ontological dualism.

Related to this is his use in the following quotation where speaking of modern machinery, Marx asserts that machines "are instruments of the human brain created by the human hand; they are the *materialized* power of knowledge". (Grundrisse, p. 594.) Here "material" means the "physically manifest" expression of human knowledge. A similar use one finds in "Capital vol. I" where one reads: "The recent scientific discovery, that the products of human labour, so far as they are values, are but the *materialized expressions* of the human labour spent in their production" (p. 74).

But the term "material" is used not only as an attribute of physical objects, but also with regard to man: "Just as philosophy finds its *material* weapons in the proletariat, so the proletariat finds its *intellectual* weapons in philosophy" (Mega 1/1, p. 621).

"Material" is sometimes used as equivalent to "naturwüchsig", i.e., emanating from nature or functioning as a natural force, i.e., unplanned and uncontrolled. Thus in the last-mentioned text Marx says that "theory can turn into a *material* force" when it gets a grip of man. Still these examples imply common-sense dualistic notions. The expression "material force", however, is often used synonymous with "productive forces", i.e., forces in the process of "material" production, as distinct from the process of production of knowledge.

Therefore, it is more often in his analysis of *society* than in his analysis of *human nature* that the word "material" appears. Marx talks about "material life", "material production", "material means of production", the "material requirements of human life", "material wealth", "material powers of production", etc. He also speaks of the low level of the productive power of labour as "material limitations". In all these quotations "material" is used in the restricted sense of past and present common-sense language (where we, e.g., speak about "material wealth"); a usage concerning physical objects or that which can be transformed into physical objects.

Further, the word "material" is used by Marx to underline what most people do during their life time, i.e., "material work", and those everyday activities that are central for societal analysis. This choice of emphasis also has a polemical side. Physical work was, and still often is, downgraded by a "leisure class" to use T. Veblen's expression, and by those doing "intellectual" work. This contempt for manual work was in Marx's time shared by an academic minority who in their ivory-towers, "philosophized" about the deepest "problems of life". "Interpreting the world" was considered more valuable than the drudge of daily manual "material" labour in order to change the world. Marx, on the other hand, maintained that it was through this process of "material" labour the world was produced and changed. For a science of history and society therefore, "the point of departure is the societally determined production of individuals" (1953, p. 5) in and through the *material* process of production.

I think we can conclude that the predominant way Marx uses "material" has nothing to do with ontological questions concerning the nature of reality. The ontological implications the term may have, when it is used in contexts discussing human nature are restricted to those implicit in common-sense language.

Therefore one can accept, as his own words show, Marx's "materialistic" position without resorting to the "philosophical clichés of the materialists about materia" (Mega 1/5, p. 83).

1.4.4   *Some additional methodological theses*

So far we have presented only one necessary tenet to our methodological position.

We will summarize some other theses briefly here.

1. The point of departure for societal analysis is the daily life process, a process of production through which the existent is transformed. This process can be subdivided into the production of material objects ("material" in the sense of threedimensional, solid, enduring), the production of knowledge and ideas, and of social institutions. One task is to identify the producers, the "raw material", the tools or means and the products. Another task is to analyze the relation between the various processes of production. A third is to identify the "driving forces" behind ongoing change, i.e.,

social conflicts organized around groups and classes, e.g., those stemming from the distribution of scarce resources.

All of these producing and transforming activities can be comprehended under the label "praxis", a term which must be analyzed further. This thesis as stated here is opposed to methodological idealism.

2. Praxis is the process of transformation and transcendence. What means are utilized in this process? In answering this question we take recourse to the early Hegel as interpreted by Habermas (1968a). The latter speaks of three media: *work, language and morals* (Sittlichkeit). In work man's dependence on nature is manifested, and through labour, used in the Marxian sense of the "material" process of production, man and society are produced and reproduced. Language signifies man's dependence on man. Through language human interaction is instigated and made possible. Work and interaction are indissolubly related to each other. Through morals as manifested in politics and power finally, man's dependence on common goals and the means to reach them is manifested.[18]

Again work and morals are closely intervowen, as are language and morals.

This thesis is opposed to an atomistic scientific position, one that disregards interrelationships within a totality, as well as against a position which excludes values and, therefore, morals from the domain of science.

3. Language in the previous thesis was viewed as a means of praxis. Work and morals can be viewed both as general forms of praxis, *and* as historically concrete processes. The same holds true for language. The concrete social processes, e.g., the daily production of our life, presupposes language as a means of interaction. Language, on the other hand could not provide meaning for what we do and think if it were not related to these concrete manifestations of general praxis. Thus, there is a close interrelationship between language and its general logic and other concrete social processes. This leads to another consequence. Language is not only about the social world; it is an integrated part of it. To deny this is to uphold an "*artificiality* between social reality and the language of description of social reality. The language is constitutive of the reality, it is essential to its being the kind of reality it is". (Ch. Taylor 1971–72, p. 24, my ith.)

Being a user of language is as constitutive for man as being user of tools. Both are necessary for the production of life and the reproduction of the species. This thesis is opposed to a dualistic position in which language and reality are set apart.

4. The use of language presupposes intersubjective understanding. Speaking a language means to have shared meaning. If I tell a small child: "Don't take this toy, it does not belong to you", he rarely will ask "what does it mean 'it belongs' ". If he has not yet learned what it means to say "it belongs", he will learn it through my and his own actions, i.e., through interaction. This is just another way of saying what has been asserted in thesis 3: Language and concrete social processes are interrelated. At the level of the individual this means that language in terms of speech acts and acting in general cannot be separated.

Various explanations have been proposed regarding this presupposed intersubjectivity. Schutz (1950) speaks of common-sense language as comprising concepts which function as preconstituted types. As a consequence, he speaks of "typification" as the process of assuring the intersubjectivity of meaning. Wittgenstein, holds that if people use language in order to say what is true and false and to reach agreement, this agreement is not a matter of opinion but an agreement "in form of life" (1958, §241). Zinkernagel (1962), maintains that there exists a basic and general logic of language, composed of rules which we must follow, if we want to speak in a meaningful and non-self-contradictory way. Originally he called these rules "conditions for description" and maintained they could not be explained. Neither could it be explained why we follow them since all the explanations presuppose these very rules. What we can do, however, as pointed out before is to "test" the validity of these rules by violating them. We have already in section 1.3.4 and 1.3.5, presented an introductory discussion of problems connected with "conditions for description", and we will return to this problem several times. Here we may restrict ourselves to stating that a general logic of language provides the means to intersubjectivity, which then can be presupposed for all social action. If this is so, it will have deep-going consequences for the social sciences. The thesis concerning a general logic of language can be called "the principle of methodological socialism", as opposed to the "principle of methodological solipsism". This second principle, which accepting perception and sense-experience

as the basis of knowledge, states that we are in principle locked up
in our private world, though intersubjectivity may be established in
terms of conventions, etc. Our principle in contrast makes language
the basis of epistemology.[19]

5. It is a constituting characteristic of man that he is always
inside society. He cannot place himself outside as an disinterested
spectator. If he seems to be a disinterested spectator or tries to be
one, the very attitude itself is social in its origin, as well as with
regard to the consequences it may lead. That which is true for man
is also true for the social sciences, i.e., the sciences about man.
They not only are about society, they are a part of society, and
their specific scientific activities are regulated by social norms.
Therefore, the idea of a detached, neutrally observing social
science, discloses a lack of reflexion on its own positions and
activities. This thesis is directed against the central notions of a
positivistic social science.

6. As corollary to thesis 5 we repeat what we have said before.
The social sciences do not reflect the social world: they contribute
to its construction, maintenance, and change. This thesis is related
to an epistemological position that assumes knowledge in the sense
of cognition is a relation. A relation in which the subject is
cognitively productive and is, at the same time, a product of his
own creations. This thesis is directed against the notion that
knowledge is a reflection and, consequently, that interpretation of
Marxian epistemology which sees the process of obtaining knowledge as a reflection or mirroring.

7. Man as the object of the social sciences is not, and ought not
be treated as an object alone. He is an object and at the same time
a subject. One of the reasons for this has been stated before: The
knowledge I have that I am a person, presupposes that there exist
others about which the same can be said. To deny this amounts to
saying that I know I am a person, but I do not know whether the
same can be said of others.

To be a person means being able to use language to act, to
think, and to relate oneself cognitively to the world. In other words;
to be a person, as stated here, means to be a subject. But I am not
only an active or acting person. I am also the *object* of others'
actions. Thus I am an object as well as a subject.

It is a central methodological standpoint of a positivistic social
science to view the *object* of its study, namely man, as an *object*

and nothing more. The extreme of this position is expressed in the metaphysics of behaviourism. To view and to treat man only as an object, not only has consequences for the results of science, which necessarily become distorted (e.g., one may observe the verbal responses of others without investigating their meaning). It also has consequences for the way the social sciences are conducted. If we accept that the other is a subject, we must concede to him the right of reciprocity, since our actions carried out in the name of scientific research will affect him. Therefore, if we view man as an object only scientific research will, in the long run, amount to the manipulation of others. In other words social scientific research cannot be divorced from political and moral considerations.

8. As a consequence of our previous thesis, we claim that a social science which at the same time is not also *moral* (or political) science, is a contradiction *in adjecto*. And by "moral science" I do not mean a science which only analyzes moral language and/or observes moral action from a detached, elevated position, for in this case it *has* accepted the view of the other as an object only. But this also is a moral position, as we can observe, ending up in manipulative social technology. Our claim also implies that moral and political values cannot be eliminated from the social scientific endeavour.[20]

9. We have previously (p. 37) spoken of the human predicament of relating ourselves cognitively and interpretatively to a world existing independently of ourselves. Thus our relation to the world is intrinsic and intentional. But saying this does not imply that the ways we relate ourselves to the world are subjective, i.e., only understandable from the point of view of the cognitizing subject's situation. This situation is important, but the cognitizing subject is a social subject. He is an element in a network of relations existing within a historically and socially formed structure. The fact that language presupposes, and makes possible, intersubjectivity is one reason why we cannot restrict our epistemological analysis to the description of the acting and cognitizing subject's own situation, as described by him. Also, his own situational description is a socially determined description. As a consequence, epistemological problems are the problems of the already socialized individual. In the following chapters we will return to our methodological rules within various contexts. We will also add some others, but this can only be done after we have presented the central ideas of dialectics.

NOTES

1. A.N. Whitehead has launched an interesting attack against traditional ontological conceptions of materialism. He was convinced, that in spite of the enormous development in modern physics our common sense thinking was, and still is, strongly influenced by classical mechanical materialism. Though his reasoning sometimes is difficult to follow it is worthwhile to know some of his arguments, especially what he terms the *fallacy of simple location* and the *fallacy of misplaced concreteness*. (1948, p. 50, ff.). His position though being not dialectical, touches some of the presuppositions of dialectical thinking. Therefore we will present him here briefly.

When one speaks of matter or material, Whitehead asserts, one usually commits the *fallacy of simple location*. "By simple location I mean one major characteristic which refers equally both to space and time ... the characteristics common both to space and time is that material can be said to be *here* in space and *here* in time, or here in space-time, in a perfectly definite sense which does not require for its explanation any reference to other regions of space-time" (op. cit., p. 50). Thus the idea of the "material" or "matter" as a substance presupposes the assumption of something—*a thing*—being simply located here and now.

What notions does the fallacy of simple location exclude? If "material" or "matter" is characterized by simple location in *time*, i.e., *now*, it excludes the notion of ongoing processes, being of importance for dialectical thinking.

Since "matter" or "material" is the ultimate substance it cannot itself undergo an evolution (Whitehead, òp. cit., p. 109). Time is accidental and external to the configurations of "matter". The configurations exist at each instant and the world becomes a succession of instantaneous configurations.

If "material" or "matter" is characterized by simple location in *space*, i.e., *here*, such a notion excludes the idea of an organism or a structured configuration, a whole, being itself part of larger "organisms" which in turn are organized in still larger configurations. Thus it excludes the notion of the "whole", of "totality", of "structured systems" being composed of sub-systems in an hierarchical or another order.

Again, the notion of totality is, as we will see (p. 62), basic to dialectical thinking.

The idea of simple location is only understandable as a highly abstract construction. Let us take the notion of space. In the context of simple location space is not understood as an organizing principle but in either of two ways: (1) as a substance, e.g., a kind of ether in which all things are emerged or (2) which probably is more usual, as a quality which material bodies have in common, e.g., the quality of expansion. To think, however, of space in either of the two mentioned ways is an highly *abstract* construction, being mistaken for a *concrete* fact. Whitehead, therefore, talks about the "*fallacy of misplaced concreteness*" (op. cit., p. 52).

In addition to the presupposition of simple location, there are two other assumptions underlying this type of materialism: the notion of substance and of quality. "It is the way in which we think of things, and without these ways of thinking we could not get our ideas straight for daily use", Whitehead admits (op. cit., p. 53). Nevertheless the two terms are highly abstract, but considered to be highly concrete. There seems to be two ways of looking at reality. One is characterized by the search for *substances* and *entities* as well as *qualities*. The other is characterized by the search for *processes, functions* and *relations.*

These two contrasting ways of looking at reality could be characterized, on the one hand, as a *static, atomistic, substantial* view of the world, and as a *dynamic, holistic, relational process* view, on the other. These problems will be dealt with in the second chapter. So far it may be sufficient to say that the first view puts emphasis on substances and attributes, on logical orders and systems of categorization. The other stresses processes, transformations, interactions leading to change, and dialectical relations.

Whitehead adds that the ontological position of mechanical materialism has been outdated by the achievements of modern physics and biology, as represented in the doctrines of evolution, of energy and by the molecular theories. Whereas traditional materialism was in agreement with common-sense thinking "the new situation in the thought of today arises from the fact that scientific theory is outrunning common sense" (op. cit., p. 115).

2. Logical positivists endorse a methodological rule asserting that a statement is meaningful if, and only if, it can be empirically verified. Its meaning *is* the way it is verified. This is a rather restricted way of talking about "meaning". Another broader use of the term equates it with "sense". A statement has "meaning" or "makes sense" in a specific context in which it is used. An order given by an officer has "meaning" for soldiers when they understand it. A prayer has "meaning" in a religious context, etc.

3. Different versions of "materialism" and of the identity thesis as well as arguments in support of it, can be found in D.M. Rosenthal, op. cit. A critical analysis of the thesis is presented by Ch. Taylor, 1967.

4. The term "epistemology" is often used in two senses. In the first sense, usually employed in French discourses, it refers to what in Anglo-Saxon literature is often called "philosophy of science". It is mainly concerned with conditions of obtaining scientific knowledge. In the second sense it refers to what in German is called "Erkenntnisstheorie". It refers to problems of the possibility of knowledge in general (not only scientific knowledge). In this use of the term it is difficult to separate epistemology proper from linguistics and the theory of language. We will use the term in the second sense, as "theory of knowledge". The German distinction between "Wissen", i.e., knowledge, and "Erkenntnis", i.e., the process of cognitizing by which knowledge is produced, will be taken up in chapter 4.

5. Feyerabend (1975) has a long and interesting analysis of Galilei's defence of the heliocentric view in spite of common sense and contemporary scientific resistance which seemed unable to differentiate between "apparent" movement and "real" movement. In his analysis, Feyerabend shows how Galilei tried to defend his view by refuting the "tower

argument" (a stone thrown down from a tower), and how he violated all those rules which today are declared as necessary for guaranteeing "Science" and the scientific business by Popper and by positivists.

6. Assume a person would maintain that the world is a dream. Assume furthermore that we would take a bat and hit him over the head. We would then ask him: "Have you been hit? And was it by an object? Or was it just a dream?" If he would still maintain that it was a dream, we could continue hitting him. He probably would say "stop my head is hurting". We could then respond that in order to feel pain in the head, one has to admit that at least the head is not a dream, etc. Would that not constitute an empirical test? I think one has to be pretty stubborn, and/or unreasonably convinced about the thesis of the world being a dream in order to deny that this would be an empirical test.

7. The refutations of the idealistic epistemological position have been numerous in philosophy. There is G.H. Moore's famous analysis (1922) and Bertrand Russell's refutation of Bishop Berkeley's version of idealism (1968). In short, the position held by Berkeley is that there is nothing in the world except minds, and that it is impossible to know anything else than our ideas. This argument, as Russell showed, does not distinguish between the act of apprehending something and that which is apprehended, between consciousness and the object of consciousness. It uses the expression "being in the mind", in an ambiguous way. As Russell argued, in his essay published in 1912, to say that "I have a certain person in my mind" refers to the thought of the person, but not to the person himself.

Another refutation of idealism has been given by P. Zinkernagel (1962). We will make ample use of his arguments.

8. In his *Philosophical Investigations* (1958) L. Wittgenstein says: "The essential thing about private experience is really not that each person possesses his own exemplar, but that nobody knows whether other people also have *this* or something else. The assumption would thus be possible—though unverifiable—that one section of mankind had one sensation of red and another section another" (p. 95).

9. The relation of interdependence is often symmetrical, but does not always need be so. The relation between the concept of "person" and the concepts "states of consciousness" and "intentions" respectively, is symmetrical. We cannot talk of a person without states of consciousness or intentions whatsoever (though we can in an abnormal situation, where somebody is in a deep state of coma or is "brain-dead"), and we cannot talk about states of consciousness and intentions without ascribing them to persons.

The interdependence of the concept "person" and the concept "body" is not symmetrical. If we, however, talk about a "human living body" the relation becomes symmetrical.

10. The reasoning in this section, as well as in the previous one, is heavily influenced by my discussions with Dr. Peter Zinknagel, though eventual mistakes are mine.

11. The observant reader may have recognized that I have shifted from using the word "true" to the word "correct". The reason is that later

on there will be a distinction introduced, such that we will talk about "true statements" only when they, according to accepted decision procedures, have been proved to be so. The expression "correct statements" will be used for such propositions whose denial would be meaningless. Furthermore, the knowledge of "correct" is seen as a precondition for developing decision procedures for the judgment of true propositions. Thus, "correct" in this sense is a more basic notion than "true".

12. A similar idea is expressed by Volosinov (1973): "Thus side by side with the natural phenomena, with the equipment of technology, and with articles for consumption, there exists a special world—*the world of signs*", and furthermore, "Every ideological sign is not only a reflection, a shadow, of reality, but is also itself a material segment of that very reality ...", and finally, "*consciousness itself can arise and become a viable fact only in the material embodiment of signs*". (p. 10 and 11).

13. The view of alternative scientific theories and meta-theories has been developed, e.g., by A. Naess (1972) and P. Feyerabend (1975). Naess thus writes: "Whatever the proofs put forth for the impossibility of a kind of happening or process or thing, do not always reject an invitation to inspect an argument for its existence: it may exist. Anything is possible" (p. 76). This antidogmatic fanfare is similar to Feyerabend's "Everything goes". The difference between them seems to lie in the fact that Naess does not as radically question the very notion of "science". Both, however, can be viewed as opponents to Kuhn's notion of a "normal science" (1962).

14. " 'Materialism' or 'realism' will refer to any consistent doctrine of the objective world *external* to cognition, ontologically and epistemologically prior to cognition" (R.S. Cohen 1963, p. 105, our ith).

We will later on argue that the epistemological position we assume excludes the notion of *external* world, but not of a world *independent* of the subject. To avoid misunderstanding we will not talk about "internal" and "external", but about "intrinsic" and "extrinsic".

15. Hegel saw a basic contradiction between the Spirit's tendency to perfection and its attempt to achieve self-consciousness. The Spirit had to externalize ("entäussern") itself and to become embodied. But since the externalization destroyed its unity and therefore its perfection, the Spirit tried to overcome this alienation and to return to unity. Then this dialectical process would be repeated on a higher level, where the goal of self-consciousness demanded externalization which conflicted with the strivings for perfection.

16. We do not, however, totally exclude historical relativism, implying that, due to an epistemological revolution, which in turn can be the consequence of scientific discoveries, our world picture and ideas concerning necessary basic conditions, may change.

17. "The difference between Marxist and bourgeois philosophy does not concern the metaphysical quandary whether consciousness precedes matter or vice versa: on the contrary, the difference is between dynamic, creative philosophy which explains man's making of himself by making the object and contemplative philosophies which contrapose an abstract subject to an abstract object, both equally inert" (P. Piccone 1971, p. 16).

18. Mao Tse-tung speaks of three means for praxis: Work, scientific experiments, and class-struggle. Class-struggle is the manifestation of what we called morals: the goals to abolish the exploitation of man by man and to assure the creation of a socialist society with its moral goals.

19. Wittgenstein has argued that intersubjectivity can be explained in terms of "obeying or following rules". It does not make sense to talk about obeying or following a rule only once in one's life, or that it would be possible for *one* man only to do it (1958, §199). See also P. Winch (1958) about this problem. Apel (1972) defines methodological solipsism as "the *apriori presupposition* that one person alone could follow a rule".

20. The claim that social science is at the same time a moral science can even be analyzed by departure from our second thesis, where morals has been analyzed in terms of a means for praxis and as a consequence of man's dependence on common goals. The moral nature of social science cannot be established by empirical scientific methods. It has to be accepted as a methodological rule. To deny this is self-contradictory: To say, my way of conducting science is not political *is*, in itself, a political (and/or moral) position, which usually (indirectly) gives support to the existing power structure.

Many Marxists assert that *all* science is class-related: The results of scientific activity depend on the class-belongingness of those who conduct science. This thesis can both be false and correct.

It is false if it is maintained that *all* science and its results are a consequence of the factual class-belongingness of those who have produced it, since *everything* we say, and think is a consequence of class-belongingness. To state it in this way is to beg the question: If everything we do is class-related how should we be able to show that such may not be the case.

In addition, if everything, including all the statements we pronounce, is class-related, i.e., relative to the class-belongingness of the person who pronounces it, what then is this very statement? If it is class-related it cannot be generally true, but only valid within the borders of a certain class. If it is not generally true, the question becomes why we should accept it.

Thus, we must accept that certain statements are generally true (which is a consequence of the position discussed in section 1.3.4 and 1.3.5), independently of class-belongingness. If this is so, we can meaningfully assert that *some* knowledge is class-related. This would hold especially for social scientific knowledge, because society is so complex, that any description we give of it can easily become class-related. Therefore, it would be incorrect to deny that much scientific work has been produced for, or has been used or abused by, a ruling class.

2: On Dialectics

Der Mensch realisiert sich, d.h. er vermenschlicht sich in der Geschichte. Die Spannweite dieser Realisierung ist so riesenhaft, dass der Mensch sein eigenes Tun als *unmenschlich* charakterisieren kann, obwohl er weiss, dass unmenschlich nur der Mensch zu handeln vermag.

Karel Kosik

2.1 SUMMARY

In the last chapter, we tried to argue that the discussion concerning materialism and idealism touches three problem areas: Ontological, epistemological, and methodological. This distinction, however, is purely analytical. In a meta-theoretical discourse the problem areas are closely interrelated. Thus, if one takes a definite stand, e.g., regarding ontological problems, one establishes logical connections to the other problem areas. This should be understood such that one is not necessarily forced, in taking one definite position, to also accept another one. The acceptance of one position usually *excludes* the possibilities of certain others, but does not necessarily imply one definite choice. This is just an application of the principle of negativity.

When we, on the ontological level, reject dualism, e.g., the body–mind dualism, we cannot, on the epistemological level, accept a sharp dualism between subject and object and base epistemological analysis on perception and sense-data. But, if we accept, e.g., the use of language as the basis for epistemological inquiry, then we cannot uphold an ontological dualism between language and reality. Rejecting certain ontological and epistemological positions has immediate effect on the methodological level. The rejection of the body–mind dualism obviously has compelling consequences for the methodology of psychology. The rejection of the sharp distinction between subject and object on the epistemological level, excludes positivistic methodologies in sociology, as we tried to indicate in the last chapter.

In this chapter, we will have to show that dialectical thinking excludes the materialism-idealism dualism on the ontological level. Dialectics is based upon the notion of totality, a notion which is in need of clarification. The word "dialectics" is often used in a loose and ambiguous way. As a concept it is vague. This state of affairs prevents clear thinking. We, therefore, try to embark on a conceptual analysis in order to clarify what we are talking about. But this conceptual analysis leads us into a dilemma. Conceptual analysis cannot be carried out in a "dialectical way", because it is static and abstract. Therefore, we cannot *grasp* dialectics through conceptual analysis. On the other hand, we cannot *understand* dialectics without conceptual analysis. The use here of the words "grasp" and "understand" refers to Hegel's distinction between "Vernuft", i.e., reason, and "Verstand", i.e., understanding. We can reformulate our dilemma: in order to use dialectical *reason*, we have to *understand* the meaning of the basic concepts or categories of dialectics. But, in order to obtain an *understanding* of the meaning of its concepts, we have to *grasp* dialectics, i.e., the context in which the concepts are used. Now this *is* dialectics and, at the same time, it is what dialectics *is about*.

Dialectics begins with certain presuppositions. We will outline them. These presuppositions are concerned with the use of certain *basic categories*, namely, the categories of *totality*, *intrinsic relations*, *process*, and *relatedness*. These four categories can be more easily described with reference to what they negate. The category of totality negates the notions of dualism and atomism; the category of intrinsic relations negates the category of extrinsic relations; the category of process negates notions of an unchangeable, given structure; the category of relatedness, finally, negates a position favouring the treatment of social facts as things.

The four mentioned categories are all necessary to the language of dialectics and presuppose each other. The same can be said by maintaining that these four categories are complimentary to each other.

In the following pages each category is discussed, explicated, and its role for dialectical analysis demonstrated. "Totality" is analyzed in section 2.3. It is first shown that the categories of "totality" and of "concreteness" are interrelated. Marxian methodology is presented as an exemplification of this interrelation. The terms "concrete" and "abstract" are used, in a dialectical context, in a different way than their traditional use. "Concrete" means placing something in the context of a totality, and taking into consideration many determining characteristics and interrelations. "Abstract", in this context means to treat something as isolated from the context of totality. Marx's methodology assumes that science should present its results as "thought-concreteness". This term is discussed, and it is shown that it presupposes four pairs of notions: mode of inquiry and mode of presentation; appearance and essence; reason and understanding; and finally, the immediate given and the mediated.

Thereafter, we present the notion of a concrete totality and delimit it from other notions of totality. A central principle is stated. To view the world as a totality does not imply that we can have total knowledge of the world. It only implies, that the limited knowledge we may have, should be placed within the context of a totality.

In section 2.4, we treat the distinction between intrinsic and extrinsic relations. Traditional social science attempts to formulate its concepts such that it can establish relations between independent and separate variables, i.e., external or extrinsic relations. Dialectics, on the other hand, is based on the category of intrinsic relations. Another principle is stated: All dialectical relations are intrinsic relations, but the reverse does not hold true. Intrinsic relations are characterized by their relata being separate but interdependent, in an opposing and complimentary way, and in that they form a unity or totality. Dialectical relations, in addition to the mentioned characteristics, are such that the relata are contradictory in either of two ways, and, at the same time, have something in common and, in this sense, are identical. This leads to a detailed discussion of the notion of identity. Before that, the opinion that intrinsic relations are logical-conceptual relations only is rejected. If it were accepted, a dualism between language and reality would have to be introduced, a dualism which we must reject.

The discussion of "identity" is central in this chapter. A distinction is made between the notions of, "to identify something *with*" and, "to identify something *as*," and their interrelationship. Acknowledging this important distinction not only overcomes a traditional ambiguity in our use of the concept "identity", but also leads to deep-going consequences for defining what it means "to use language".

In section 2.5 the notion of "process" is analyzed. It is shown that process refers to change, transformation, and transcendence. This notion of transcendence, which is of central importance for dialectical thinking, has been analyzed previously in section 2.4, where, also, the notion of a dialectical movement is clarified. This clarification is now applied in the analysis of process. Process as transcendence is praxis. It is shown that praxis is a central concept in dialectical thinking, and that it has a meaning different from usages in everyday language. It is understood as the dialectical unity of producer and product, subject and object, determining and determined. These problems are dealt with in an extended way.

Thereafter, it is shown that praxis cannot be reduced to work or to production. Instead, work, in the sense of the process of production, language, in the sense of communication and precondition for communication, as well as morals, are viewed as basic aspects of praxis. It is finally shown, that praxis has an ontological, as well as, an epistemological reference.

The last problem discussed in this section is concerned with one aspect of dialectical process, namely, inversion. This means that praxis not only produces the transcendence of the given, but that in this process, subject and object are inverted. This is clarified by reference to Hegel's master-slave relation, and to Marx's notions of the fetishism of commodities, and reification.

In section 2.6, finally, the category of relatedness is discussed. It is shown that Hegel and Marx used the notion of "category" differently from the way Kant used it. They consider a category as an historically limited way of determining our thought and language. As such, a category is itself an aspect of reality, though only in a one-sided and abstract way. Thus, our rejection of the dualism between language and reality is viewed from another angle. Reality is the unity of the world of objects and the social world, which, though different, are in certain aspects identical.

Relatedness, then, is the attempt to analyze societal phenomena not in terms of things, but in terms of relations and their relations to other relations. Thus, it is shown, that the category of, e.g., "capital", is not a thing, but contains in itself many relations. When it is related to other categories, i.e., "wage-labour", also is not a thing, but a category made up of many relations. Thus, an analysis of societal processes in terms of relatedness gives a rich and many-sided picture of relations that are related to each other.

It is then shown that the four categories: *totality, intrinsic relations, process, and relatedness*, are themselves interrelated, and make up the dialectical framework of dialectics.

In the final section, a distinction is made between the category of relatedness and the notion that social psychology should analyze persons, not in terms of properties, traits, and substances, but in terms of interactions and situations. Also, a distinction is introduced between societal and social relations. This distinction, and the relational rule, together, make it possible to formulate the task of a dialectical social psychology, and to delimit it from the meta-theory of behaviourism.

This chapter is central to the book. It is here that an attempt is made to clarify the basic and necessary categories of dialectics. At the same time, basic dialectical processes are explicated, and illustrations used to make these ideas concrete. The rest of this book depends on this chapter and, therefore, an understanding of it presupposes the comprehending of this chapter in its various aspects.

2.2 BASIC ASSUMPTIONS OF DIALECTICS

We start with an attempt to analyze and reflect about the preconditions of dialectical thinking. We do this in order to discover implicit assumptions of an ontological and epistemological kind.

Reflexions of this kind imply criticism, in the sense of opposing prevailing positions. These negate dialectical thinking and its preconditions.

Such criticism can be carried out in at least two ways: (1) Through rather detailed critical analysis of basic categories or concepts, each taken for itself. This is what analytical philosophy does and what gives it its strength in developing tools for semantic analysis and dissection. Through such an analysis, we may reveal the ambiguity and vagueness of our language, and dissolve misunderstanding and pseudo-problems; (2) Through a critical analysis of hidden or explicit, often normative, presuppositions of a given theory viewed as a totality (see, e.g., J. Israel 1972).

These two types of criticism combined, may help us to *understand* what we are talking about, e.g., when we talk about dialectics. They may, however, not be sufficient in helping us *grasp* how that we talk about is related, forms a whole, and, what is especially important, which obstacles may be encountered in the functioning of a whole. Thus, a *second type* of criticism must be employed, reflecting about obstacles and constraints existing as human products, leading to "distorting pressures to which individuals or a group of individuals, or the human race as a whole, succumb in their process of self-formation" (P. Connerton 1976, p. 20).

In order to *grasp* how what we talk about functions, and the categories we want to understand, we ought to look at the obstacles that prevent functioning in the intended way. This is another aspect of the principle of negativity (see p. 30), as well as an emphasis on the inclusion of values, in terms of future goals to be achieved.

This type of critical analysis, concentrating on an identifiable subject—individual as well as aggregates—is based upon notions of change and transcendence in two senses: it looks at constraints as processes, and it has the intention of contributing to their removal.

Since however, change, transformation, and transcendence has to be supplemented by continuity and preservation, a *third type* of criticism has to supplement the previous one.[1] It implies the *reconstruction* (see P. Connerton, op. cit.) of the preconditions of possible knowledge, which we use in order to understand, as well as to grasp, our subject of study. This kind of epistemological critical reconstruction has been attempted in the previous chapter by reference to a general logic of language. It will be taken up again in order to demonstrate the interconnectedness of dialectical thinking and common-sense language use.[2]

We will start with the analysis of four categories and presuppositions of dialectics and formulate them in two ways, namely, what they assert and what they, consequently, negate:

1. Dialectics begins with the category of *totality*. Hence it negates all kinds of dualistic bifurcations such as "material" and "spirit", "body" and "mind", "language" and "reality", etc.[3] Dialectical reasoning, however, operates with opposing concepts of the type mentioned above. But it treats them as different and interrelated relata in a dialectical relation which transforms them

into a unit or whole. Hence, the notion of totality does not imply that dialectical reasoning attempts to overcome a dualistic ontological position through a monistic reduction. Reduction implies the explanation of one phenomenon (e.g., mind), being conceptualized in one language (e.g., the language of psychology), in terms of the language employed for the analysis of the other phenomenon (e.g., body and the language of physiology).[4] Reduction also implies the substitution of dualistic notions by monistic ones. But dialectical thinking is not monistic. Dialectical reasoning attempts to transcend dualism as well as monism, by operating within a "unified" framework, one that presupposes the category of *totality*. What this unified framework and the category of totality refer to will be the task of our continued analysis.

2. As stated above, the rejection of dualism and monism implies that dialectics, can and must operate with *dual notions* designating opposites, such as "subject–object", "worker–capitalist", "psychological–physiological", etc. This utilization of opposites is basic to dialectical thinking. But it does not lead to dualistic theorizing, due to the specific way relations between opposites are conceptualized. Whereas in traditional empirical science, relations between those relata which make up the relation are conceptualized as *extrinsic* relations, in dialectical thinking they are conceptualized as intrinsic relations. This will be clarified in a very detailed way. In this introductory presentation, we just want to say that all dialectical relations are intrinsic relations but that the reverse does not hold true.

The category of totality, as unifying and being unified, presupposes the category of intrinsic relations.[5] On the other hand, intrinsic relations cannot be thought of independently of a totality or a whole.

3. The third category is concerned with the presupposition of basic units, by which the dialectical process is described. In every day language we speak about *things* and *relations* between things. If we analyze societal processes in a dialectical manner, however, the notion of "thing" has no predominant place. Instead, we think of the basic units of societal processes as relations, which in turn are interrelated with other relations. For example, in the Marxian analysis the notion of "capital" does not refer to a "thing", but contains several relations as "variable capital" vs "constant capital", and so on. All these relations are interrelated in

themselves and with their opposites. Thus a basic category in dialectical thinking and the analysis of societal processes is "relation" being (intrinsically or dialectically) related to other relations. This notion of the relation of relations will be called *relatedness*.

4. Relatedness as a basic category presupposes the category of *process*. A relation of a relation is something which goes on, which is changing and changed, transforming and transformed, transcending and transcended. The general category of process refers to all these notions. Opposed to a process view is a static structuring approach. Relatedness and process presuppose each other and both presupposes the notion of totality. Thus we can summarize: Dialectics is based upon the categories of *totality*, *intrinsic relations*, *relatedness*, and *process*, all of them are necessary and interrelated notions. Whether they also form *sufficient* presuppositions for dialectics cannot be stated. The use of dialectical thinking and the dialectical imagination will decide whether these four notions also are sufficient.

If we wish, we can characterize what these four categories refer to as the ontological preconditions of dialectics. It will now be our task to substitute the labels by an analysis which, hopefully, will allow us to present basic ideas of dialectics, *as well as* be dialectical itself in presentation.

2.3. TOTALITY

2.3.1 *Totality and concreteness*

In our daily activities, when we eat our food, when we perform our work, when we talk to others, when we, in general, do what we do daily, and in a routine manner, we usually do not reflect about what we do or about how we act. This, in fact, may be taken as a definition of "routine". Thus man is not primarily a being who reflects and speculates about the world, i.e., looks at it as something strange, in the way we do when we visit a foreign country with a "strange" culture.

Man, primarily, is an acting and language-using being, involved in his daily activities, guided by intentions, desires, goals, inclinations, and purposes. In addition, all his actions form part of a social network with a history of its own that is continuously changing.

Thus man in his daily life is an active and acting being. His notions of the world are intimately related to his daily experiences. This, I think, is the idea Marx wanted to stress when he criticized the epistemological position of Feuerbach in his well-known 11th thesis: "The chief defect of all previous materialism (including Feuerbach's) is that the thing, reality, sensuousness, is conceived only in the form of the object or the perception (Anschauung), but not as a *sensuous human activity*, as praxis; not subjectively" (Mega 1.5).

For Marx, the analysis of the process of producing knowledge has to be based upon the actions of the common man, on his daily praxis. This means, also, that the subject's role in this process is stressed. The ambiguous expression "not subjectively" can be interpreted in this sense. It is the actions of the human *subject* which form the basis for the analysis, but not an autonomous, isolated, subject. It is rather the already socialized subject whose actions are social actions. Therefore, Marx rejects the idea of basing an analysis of the process of the production of knowledge on perception. Perception is in essence private, whereas action, and especially language-acts, are public and social.

Thus we can summarize: Man, as an acting and language-using subject, in his concrete daily activities, must be taken as the basis in all analysis of the process of knowledge. Further he must be seen in a double sense: as the producer and, at the same time, as the product of his own production.

We have used the phrase "concrete daily activities". What does the word "concrete" mean here?

Traditionally, for example in the language of analytical philosophy, the word "concrete" designates well delimited details that are often presented as isolated *facts* taken out of their context. The word "abstract", on the other hand, usually then refers to general characteristics which can be established by ignoring the specific and the detailed.

In Hegel's language—and Marx followed Hegel in this respect—the words "concrete" and "abstract" are used differently and, in fact, in the opposite sense. The word "concrete" designates that which is presented (or presents itself) within a totality, that which is distinguished by its many determining and defining characteristics (Bestimmungen). The word "abstract", on the other hand, designates that which has been taken out of its constituting context and isolated. It is analyzed, talked about, or perceived, as something "for itself".[6] Thus a single thing, taken out of its context, is in this language characterized as "abstract".[7]

In order to understand something as something specific, it has to be taken out of its context. The context not only provides the background against which the single thing stands as a figure. The meaning which we assign to something making it something specific, and our perception of it as something specific, this meaning is also conveyed within and through the context.

Thus, Marx asserted that we move from the concrete whole to the isolated and, in this sense, abstract. The starting point is the concrete whole of phenomena. In other words, we face, in our daily activities, a concrete reality produced by man in two senses: through his hands and through the ways we talk about it. The point of departure thus is, to speak in Marxian terms, *empirical concreteness:* The common-sense world of our daily practical activities, according to Marxian methodology, also holds as starting point for the activities of science.

Scientific activity, as a process of production of knowledge, has been analyzed by Marx (1953) as comprising *three steps*, which in turn can be divided into *two movements* or *phases*. The first step is the description of concrete reality in its appearance, i.e., how I observe it empirically. Marx using an example from economics, says: "If I therefore start with the population it would be a chaotical representation of the whole and through closer determining definitions I would analytically more and more reach simpler concepts; from the conceived concrete to increasingly thinner abstracta until I would arrive at the simplest determining characteristics" (op. cit., p. 21).

Thus, the two first steps comprise the movement from the unsystematic, but not unorganized, level of empirical concreteness, to the level of abstraction. Traditionally social science sets a stop here. This is probably due to the fact that abstractions, as mentioned before, are conceived as general and valid concepts for the description of the more detailed concrete conditions. One reason for this is an inherent *atomistic* position. Inquiry begins with facts, the immediate given, conceived of as isolated phenomena or events. Through abstraction one then attempts to construct interrelations between independent and isolated facts.[8]

The alternative position starts with the notion of an organized, though so far unsystematically, totality, in which things are related to each other. However, it is not yet understood how these interrelations are formed, or how they function. This is, as mentioned, the level of *empirical concreteness*.

The production of scientific knowledge moves from this first level through the level of abstraction to its third level. From "low down" in the thin spheres of abstraction, the travel goes upwards until one has ascended to a concrete level again (Marx, in fact, speaks of "ascendance" from the level of abstraction, whereas in the traditional use of the word, "abstract", is conceived as the most elevated). In Marx's own words, one has to travel "until I finally would arrive again at the population, but this time not by a chaotic presentation of the whole, but *a rich totality of many determining characteristics and relations*" (op. cit., p. 21, my ith).

The third level, then, can be called the level of *thought-concreteness*, as distinguished from the first level of *empirical concreteness*.

In the thought-process, the production of this totality—the thought-concreteness—is, or may be, experienced as the outcome of the whole process. But Marx asserts, that what *appears* as the outcome or the result of the process, is, in fact, its point of departure. Marx maintains this position because he does not accept dualistic notions concerning reality or our speaking and thinking about it. Knowledge is expressed in our language and is about reality (though it may not always be correct).

If the level of thought-concreteness is not the outcome, but the point of departure for the process of producing (scientific) knowledge, why, then, is it not directly accessible to the acting and perceiving individual?

The process of production of scientific knowledge, moving from the levels of empirical concreteness to abstraction, and from there to the level of thought-concreteness where it starts again, comprises not only three levels but also *two phases*. The first two levels, taken together, are called the "*mode of inquiry*" (Forschungsweise). The transition from the second to the third level—the level of thought concreteness—also implies the transition from the mode of inquiry to the second phase, the *"mode of presentation"* (Darstellungs-weise).

"Of course the mode of presentation must differ in form from that of inquiry. The latter has to appropriate the material in detail, to analyze its different forms of development, to trace their *inner connections*. Only after this work is done can the actual movement be adequately presented. If this is successfully achieved, then the life of materia is mirrored in ideas and therefore it may appear as if one had to do with an a priori construction" (K. Marx 1965 p. 27).

The task of social science is conceived as two-fold: inquiry and presentation. Presentation must be concrete, in the sense of placing the results of the inquiry into the context of totality and—which is in fact the most important task—in outlining the complex interrelations in terms of ongoing processes.

"The concrete is concrete because it is the summing up of many determining characteristics (Bestimmungen) and therefore the unity in the manifoldness" (K. Marx 1953, p. 21).

We can now view the object of inquiry as a totality of interrelated elements and look upon it from various angles and perspectives, bringing out the manifold determining characteristics and their interrelations.

Marx maintains furthermore that if this complex concrete totality would be available to common sense understanding, science would be superfluous.

The distinction between mode of inquiry and mode of presentation as well as the assertion that what seems to be the outcome of the scientific process is, in fact, its point of departure, has to be related to another distinction. We do not grasp the complex, concrete totality, from which we must start, because when we begin, we must distinguish between that which is *immediately given*, and that which is *mediated* through the process of inquiry. The immediately given are *appearances* or *manifestations*. The mediated, the produced, are the *essence*. Thus we must distinguish between appearance and essence.[9] This distinction is of fundamental significance for Hegelian-Marxian epistemology. It amounts to the rejection of an epistemological position based upon perception and sense-data.

2.3.2 *On appearance and essence*

In German the word "appearance" has a double meaning; the German word "Erscheinung" means "appearance" as well as "illusion". When is an appearance or phenomenon an illusion? I think Hegel's answer can be formulated as follows. If a person accepts the idea that what appears to us through perception is "true knowledge", then he nourishes an illusion. If he, on the other hand, is aware that appearance (or sense-data, if we want to use a more modern word) are just appearances, and do not give us knowledge which cannot be disputed, then he does not nourish any illusions.

Why then should appearances be illusions? Because they are, according to Hegel, constraints forced upon us be existing social and natural conditions. Reflection about that which is immediately given in appearance thus may have a liberating function. In this sense, reflexion becomes, as mentioned earlier (see p. 60), a form of criticism of the existent. If its essence is grasped we have a chance to overcome the constraints. Thus to the worker in a capitalist society, objectified labour, i.e., his labour transformed into objects which can be transformed into capital, does not appear as a power which may dominate him. Socially created constraints—through, e.g., indoctrination—may prevent him from understanding the *essential* nature of capitalism.

When he starts reflecting about what appears to him as given or "natural", then it loses its character of being immediately given and as such difficult to change. Instead it is understood as produced and therefore accessible to change. Reflexion becomes the process which amounts to stripping appearances of their character of "immediately given or accessible truths". It reveals them as *manifestations* of something more basic, namely, the essence. Essence in turn, cannot be grasped directly. It must be through a process of the production of knowledge in which reflexion about the immediately given is one important aspect. But, in order to be able to reflect, one has to understand, and to overcome, the constraints which the immediately given sets up for reflexion. That which is immediately given is unproblematic. It appears as self-evident. Overcoming this constraint of the given is to make what is unproblematic problematic. To make the self-evident questionable. (A similar position is found in the late Wittgenstein.)

Essential knowledge, hence, is not, and cannot be, immediate knowledge. It is knowledge mediated by a process of production of knowledge. It may demand straineous effort. Furthermore appearances, as manifestations, provide only isolated, i.e., abstract, fragments of knowledge. Grasping the essence is a consequence of the process of production of knowledge, where a totality with its many-sided interrelations is established. Thus, the distinctions between (1) "immediate" and "mediated"; (2) between "appearance" and "essence"; (3) "mode of inquiry" and "mode of presentation"; (4) "abstract" and "concrete", and (5) "reason" and "understanding", are all related.

In the process of production of knowledge, the *mode of inquiry* deals with *appearances*, which means the *immediately given*. It ends up in abstractions, i.e., isolated fragments of knowledge which only make possible *understanding*. Overcoming this constraint leads on to the next stage in the process of production of knowledge: the *mode of presentation*. Here, the *essential nature* of the things are presented. This means they are *mediated* by reflexion, which overcomes the disparate and isolated fragmentary knowledge, by putting it into the context of a *totality*. (This does not imply that we achieve total knowledge, but that the limited knowledge we have, is placed in the context of a totality with its interrelations.) This makes it possible to move from *understanding* through reflexion to *comprehension*. Through comprehension (reason) we grasp the essential nature of the totality.

The five pairs of interrelated concepts mentioned above, thus present themselves as opposed relata in a dialectical relation: they are different, but belong together and compliment each other. Their use amounts to, (1) A rejection of a phenomenalistic or sensualistic epistemology, i.e., one based on perception and sense experience. This does not, however, exclude empiricism. It only denies the supreme status of empirical data. It reduces them to the first stage of the process of production of (scientific) knowledge. (2) A rejection of an atomistic, inductive science, and its substitution by an emphasis on interrelated and many-sided determinations within the framework of a totality. (3) It places emphasis on the productive aspect. Knowledge is produced which, in turn, brings the subject into focus. Marx, as distinguished from

Hegel, saw as the central process of production what he called the process of "material production" or "the life process". But, he made it clear that this process is intimately related to the process of production of knowledge, two processes that can be analytically distinguished, but which, in fact, are closely interwoven.[10]

Let us, for a moment, apply the previous reasoning to society. If society, or the social world, is not something which is immediately given, then it is mediated, i.e., produced by man. But something which is produced can also be changed. It can no longer be conceived as something existing independently of the producing man, or as imposing on him the inner lawfulness of its own goals. The notion of active forces in society to which man is submitted—e.g., the notion of technology imposing its inherent goals upon us—can be revealed as an appearance whose essence is the process of reification, i.e., the transformation of man into an object. Furthermore, if we comprehend reification as a process inherent in the capitalistic system of production, we can also begin to grasp how by overcoming the posed constraints to change it. This presupposes understanding of the given as something produced, produced through praxis in all its forms. "When existence is revealed as mediated, it will be conceived as product" (H.J. Krahl 1970, p. 142).

We act upon the physical and the social world. We interfere, transform, and transcend. In doing this, we not only produce the physical and social world. We also produce new knowledge, which, in turn, can be employed in further transformations.

The production of knowledge is intimately related to other processes of production. It is not an arbitrary process. It is a relation between the producing subject and its object. In German, the word "object" can be translated into "Gegenstand", i.e., something standing against and opposite us, upon which we act. Therefore, that which stands opposite us is changed through our interference.

Assume you are standing in a locked room without having a key. You decide to thrust yourself against to door to force it open. "You have a sense of resistance and at the same time a sense of effort. There can be no resistance without effort; there can be no effort without resistance" we are told by Ch. S. Peirce (quoted after R. J. Bernstein 1965, p. 73). To put a shoulder against a locked door is a way of actively relating oneself—to make an effort—to something which stands against us—a "Gegenstand", or object which resists. Without acting through effort there would be no subject. But, there would be no effort without a resistance "standing against", i.e., that which makes an object into an object. By increasing our effort the door bursts open. The object is changed and so is the subject, since his efforts have to change.

The metaphor used by Peirce can now be applied to the production of knowledge. Knowledge can be viewed as a relation between an acting, producing subject and a continuously changing object. This relation is reciprocal. We not only act and produce, but are ourselves changed by the products of our production.

The close interrelation between various processes of production makes "praxis" a central notion for epistemology: "For man to be able to recognize how things are independently of himself, he has to subject them to his praxis; in order to determine how they are without his intervention he has to intervene into them" (K. Kosik 1967, p. 21).

The central role we attribute to praxis in knowledge and other production processes makes it necessary to analyze the concept. This will be done on p. 118.

Let us finish here with some remarks concerning the role of science. In the production of scientific knowledge we have distinguished: (1) between three levels, the level of empirical concreteness, of abstraction and of thought-concreteness; (2) between the mode of presentation and the mode of inquiry and (3) related this distinction to the one between the immediately given and the mediated, which is always produced.

The last mentioned distinction, again, is related to the distinction between appearance and essence.

Marx's conception of the role of science can be illuminated by a quotation: "All science would be superfluous when the form of appearance and the essence of things immediately would coincide" (1965 vol. III, p. 825). He also maintains, as mentioned before, that appearances are produced spontaneously, whereas the essence has to be discovered by means of scientific production of knowledge (see e.g., 1965 vol. I, p. 564).

There is one problem which these quotations raise, and which we want to discuss. When Marx speaks about the role of science, as compared to common sense, does he formulate some general conditions independent from given historical conditions?

In agreement with his thinking in general, Marx probably refers to the role of science in a given society, with a certain structure, and in a definite historical period. The sharp division between intellectual and manual work activities that characterize our social system, may be one of the historically specific conditions affecting the role of science. This division may prevent those restricted in their daily activities to manual work from carrying out the intellectual operations necessary to reaching the level of thought-concreteness. A consciousness-producing mass-media industry, may have an additional hampering effect. It may contribute to the transformation of the world of empirical concreteness into, what K. Kosik calls, a "world of pseudo-concreteness". Kosik also believes that this pseudo-concreteness can be destroyed by "a revolutionary-critical praxis of humanity, which is identical with the humanization of man ... the decisive steps of which are social revolutions" (op. cit., p. 19).

This societal division of labour also hampers those divorced from the manual activities of the process of material production, who deal only with intellectual activities. They tend to lose contact with central problems of the social world and their work may end up in abstract constructions. "Abstract" is here used in the Hegelian sense of being isolated from, and taken out of, the context of the totality of the social world. They also face the difficulty of getting at "the essence".

Why is this so? Because essence cannot be established in a contemplative or speculative manner within the confines of an ivory-tower; or in the disengaged manner of a posivistic scientific establishment, which is aloof to its "objects".

In order to reach "the *essential*", social science must be more than *about* the social world. It must be a part of it, both as producer and product of the ongoing change in this world. Furthermore, it must be aware of this role and actively accept it, in order to get at the essence.

Thus, as a consequence of the historically developed division of labour, some people are engaged in the daily practical activities of the process of material production. This is the majority. Others are engaged in the process of production of knowledge. But praxis, as the activity of change, requires the unification of practical and theoretical activities.

So far, we have tried to present some of the problems of totality on the *methodological level.* We gave an indication of the process of production of knowledge as a movement, from empirical concreteness, via abstraction to thought-concreteness and, from there again, on to higher levels of empirical concreteness This implies in spite of the fact that we, as mentioned before, are unable to obtain total knowledge, should strive to place the knowledge we can produce within the frame of concrete totality. This will illuminate its manifold determining characteristics and interrelations.

The *principle of methodological totality* presupposes that we reject ontological atomism and replace it with an ontological holism. We will discuss this problem next. There remains, also the problem of totality on the epistemological level, which we will return to later on.

2.3.3   *Concrete totality*

The prior analysis, concerning the production of scientific knowledge discussed methodological problems such as the distinction between the mode of inquiry and the mode of presentation. Implied in the notion of the process of production of scientific knowledge as a movement, where empirical concreteness via abstraction is *transformed* into thought-concreteness, is the ontological notion of totality. The answer to the question: "what is reality" presupposes, and affects epistemological principles and methodological rules. *Reality has to be conceived as a concrete totality.* This means that it is (1) organized and structured as a whole; (2) the structure is built up hierarchially and comprises sub-totalities (cell, human organism, family, class, nation, etc., are exemplifications of possibilities for hierarchical structuring within a totality), (3) that it is not unchangeable, but undergoing a continuous process of transformation, a well as, of transcendence; (4) that it is produced, and that it is producing within itself; (5) that its organization does not imply a harmonious co-operation or co-ordering of sub-totalities or elements within this totality, but rather, the existence of contradictions, viewed as "the driving forces" of change, transformation, and transcendence.

In this short account, we can recognize that the notion of totality presupposes the notion of process. If we confine ourselves to the totality of the social world which we will do here, we can view it as something given and at the same time, as a historical process "the product of man acting on antecendent natural surroundings" (M. Marković 1974, p. 28). One could, therefore, speak of "totality" as an ongoing process of "totalization", in which the given is transformed and transcended.[12]

In order to clarify the implications of the postulate of concrete totality, we will try to outline what it negates, and which philosophical positions it excludes.

2.3.4 What the notion of concrete totality negates

On the ontological level this postulate negates all kinds of dualism, i.e., the bifurcation of the world into sharply separated and extrinsically related entities or events.[13]

Furthermore, it negates atomism. Atomism starts from simple elements and tries to build up increasingly complex systems through ordering, categorizing, and relating these elements. Atomism can be reversed into a holism which is, however, basically different from the notion of concrete totality. This holistic approach starts from the whole "viewed as the outcome of some sort of emergence, vaguely conceived as a law of nature and not further analyzed" (J. Piaget 1971, p. 8). Let me exemplify this. Assume a social–psychological study of dyads where certain regularities are formulated as a "law". Assume that this "law" also holds if we add a third and fourth person to the dyad. If we add a fifth person, however, the "law" breaks down, and a new law has to be formulated. We thus have a state of *explanatory emergence*. The new "law" emerged as a consequence of the totality comprising five interacting persons.[14]

Thus, "emergence" here means that the whole adds some new characteristics to the elements, which cannot be explained in terms of the functioning of the parts. They "emerge spontaneously", as a consequence of the functioning of the whole.

This notion contradicts the idea of dialectics concerning a whole which is produced and produces itself. (The social world is a product and produces its producers).

Whereas in atomism, the characteristics of the whole emerge as a consequence of the relations between parts, in this "false" holism, the process is only reversed. Parts receive characteristics which they do not have as isolated elements. Emergence thus is taken for granted.

On the *epistemological* level, the notion of totality negates the position that knowledge is a summation of facts. As a consequence, it is maintained that we, for that reason, can never give a total description of reality. There are always additional facts which can be added. We have already given reasons—in terms of innumerable ways of relating oneself to reality—for the claim that a total description of any sub-totality or reality is not possible. But this does not imply, as Popper, Hayek, and others maintain, that the ontological position of a concrete totality is mysticism (see, e.g., K. Popper 1957).

"The dialectics of the concrete totality is not a method which naively pretends to grasp in a definite way *all* aspects of reality and to present a 'total' picture of reality" (K. Kosik op. cit., p. 37).

Totality is not the sum of all facts. Summing up facts does not, as such, give knowledge of the world. The postulate of the concrete totality implies that the limited number of facts we have of the world can only be transformed into knowledge that *grasps* the world, as opposed to merely *understanding* it, when these facts are placed within the context of a structured concrete totality.

Another type of totality is criticized by K. Kosik (1967, p. 57–8), where one, as in the structuralist interpretation of Marxism, views the world as the sum or configuration of autonomous structures influencing each other. In this case, man, as the acting concrete subject, the "executor" of praxis has been substituted by "a mythologized, reified, fetishized subject: the autonomous movement of the structure" (ibid).

The double movement from the producer to the produced, and from the produced to the producer, where man is the creator, has been substituted by "simple" or complicated movements "of autonomous structures, i.e, by the products by means of the reification of tangible-intellectual human work" (ibid).[15]

On the methodoligical level, the idea of a concrete totality cannot be reduced to such banalities as the statements: the whole is more than the sum of the parts, or that in a whole everything is related to each other. (For a semantic analysis of the term "totality", as used in a more traditional contexts, see E. Nagel 1968.)[16]

2.3.5   *The developing concrete totality*

Though we must in our thinking presuppose the totality as given, dialectical thinking cannot take this *given* totality as *unchanging*. The given totality has *become* what it is, and continues to develop. Marx expressed this idea in the following way: "When in the accomplished bourgeois system every economic condition presupposes the other in the bourgeois-economical form and if thus everything posited at the same time is a precondition, such is the case with every organic system. This organic system itself as a totality consists exactly in the subordination of all society's elements under it or in the creation out of itself of those organs, which still are missing. In such a way it becomes historically a totality" (1953, p. 189).

The phrase "out of itself" should perhaps be replaced by "within itself" in order to avoid any structuralistic misinterpretation.

This process, the production of the totality, cannot be grasped if one holds an ontological position in which knowledge of reality is understood as the knowledge of the sum of a progressively increasing number of interrelated facts. There stands the notion of a linear adding of facts, which at a certain point, may lead to a restructuring as against the notion of a concrete totality. Here, a given fact is a relative point of departure which has to be placed within the context of the whole, in order that its meaning and function can be grasped.

Kosik (op. cit., p. 45), points out that there are three basically different conceptions of totality:

(1) the atomistic-rationalistic conception, which understand the totality as a system of simple elements or facts (a conception inherent in a tradition reaching from Descartes to the Wittgenstein of the "Tractatus");

(2) the organismic and organismic-dynamical conception, either in the Aristotelian version where the world is understood as a purposive, anthropomorphistic whole, and everything has its pre-determined place; or in the expressive, self-realizing totality of the German Romantic philosophy;

(3) the dialectical conception of the developing, producing and produced, structured totality. In the first version one can use the picture of linear related facts. In the dialectical conception, one cannot talk about the summation of facts, processes, or structures,

but about genesis, transformation, and structuring. Therefore, if we ask what the social world is, we must answer with how it is formed and transformed.

The dialectical conception can be pictured as a spiral formed movement, where parts contribute to the formation of the totality and are transformed by it. For example take the notion of wage–labour. Viewed in isolation its meaning and function cannot be understood. Placed within the total context of the capitalistic system, we can understand how it contributes to the reproduction of this system. But we also must see how it forms change, since reproduction is not a simple re-shaping of given conditions. It is extended in the sense that new aspects are added which eventually lead to a restructuring within the system.

These transformations are viewed as a consequence of internal contradictions: "A totality without contradiction is empty, contradictions without a totality are formal and arbitrary" (K. Kosik op. cit., p. 56). To say that there exist contradictions between workers and capitalists is an arbitrary statement. To say that there exist contradictions between workers and capitalists within the capitalistic system, due to the appropriation of surplus labour by the capitalist, is a starting point for the exploration of this contradiction placed within a totality.

A societal phenomenon, for example the contradiction between workers and capitalists, can be grasped as an *histortical fact* when we understand that it has a mediating function, and is mediated at the same time. A societal fact mediates the functioning of the whole—in our example, the capitalist system. At the same time, it is reproduced by the processes going on within the system. Thus, a societal phenomenon can be viewed as having a double function, which makes it into a historical fact: "On the one hand, it defines itself, on the other, it defines the whole; to be producer and at the same time product; to be determined and at the same time to determine; to be revealer and at the same time to decipher itself; to achieve real meaning and at the same time to confer meaning on something else" (K. Kosik op. cit., p. 43).

The double function of a part within a whole not only makes us see the necessity of a historical analysis. It also raises a question concerning the meaning of "relation" in a dialectical context of parts within a totality. We will discuss these problems in section 2.4.

Before proceeding to this analysis, we should point at the fact that Marx not only understood the social world, as such, as a process, but also saw the basic concepts, through which we talk about this social world, as undergoing change and transformation.

2.3.6   *The historicity of basic concepts*

In a letter to Annenkow, Marx wrote that man not only produces societal relations in accordance with his productive forces, but, also, "the ideas, the categories, i.e., the abstract, cognitive expression, of exactly these societal relations. The categories are, consequently, just as little eternal as the relations which they express. They are historical and passing products" (Das Elend der Philosophie 1960, p. 15).

Marx, considering "categories" as basic to our thinking and talking (see also p. 88), maintains in this quotation, that they are not eternal or transcendental, but related to historically given conditions, and therefore, themselves historically limited. Categories and concepts, therefore can be analyzed in terms of their historical anchorage, their relations to existing "material" conditions, to their change, and how this change is partly determined by changes in our way of thinking. Since societal systems are undergoing change and transformation, the theories about society, i.e., the attempts to explain the function of society, consequently have to be transformed. The same holds for metatheory, which can be considered to be adequate only in a given period. Knowledge about the world influences our metatheories and they, in turn, may have a profound influence how we theorize (see also p. 81 and P. Kemp 1975, H. Reichert 1970).

Furthermore, theories about social systems cannot be formulated independently, and/or prior to, a certain developmental level of society itself. The Marxian analysis of the capitalist system in "Capital", could not have been developed before capitalism itself was sufficiently well developed. This may seen obvious and even trivial.

But on second thought, it is not. First, the level of development of a societal formation is only a necessary, but not a sufficient, condition for developing theories about it. Second, things seem to be different for the natural sciences. Thus, Newton's law of gravity could, *in principle*, have been formulated earlier. (Why Newton's

physics was developed in the 17th century, and what the societal
context and pre-conditions of this development were, is quite
another problem.) Marx's theory of capitalism could not, *in
principle*, have been developed much earlier and in a different
cultural context. (It has been criticized also for being too
"ethnocentric". See A. Abdel-Malek 1968.)

Marx gives an example of the interrelationship between the
development of concepts and societal relations. Speaking of
categories as thought-positing (Denkbestimmungen), he wants to
compare "simple" categories, having a few determining characteristics, with their later use, when more characteristics have been
added as a consequence of an increased complexity in society itself.
Simpler categories may be "expressions, in which the undeveloped
concrete may have manifested itself" (Zur Kritik, p. 249).
Potentially, there is already contained in this simple category
"more many-sided relations and conditions" being expressed by a
more comprehensive and, therefore, more concrete, category.
According to Marx, it is possible that the more developed category
preserves the more simple category as a "subordinated relation"
(ibid). Therefore, "the more simple category can either express
existing conditions of an underdeveloped whole or subordinated
conditions of a developed whole" (op. cit., p. 249–50). To the extent
that the social world develops into greater complexity "the
development of abstract thinking, ascending from the most simple
to the combined, corresponds to the real historical process" (ibid.,
p. 250).

This type of analysis also indicates that Marx could not make
the erroneous, dualistic distinction, between language and reality.
Language for him was as much a part of reality as other social
relations and conditions.

2.4   INTRINSIC AND EXTRINSIC RELATIONS

2.4.1   *Negation and transcendence*

An exposition of the way one talks about "dialectical relations"
can start with a brief look at Hegelian logic. Hegel did not use the
world "logic" in the sense of a formalized and axiomatic system of
rules. Instead, he attempted to present ontological problems in the

context of his logic: to present them such that they are logically compelling. This is not accomplished by a strict formalized, deductive system. But by proceeding from single concepts with few determining characteristics, he moves, through negation and transcendence to more and more complicated notions, and in a way that is persuasive.

Hegel begins his logic with the concept of "being". His reasons are as follows: What is "being", taken as a most elementary and primitive concept? Let us construct it such that it has no characteristics or properties. Let us think of "being" as something without colour, shape, or location in time and space—stripped of every determining characteristic. It is, to speak with Hegel, "the undetermined immediately given". If we strip the category "being" of all its determining characteristics, its properties—we *negate* it as a basic category of our thinking, since in its traditional use the category of "being" has plenty of properties.

When we strip "being" of all its properties, we contradict it in the literal sense of the word. By negating "being" it turns into its opposite, into "not-being", in the sense of emptiness. Hence, by negating the concept of "being" in the way we have attempted, we relate it, in a logically compelling way, to "not-being".

However, this operation has an interesting consequence. Having stripped "being" of all its determining characteristics, and thus having it negated into "not-being" in the sense of emptiness, we, in fact, endow "being" with *one characteristic* or *property*, namely the one of emptiness or not-being. But what does this amount to? It amounts to the negation of the original negation. In other words, "being" when stripped of all its properties is negated as a category of thought. This leads to its opposite, "not being", which negates the negation since "being" now receives one property. Through this negation of a negation, the original pair of categories has been transcended. It is no longer the being as non-being and the non-being as the being. It has *become* something. Hence, the transcendence of the two original categories, through negation of the negation, leads to a third category: that of "becoming". "Becoming", in one sense being *change*, can, therefore, be posited as that which characterizes "Dasein", i.e., existence. In other words, existence is becoming, is ongoing change. "Dasein", in this context, is a totality comprising as *separate*, but *interdependent* and *intrinsically* related concepts, "being", as well as, "non-being".

It also establishes "becoming", ongoing change, as a basic ontological category.

This example points at various aspects of dialectics:

(1) We start with one element (not necessarily a concept) and look for its opposite (this notion will be clarified later).

(2) This can be done, e.g., by using the operation of contradicting.

(3) The original element and its opposite have meaning, or make sense, only in relation to each other. They are different and, at the same time, interrelated. This relation is internal, e.g., where two concepts define each other.

(4) The operation through which we produce the opposite to the original element amounts to its *negation*.

(5) The dialectical process does not, however, stop here. By joining the two elements, we go a step further and negate the original negation. This amounts to the formation of a totality in which the two elements still exist.

(6) Here we get a hunch why Hegel says that something can be different, even contradictory, and, at the same time, identical. First of all, "identity" refers to the new whole. This will be explained further, when we explicate the meaning of the word "to identify". Second, it refers to each element making up the whole.

(7) The operation of negation of a negation is equal to *transcendence*. In German, the word as a verb is "aufheben". "Aufheben" has three meanings, all of them are utilized, though not always explicitly, when Hegel talks about "Aufhebung": (1) to preserve something, (2) to do away, and finally (3) to elevate something. Thus if we return to our example, "being" is preserved in the new concept of "Dasein", but it has, at the same time, been done away with through its negation. Finally, the new concept "Dasein" is the solution to the contradiction on an elevated level. At the same time, it is the point of departure for the continued dialectical movement.

Thus, in general, the process of transcendence implies that something of the old is preserved. Furthermore, that some of its essential characteristics are eliminated, and that the new is formed on an elevated level.[17]

Does this dialectical movement only apply to very abstract conceptual analysis? Let us attempt another example.

Capitalism means the private ownership or control of means of production, i.e., the means of production are controlled by a few, whereas they are used by many in a societal process. The negation of private ownership is public ownership. This does not, however, imply socialism as many have thought. Negation of private ownership by public ownership can mean that the means of production still is controlled by a few, though at this time by state-bureaucrats. Thus, the negation does not solve the contradiction between control by few and use by many in a societal process.

Therefore, the negation has to be transcended, i.e., negated, which, for example, implies ownership and control by "the associated producers". We can explain transcendence such that the use of the means of production is preserved, control by few negated and the new forms of co-operation have elevated the problem to a new level. Here again the dialectical process starts.

In this example, different from the one borrowed from Hegel, we deal with the conceptualization of certain aspects of the social world. We maintain, however, that the very process of the socialization of means of production, and its conceptualization, are only separate, but inter-dependent aspects of one unified process. Societal processes, as observed in the actions of man, and the conceptualization of these processes in the speech-acts of man, together form a totality. The relation between the societal process and their conceptualization is intrinsic. What this means will have to be analyzed more precisely.

Before doing that, I like to clarify one thing. The example, borrowed from Hegelian logic, was used for a didactical purpose only: to explain the notions of "negation", "negation of negation" and "transcendence", within the context of dialectical reasoning. (An additional analysis of the word "negation" is to be found at p. 226.) Thus, in our theoretical framework, we have no use for the Hegelian concepts of "being", "non-being", or "existence". As our example, concerning the notion of socialization of means of production, was intended to show, we can make use of Hegelian dialectical "logic" without being tied to the concepts he used.

This is in agreement with a basic idea Hegel held himself. Namely, not only science and its results are historically limited, but also, in the sense meant by Hegel, metascience: the philosophy of science or logic. This too develops and transforms as the world changes. There is, furthermore, a relation between the change in science and the change in metascience and logic. They influence each other (take for example the impact of quantum mechanics on epistemology. See M. Jammer 1966).

There is one additional point to be mentioned in regards to Hegel's logic. Logic, for him, implied that there were necessary relations between concepts. Thus, the use of certain concepts is intimately related to the use of other concepts, and to deny that does not make sense (we have treated this problem on pages 27 ff.). Thus, in this aspect we approach Hegel's own position. What we do not accept are the reasons Hegel gave for his way of thinking, and the ontological assumptions he made in introducing the idea of absolute Spirit. However, his assumptions, and the motivations for his thinking, must be understood in an historical context: in the situation Hegel found himself, against whom he argued, and the political and social situations were in which he worked and took his stand (for that see W. Kaufmann 1966, Ch. Taylor 1975 and for his political stand J. Elster 1976 and P. Kemp 1975).

Characterizing very briefly his situation we can remind ourselves that Hegel lived in the epoque of the French revolution and its aftermath. He finished his *Phenomenology*, in Jena "the night before Napoleon finished the Holy Roman Empire, which had lasted over a thousand years, in the battle of Jena" (W. Kaufmann 1966, p. 33). He witnessed the beginnings of the process of industrialization, the development of science and, as a consequence, of what Romantic thought had presented as the splitting up the world.

2.4.2   *Intrinsic and extrinsic relations analyzed*

In traditional science, concepts usually have the task to institute *classifications*.

One purpose of classification is implied in the ontological position expressed in the following quotation: "A century ago Mill stated as the requirement of a scientific valid concept that it should identify properties which are causes or 'sure marks' of many other properties. Nowadays this *requirement is formulated* as calling for *statistical relationships*, rather than strict causal connections. We *conceptualize* a subject-matter in ways which we anticipate (or hope) will yield *significant inter-correlations* ... *The function* of scientific concepts is to mark the categories which will tell us more about our subject-matter than any other categorical sets" (A. Kaplan 1964, p. 51–2, our ith.). This quotation stems from a widely used text that says to present *the* methodology of the behavioural sciences. Let us look for a moment at what it states: (1) Concepts institute classifications; (2) Good classifications are usually those which ensure statistical intercorrelations. Statistical intercorrelations are the prototype of extrinsic relations. They presuppose the independence of measures, used as translations of concepts. It is not mentioned that this type of reasoning presupposes a dualistic and/or atomistic, as well as, a static ontological position. One of the reasons for this lack of clarification is that traditional empirical, positivistic social science does not reflect on its presuppositions. It takes them for granted, for SCIENCE.[18] Other examples of extrinsic relations are accidental connections, thus, when two cars are parked side by side; or temporal succession, when e.g., two arbitrarily chosen television programmes are presented one after the other.

An extrinsic relation between two relata exists when each of them *can*, and in certain cases—when e.g., using correlations—*must* be viewed as independent from each other. Something is what it is, independently of whether the other is, or is not (Østerberg 1966, p. 9). Relating two things to each other in an extrinsic relation does not change them, neither in what they are nor in their function. The relata in an extrinsic relation do not "refer" to each other, neither when they are defined, nor when acting or being acted upon. When two cars are parked side by side, nothing more happens. Take as an example, pearls separately, and thereafter joined by a thread (see Østerberg for this example).

Each pearl is independent of the other. A pearl can be defined without reference to the thread. If they are joined by a thread just in order to store them, the thread establishes an extrinsic relation. They are separate and kept together as two variables are joined by a statistical correlation.

If, however, we transform the pearls into a necklace, they change their identity. They form a whole. Their relation to each other is no longer extrinsic.

Take another example. A watch is placed on a table and all its parts are separated and displaced. The relation between each of the parts is extrinsic in the spatial sense. Then, we join them such that the watch can function. The parts become intrinsically related to each other. They supplement each other in a *working* and *functioning* whole.

An intrinsic relation is a relation between two or a set of relata in which *both or all* are what they are in relation to each other. They refer to each other and form a unity or a totality (D. Østerberg, ibid.).

Since in an intrinsic relation the elements form a totality, they are necessary elements. They do not "function" or "exist" independently, but only in relation to each other. Conceptually this means that a pair in an intrinsic relation cannot be defined without referring to each other. The meaning of the word "subject", e.g., has to be established by referring to the word "object", and vice-versa.

The totality, which is formed through the elements being related to each other, can be said to be more basic than the elements taken themselves. This means that the point of departure is the totality, from which the elements can be abstracted and in this sense, isolated. This leads to an important principle of an epistemological kind, namely: "One divides into two". Its use will be elaborated in chapter 4, p. 222.

An intrinsic relation has at least three characteristics: (1) the relata make up a unity or totality, (2) they are separate and different, (3) they are interdependent.[19]

We want now to state a basic principle: *All dialectical relations are intrinsic relations, but all intrinsic relations are not necessarily dialectical relations.* The three characteristics by which we have described intrinsic relations are also to be found when we describe dialectical relations. They are, however, not sufficient for describing them. Before we can analyze what we mean when we speak about dialectical relations, two problems have first to be clarified. The *first* problem has to do with the use of the word "intrinsic relation". The *second*, with the clarification of what we mean when we speak about "identity", since this concept is important in the analysis of dialectical relations.

2.4.3 *On conceptual matters*

We have, in the previous text, consistently talked about "intrinsic-extrinsic" relations, deliberately avoiding the terms "internal–

external". We have done this in order to avoid an expected confusion.

In traditional philosophical discourse, the term "internal" relation has been used to describe *logical-conceptual* relations. The example we used in the previous section to illuminate Hegelian logic, may be sufficient to bring out the meaning of an *internal* relation within a logical-conceptual context. The concept of "being" is defined such that it is, in a logical compelling way, related to "non-being". From this example, however, we should not draw the conclusion that all internal relations are of a logical-conceptual kind.

If we support such an assumption, we also have to accept a traditional bifurcation between language and reality which implies that internal relations are logical-conceptual, i.e., refer to matters of language, whereas relations within "reality" are *external*.

If we accept the bifurcation upon which the mentioned use of internal–external relations is based, we abandon the basic dialectical category of "totality", analyzed previously. Furthermore, if relations within "reality" are external, then we can choose between either of two possibilities: Since we have defined all dialectical relations as internal relations this definition is false. Or, accepting this definition, then dialectical relations have nothing to do with "reality", but only with logical-conceptual matters. Furthermore, we are unable to maintain that the relation between language and reality is dialectical, or can be grasped within a dialectical framework. If this is the case, we have to abandon our project because the relation between language and reality is conceived of as a dialectical one and this conception, in turn, is necessary for our reasoning.

We have mentioned why we reject the bifurcation of language and reality on previous pages (see p. 33) and why we refuse to understand their relation as *external*. We will return several times to a discussion of this problem (see e.g., p. 93).

Now we must give reasons why we consider the relation between language and reality as *internal*, but not as a logical-conceptual relation. (In order to avoid the mentioned semantic confusion, we will, from now on only use the term "intrinsic" and "extrinsic" and no longer talk about "internal" and "external".)

Let us start with the notion of "concept". As mentioned, in our traditional way, concepts are understood as classifications through which we abstract from reality in order to be able to explain reality in terms of general abstract principles.

There is another way of viewing concepts, having its roots in Hegelian philosophy. In this view one of the basic assumptions is that the world is the external manifestation of Spirit and is posited as its rational necessity. What does this mean? We can perhaps better understand it, if instead of the Hegelian notion of "Spirit", we use the more common notion of human knowledge. The world as we know it is thus a manifestation, in the sense that we have constructed it in our head according to principles of rationality, which make our constructions not only plausible, but also logically compelling. (It is for this reason Marx, in his criticism of Feuerbach's epistemology, could say that the active part of man in the production of knowledge was understood by idealistic philosophy. Though, what this philosophy did not understand was the way man "materially" constructs the world, and how the process of production of knowledge is intimately related to "material" production.)[20]

Concepts, in this process, are not something through which we characterize the world in an abstract way. They are for Hegel, the tools through which the Spirit brings about the world. Concepts are the underlying necessary building-stones of the world. Thus, Hegel could speak of true and false concepts (where we speak of true and false statements or judgments). True are those concepts which posit the world in a way that clarifies its rational necessity.

There is another reason why Hegel spoke of true concepts. Since the world is something in continuous change, concepts, as the tools of change, are also in a state of change. In addition they, like the world, may not be fully developed. In German there is an expression which is not translatable into English: "Im Begriff stehen". Literally, it means "to stand in a concept". Its meaning in English is "being in a state in which something is going to develop or occur"; This can be interpreted to mean one is conceptually or cognitively ready to do something. One is thinking of doing something: "things are said to be in their concept, when they are in germ, when they have just started to develop" (Ch. Taylor 1975, p. 110).[21]

There is a third reason why Hegel could speak of true and false concepts. He viewed them as being in a process of development or change. Therefore, he did not attempt to make them precise. As we have discussed before (see p. 142), his basic concepts or categories often have two or more meanings, which are not arbitrary. These different meanings of the same word, when related to each other, often become epistemological hypotheses or even statements about the world. We discussed previously the word "appearance". It serves well as an example for this double meaning of a word, since it may refer to a phenomenon as well as to an illusion.

Setting Hegel aside, how should we view concepts within the problems of dialectics?

In general, we can say that the way we view concepts depends (1) on the ontological position we have taken. This will determine what kind of concepts we are looking for and how we want to use them. (This became clear in analyzing the implications of the position stated by Kaplan in the quoted textbook, see p. 82).

(2) on the context within which we use the concepts.

(3) on our notion of what it means to have a language.

(4) on our way of looking at the relation between language and reality.

Let us first demarcate the context in a broad manner, as the one with which social science deals, i.e., the social world and its "material" conditions.

As we have discussed earlier, an atomistic position demands that we view concepts as abstract, as relatively isolated from the context and from each other, as being mutually exclusive and, therefore, independent. This is necessary in order to make possible the formulation of propositions which ensure the establishment of extrinsic relations, e.g., intercorrelations. As a consequence, we first define our concepts with a vague idea of the subject-matter and, therefore, impose a conceptual structure on social reality.

Assume, however, that we start with a holistic position, in which we take our point of departure in a concrete totality in the sense explicated in previous sections. Thus, we start with a given, but not unchanging, complex system. It comprises social phenomena, social processes, *as well* as, the concepts and expressions we use when we talk about these phenomena and processes. If there exist intrinsic relations between language and the social world, and if language, in addition, is an integrated part of the social world, then the same must hold for the specific concepts and expressions we use for talking about specific social phenomena and social processes. If social science is viewed as the totality of these concepts and expressions, we must acknowledge that social science itself is an important part of the social world.

How can this complexity be translated in order to give us rules for the use of concepts in the social sciences? I propose we follow an idea expressed by Marx: "In the study of economic categories, as in the case of every historical and social science, it must be borne in mind that as in reality so in our mind the *subject*, in this case modern bourgeois society, is given, and that categories therefore only express *forms of existence* (Daseinsformen), *determining characteristics* (Existensbestimmungen), and frequently only one-sided aspects of this definite society, this subject and that therefore *society not even in science* starts there, where only one talks about it *as such*" (1972, p. 254).

Marx talks here about *categories* as one-sided and abstract determining characteristics (Denkbestimmungen) of a concrete totality. This is the *first* point to be made. But we cannot understand what he maintains, if we do not know that he uses the word "*category*" and the expression "one-sided aspects" in the sense arrived at in Hegelian logic.

There, Hegel criticizes Kant in his use of categories. Kant distinguished between the world of objects-things as they are in themselves (Das Ding-an-sich)—and our *understanding* of them as a *phenomena*, i.e., experiences of our perception. Thus, Kant maintained a *dualistic* conception, in spite of his assertion that we never can have knowledge about the world as it is in itself. What we have knowledge about are the phenomena. But, in order to understand them, we must assume that our perception and cognition occurs within a frame of presupposed (transcendental) categories which determine our perception and cognition. These are, e.g., the categories of space, time, causality, finite and infinite which Kant declared as being opposed to each other.

Hegel's criticism of Kant concerns the introduction of a type of dualism that is opposed to an ontological position which assumes a totality.

Traditionally, epistemology distinguished sharply between the knowing or knowledge-producing subject, *and* the objective world. It assumed a correspondence between subjective knowledge, and the objective world mediated through our conceptions. These conceptions could either be understood as instruments for our knowledge, or as a lens through which objective reality is mediated.

If we accept that our conceptions, cognitions, or perceptions, are instruments or lenses for knowledge, Hegel argued, we could have knowledge of objective reality itself only if we could disregard the very instruments through which we obtain knowledge. This is an impossibility.

Also Hegel rejected Kant's demand that one should investigate the possibilities for obtaining knowledge by establishing the categories as transcendental preconditions for knowledge. He argued that it was contradictory to say we must *know* the preconditions of knowledge *before we are able to know*. It is as if one demanded the ability to swim before entering the water.

Hegel asked how it was possible, accepting Kant's assertion that his categories cannot be applied to the world as it is (because we cannot know anything about it), to apply these categories only to our subjective knowledge, i.e., to our understanding of phenomena, if they do not apply to objective reality. Hegel accused Kant of *using* the categories, neither investigating the preconditions for their choice, nor their relevance for obtaining knowledge. Kant postulated them as given, as transcendental and, therefore, universal preconditions for our knowledge. Hegel, instead, rejected the sharp dualism between the knowing subject and objective reality. He saw them both as aspects of a totality, as intrinsically related. Since this totality undergoes continuous change, he concluded, that the categories we use are not transcendental, but historically limited. They are nothing but one-sided aspects of a totality at a given point in history.

Marx took up these basic ideas of Hegelian epistemology. *First* of all, he accepted that categories are ways of trying to determine or define certain aspects of the world, and thus one-sided aspects. Categories of our thought, furthermore, cannot be separated from the totality and posed against it in a new dualism: thought or language *against* reality. *Second*, he accepted Hegel's really revolutionary idea that these categories are not eternal and transcendental, but themselves products of the development of the world and, e.g., of science as a part of this world.

For instance, the Galileian notion of motion is different from the Aristotelian notion of motion and revolutionized thinking and theories of physics. The categories of time and space in Einsteinean theory of relativity are different from Newtonian categories etc.

Marx added that basic social categories like capitalism could not be developed at all, before capitalism, as such, had fully developed. We can add, that when capitalism enters new phases as, e.g., that of state-capitalism, Marxian categories also have to be changed (which dogmatic marxists sometimes forget).

Let us summarize: Marx uses the notion of *category* in the Hegelian sense, as one-sided aspects of a *concrete totality*. *Second*, societal categories are an integrated part of society. As social facts, they have the double function of determining our comprehension, and being determined themselves. *Third*, since we cannot have total knowledge of reality, the categories we use are only abstract, one-sided aspects of the concrete and many-sided, determined totality. Fourth, what we are talking about must be *understood*, in order for our categories, to grasp what is significant. In other words: to formulate categories about capitalism in order to grasp (through reason) what capitalism is, we must first have an *understanding* of capitalism as it appears to us. But understanding, in turn, presupposes a certain grasping. Thus, the process of producing knowledge implies a dialectical relation between grasping and understanding. This process, in turn, is closely related to other processes of production—material production—and is determined by it and at the same time determining it.[22]

There is also a *fifth* reason, which is not yet clear because the translation of the quoted German text creates some difficulties. Keeping in mind that Marx talks about categories (Denkbestimmungen), and not about concepts, as we most often use the term, we quote again: "In the study of economic categories ..." But Marx uses another expression "bei dem *Gang* der ökonomischen Kategorien". It can be translated "in the matter of economic categories, taking their course". Thus, categories are not given, they take a course, are transformed as society is transformed, and contribute to its transformation.

We discussed earlier that Hegel used the expression "Im Begriff stehen", i.e., a concept or a category being in its germ. Marx adds, that it is on its way, on a certain course. This is not strange if the social world is grasped as a process, and categories as integrated parts of the social world.

Finally, we must ask the same question as when we discussed the consequence of the atomistic notion of concepts. Do we impose a structure on society, e.g., the capitalist society, in this case also? As we previously have said, the analysis of a given social system presupposes the *grasping* of central categories, which are conceived of as forms of existence of this system. But in order to grasp these categories, we must have a certain amount of advance understanding of the system. Thus again, we have the dialectics, where reasoning (grasping) presupposes understanding of what we want to grasp. This is not specific to the social sciences. It is a function of language. In order to be able to use language, we must already have some knowledge of that which we speak; though our knowledge may be extended in the course of talking about it. We will have ample opportunity to return to this subject.

Let me summarize. Dialectical relations are intrinsic relations. To maintain that intrinsic relations are only conceptual-logical relations and nothing more, implies a violation of the dialectical principle of totality, and hence introduces a dualism between language and reality. We have, alternatively, in the preceding argumentation, maintained that concepts and categories are aspects or parts of reality itself. They represent the ways we define reality for ourselves. But this cannot be done in an arbitrary way.

2.4.4   *Other contexts in which we speak about intrinsic relations*

So far, we have rejected the notion that intrinsic relations are logical-conceptual relations because such an assumption implies a dualism. This, in turn, is in contradiction to the notion of totality. Furthermore, we have tried to show that intrinsic relations, in turn, presuppose the notion of totality or a functioning whole. The elements in this functioning whole are separate but interdependent.

In chapter 1 (see page 37), we also used the term "intrinsic relation" in a different context, namely, in an epistemological one. Our task now will be to analyze the use of the term "intrinsic relation" in this context, and relate its usage here to one in the context of the analysis of intrinsic and dialectical relations. A central assertion in the epistemological context, was that the world of objects exists independently of the knowing subject, but not extrinsically to him. What does that mean? Let us exemplify by using Peirce's illustration of effort and resistance, when a man thrust himself against a locked door. The door is independent of him. But in order to act towards the door, he has to relate himself cognitively in advance. He tries to identify it, e.g., as locked door. What does that imply? The man has a *standpoint* from which he relates himself to the door. (Conversely, we could speak of the standpoint of the door in relation to the man). Depending of the standpoint he takes, he has certain cognitions and ways of interpreting the door (e.g. that it is locked). The way of cognitizing and interpreting the door is, from his standpoint, aspects of the door. Furthermore, he may have a certain *mode of orientation* toward the door, related to the value he assigns it. He could ask himself whether he should thrust himself against the door even to the risk of creating damage. Thus, *standpoint, aspect,* and *mode of orientation,* seem to be basic preconditions for intrinsically relating oneself to the world, as an act in itself, or as a step in consecutive actions (thrusting oneself against the door).

Thus, if the man identifies the door as locked, he *relates* himself actively to it, i.e., making certain choices from a given standpoint. The choices are concerned with aspects of the object, and influenced by his mode of orientation. In order to carry this out, the man and the door, though separate and independent of each other, must form a totality: his efforts are interdependently related to the door's resistance. They function together as the parts of a watch function in an interdependent way.

Hence, we view the process of cognitizing as an intrinsic relation between subject and object. The notion of knowledge-as-a-relation is opposed to the notion of knowledge-as-a copy. The latter presupposes a sharp separation between subject and object and, furthermore, extrinsic relations (see about knowledge-as-a-relation vs knowledge-as-a-copy J. Piaget & B. Inhelder, 1969, see also p. 242).

We can now relate our preliminary analysis of epistemological processes to our use of the expression "intrinsic relation". In a dialectical conceptual framework, the notion of "intrinsic relation" becomes a basic notion, since all dialectical relations are intrinsic (though, in order to understand this notion of intrinsicality it has to be completed by the notion of "extrinsic relation". Both are necessary, but "intrinsic relation" is basic in our framework and "extrinsic relation" secondary).

Such epistemological problems as the problem of knowledge cannot be excluded from our dialectical conceptualization. Therefore, the process of cognitizing has to be viewed as an intrinsic relation between subject and object. Its dialectical aspects will be discussed in chapter four.

2.4.5 *On language and reality*

There are still other arguments against the bifurcation of language and reality which, to me, seem to be of greater importance than the arguments used so far.

In order to *speak about the relation* between language and reality, or any relation at all, we evidently must possess language. To possess language partly means to follow certain rules, though we may neither be aware of them, nor the fact that we follow them. In part it also means the ability to formulate certain statements which are not analytic, but which are such that their truth cannot be denied. A denial would render these statements meaningless, since they would be self-contradictory. One example of such a statement is the one just presented: In order to speak about the relation between language and reality, we must possess language (where "possessing a language" is not identical to "being able to speak about relations").

To possess a language or, which is the same, to be a user of language, means to be able to put forward certain correct statements in a concrete social situation. Something which cannot be done without following certain rules. Some of these rules are basic, in the sense that they cannot be further explained, since any explanation of them presupposes their very existence. If we deny this statement, we are forced to accept the existence of rules which can explain these basic rules, and again, rules which can explain the second set of rules. We obtain a regression of rules *ad infinitum*.

The basic rules we talk about will be called "the basic logic of language" (see chapter 3, p. 174). The consequence is thus, we have to accept the notion that possessing language means to act in accordance with certain rules in a concrete social situation. (We do this though we may not be aware of it nor of the content of these rules.) These rules are characterized by being logically compelling, though they are not necessarily rules of formalized logic. In short, they state relations between concepts which cannot be used independently of each other. If we can speak according to these rules in concrete social situations, we are able to formulate some statements which are correct. This implies we cannot deny the correctness of these statements without being self-contradictory.

A consequence of this is that we cannot explain the meaning of "correct", since all explanations of "correct" presuppose its use.

(But this does not imply that we cannot set forward false statements. Nor does it imply that we cannot test the truth of statements. It only implies that all theories of truth presuppose a notion of "correctness", which cannot be further explained. See p. 229).

Can we explain or justify the ability to formulate certain correct statements by reference to reality? We cannot, except if we are able to formulate explanations without using language. If we say, e.g., that certain basic statements are logically compelling and, they are, in this sense correct, *because reality is such*, then we have already used language and followed those rules which we are trying to explain in that reference to reality.

We cannot, in other words, explain the use of language by reference to ontological reasons. We must abandon the bifurcation of language and reality, and accept that knowledge of these basic rules is knowledge of the *real*.

If we abandon the traditional bifurcation of language and reality do we, as a consequence, accept a monistic solution? Do we reduce reality to language or language to a natural phenomenon as in behaviouristic language theory? Is there a third possibility to dualism and monism? A dialectical solution implies that language and reality form a totality, that they are different, interdependent, and have something in common.

This has to be elaborated somewhat more. *First* of all, language and reality are different. We cannot reduce reality to language, neither can we reduce language to a natural phenomenon, e.g., in terms of stimuli, response, and conditioning. In order to be able to speak—to use language—we must be able to speak about *something*. This something is reality, e.g., the physical world. But we can also speak about language. Therefore, and this is the *second* assertion language is about reality *as well as being itself a part of (social) reality*. *The third* assertion, then, is that *knowledge* of language is *knowledge* of reality. We could not say anything about reality without having knowledge of language, i.e., how to use language, and restrict this knowledge to language alone without referring to reality and the world of objects. Thus, as in all dialectical relations, (see p. 111) we must assume that the relata—here language and reality—are different, but interrelated.

Furthermore, that they are identical, in the sense of having something in common (knowledge of language is knowledge of reality), and are opposed to each other: the notion of language and that of reality are a complimentary and, therefore, a contrasting negation (see the explanation of this expression on p. 113).

Language is a necessary condition for speaking about reality. If we abolish language and its basic rules, we also abolish reality as something about which we can speak. If we, on the other hand, deny that language is about reality, we abolish language, since language can only be understood as referring to reality (language, naturally, can also be about language. But then it is often language which is about reality). In this sense, reality is a necessary pre-condition for language.

We cannot use language without being able to use the word "correct", and we cannot use "correct" independently of "real" or "exist". That which is correct is real. For example if I say "the hands I hold up in front of me are my hands". If we identify language with reality, correct with real, we abolish both.

Thus there is a fundamental dialectical relation between language and reality. There is also one between "correct" and "real". This relation is such that the two concepts presuppose each other, and are interdependent. As we will see later on, one central characteristic of the rules of logic of language is that they state interrelations between concepts. This characteristic applies to the concepts "language" and "reality", "correct", and "real".

The fact that we can set forward certain correct statements, and that we cannot *explain* their correctness by reference to reality, is not contradictory to the fact that we use language in *specific ways* when we talk about reality. Furthermore, we can test our specific ways of talking by means of procedures which include speech actions as well as other actions.

These very complicated problems make it necessary to further explore the use of the words "language" and "reality", and the ways we relate them. There is a traditional distinction between language as a structured system of rules (langue), and language as acting through speaking (parole).

We accept such a distinction under two conditions. First, that it does not introduce another dualism. Second, that this distinction does not abstract language from its societal context. Language as a structured system of rules, is an institutionalized system. In other words, it makes up a part of society and of the totality of its institutions. It is an institution itself. The rules within this institutionalized system do more than provide the pre-conditions for making our speech meaningful. They themselves carry meaning. Otherwise, we could not understand them or have knowledge about them.

When we talk about language as speech acts, we do not view it as the expression of individuals, i.e., as idosyncratic psychological phenomena.

Speech actions are always *interactions* between a speaker and a listener, and the basic rules provide for an intersubjectivity of understanding. As actions they are social. The context in which they are performed is also social.

The interrelation between language as an institutionalized system of rules, and language as speech interactions, can be formulated as the following: basic rules are preconditions for speech interaction, including the listener's understanding. The rules, on the other hand, cannot be formulated independently of our use of language, i.e., of speech interaction. In this sense, language as a structured institutionalized system is *real.* The institutionalized rules of language provide meaning for what we say. When we say something we are always in a concrete, historically conditioned, situation. But this is only one side of the dialectic. We are, at the same time, affected by the existing institutionalized structures. Volosinov (1973), to bring out this dialectical relation, distinguishes between "theme" and "meaning" of verbal expressions. According to him, "theme is a complex dynamic system of signs that attempts to be adequate to a given instant of generative process" (p. 99). The theme, in our terminology, is that which is expressed in the concrete situation where we find or place ourselves. "Theme" is that which makes the situation *specific* (or the expression of that which is specific).

"Meaning is the technical apparatus for the implementation of theme" (ibid). It is that which is *common* to users of language. As we will discuss on the following pages, in order to express something *specific* it must have common characteristics and everything common is supplemented by something specific in this case, the concrete situation of the speaker.

We now attempt the explication of words like "real" and "reality". We can say that language is real and so are singular statements. Chairs are real. But, can we say that chairs are real in the same sense as statements? Hamlet is real. Can we say that he is real in the same sense as the present Danish prime minister?

In fact, we use the word "real" (and in consequence "reality") in various ways. A discussion of the uses of "real" and "reality" within the context of this book is impossible. In any case, we agree with J.L. Austin (1962) that the ways we use "real" are so many that a single definition seems impossible to give. We sometimes call something "real", e.g., "this is real chocolate" in order to indicate that is not artificial, a fake, an illusion: something fictional. Thus, if we say that the prime minister of Denmark is real, we may want to say that he is not fictional. On the other hand, if we say that the fictional character of Hamlet is real, we may want to say that he is fictional, but not a hallucination since we can find him in Shakespeare's work, etc.

We may also use the word "real" in existential expressions. "The chair is real" may hence mean that "it exists" or that "there is a chair". When we speak about "statements being real", we may refer to their truth-value. Thus, they may be true and, at the same time be about something being real.

We are going to stop the discussion of "real" since we are already getting involved in a multitude of difficulties.

Let me just point out one of them. When we use the word "reality", we may use it in a way different from the word "real". For example we may say "there is only one reality". We are perhaps stating an ontological assumption. In any case we do not say that "reality is real", without making a tautological statement.

When we talk about *one* reality we may implicitly assume that the descriptions we can give of "reality" do not differ from the descriptions given by others. Since we, however, can relate ourselves to "reality" in innumerable ways, descriptions of "reality" by different persons may vary.

To some extent, however, they must be the same. Otherwise we could not use language at all. Hence there are correct descriptions of "one reality" common for all and there are correct descriptions of "one reality" specific for certain individuals, groups, classes or other categories.

Perhaps we could express the same thing by asserting that there exists a difference between a person, being in a concrete social and historical situation, where he makes his correct descriptions and knowledge which exists "objectively" as collective knowledge, independent of a specific individual, but not independent of any individual. A person being in a concrete situation has necessarily limited knowledge (though he may be able to place his limited knowledge within the context of a totality). Therefore a part of his correct descriptions may vary from those being common to all.

Let me summarize. When we talk about knowledge of one reality in the most general sense then we can assume that one part of this knowledge is common to all users of language and a part is specific to certain individuals.

They may live in a special culture, using concepts not known in another language (e.g., the language of Hopei-Indians). Within one culture there may be different ways of talking about reality due to class differences, being the basis of varying language environments. Finally, there may be descriptions of reality specific for one individual (which, however, can be talked about and understood by others). For example descriptions being of special interests to psychoanalysts and their clients.

As a final remark we maintain that it is meaningful to talk about *one* reality being described as *common*, i.e., the *same* for all individuals, as well as aspects of this reality being *different* for specific individuals. Saying this is not contradictory. Quite to the contrary it seems to be a logical necessity. We are unable to speak about the "same" without implying that there is something which is "different" and vice-versa. The interrelation between the two ways of talking will be extensively treated in the next section. We here want to propose that the interrelation between the two usages is of central importance for the language of dialectics and, at the same time, for connection to the dialectics of language.

2.4.6   On identity

In section 2.4.1, we tried to present a first and preliminary explication of the notion of "intrinsic relation". We maintained that all dialectical relations are intrinsic relations, but that the reverse does not hold true.

This is because of two conditions. *First*, the three characteristics necessary for describing a relation as intrinsic (relata are different, interdependent, and make up a whole), are not sufficient for the analysis of dialectical relations. Hegel asserted—and Marx maintained this position—that the relata in a dialectical relation, not only are different and separate but, at the same time, also identical.

Second, dialectical relations, as distinguished from intrinsic relations, are characterized by their relata being opposed to each other. The term "opposed" or "opposite" is vague, however. We can distinguish three ways of using it in this context. This will be done in the next section.

Representatives of conventional wisdom have often character-ized a proposition which asserts that two things are different *and* identical at the same time, as either a contradiction, or as an example of the way language should not be used.

If we want to retain the notion of a dialectical relation, and assert that the relata in such a relation are different as well as identical, we have to clarify the use of our language. Especially, we must analyze the notion "to identify".

In our use of the language, the terms "identity", "identical", and "to identify", give rise to three serious ambiguities. The *first* has to do with the fact that we use the terms in a restricted, and in a wider, more indeterminate, sense. The *second* ambiguity concerns our use of the term in two ways which confer different meaning. The *third* ambiguity has to do with a special context in which we use the terms, namely, in the context of temporal identity (for a discussion of two of the ambiguities see P. Wienpahl 1972). In the following three subsections, we will analyze the three ambiguities separately. We will try to reach a conclusion of central importance for the relation between dialectical relations and the basic conditions of our common-sense language.

2.4.6.1 *On the law of identity*

The most restricted way of using the term "identity" is when we say "x is identical with itself". In Aristotelian logic the term has been used in this way. The law of identity states the above mentioned tautology, that "x is identical with x". There has been much dispute concerning the interpretation of this principle. Some logicians maintain that the relation of identity is reflexive, i.e., that everything bears this relation to itself. Other philosophers, Hegel among them, opposed this interpretation. They assert that it makes no sense to speak about a relation except when assuming that there are at least *two* relate, where something bears upon another thing. Since, however, nothing can be related, in the strictest, reflexive sense of "identity", to something else, the conclusion is that "identity" used in this sense, is not a relation.

We can conclude that a proposition maintaining that something is identical with itself is trivial, as well as profound. It is trivial to say that a thing is identical with itself. How could it be otherwise. Wittgenstein remarked about such a proposition: "There is no finer example of a useless proposition, which yet is connected with a certain play of imagination. It is as if in imagination we put a thing into its own shape and saw that it fitted" (1958, §216).

How can we put something into its own shape? I think this expresses exactly the dilemma of the use of "identity" in its most restricted sense. In fact, one may argue we can use the term in this sense only, if we abstract from any space and time determinations, and use it in a completely abstract way.

One of the solutions to this riddle is to introduce spacial and temporal characteristics, as when the identity relation is transferred into *numerical* identity. The classical example, then, is the statement "the morningstar is identical with the eveningstar". If we abstract from time and space determinations, we could say that there exists only one star and it is identical with itself. But, at the same moment we introduce a time dimension, we speak about "morning" vs "evening star", i.e., we introduce *different* words for the *same* thing. Thus, we seem to have a choice, either to use "identity" in the most restricted sense, abstracted from time and space, and end up in a tautology; or we introduce these two dimensions, but then, "identity" is no longer used in the same strict sense. We now talk about "sameness", e.g., when we say that the morningstar is the *same* as the eveningstar.

G. Frege, who treated the problem, agreed that to say "the morningstar is the morningstar", is using "identity" in a trivial sense, which is cognitively non-informative. To say, however, that "the morningstar is identical with the eveningstar" is not trivial, but an astronomical discovery. His solution is that we have *two* terms *referring* to the *same* object, but having a *different sense*. He distinguishes between reference and sense. In doing so, he uses words like "same" and "different". This is an important fact that leads us to our next problem.

2.4.6.2 *On the meaning of "to identify something"*

If we analyze our daily language we find that the term "identity" is not only used in the most strict sense of "identical with itself". Instead we use it in the broader sense of "sameness", "likeness", etc. This broader sense introduces more ambiguity.

In addition—and this is more important—we also use the expression "to identify something" in *two completely different*, but as we will see, intimately related senses. First, we speak about "to identify something *with* something"; second, we speak about "to identify something *as* something". The difference between the two usages can roughly be explained in the following way. In the *first* sense, when we talk about identifying something *with* something, we concentrate on what is *common, similar, alike* or *same* for two things, abstracting from that which is *different*.

When we use it in the second sense, as "identifying something *as* something", we concentrate on what is *specific, different, distinct,* or *unlike* when comparing two things. (A typical example of the use in the second sense is when we speak about "an identity card".)

The following assumption seems most important to us: In order to carry out the operation "to identify something *with* something", we must be able to carry out the operation "identifying something *as* something", and vice-versa. In other words, the two senses in which we use the expression "to identify something", *presuppose each other* logically.

We could not, e.g., speak of "identical twins" having the *same* characteristics, if we did not know that they were *different* persons. On the other hand, when we see them as *different* persons and are told that they are identical twins, we may be able to look for "sameness".

We could not say that the morningstar is the same as the eveningstar, if we did not know that we, in saying this, are referring to a *different* observation time. In reverse, the fact that we see them as *different* makes it possible to understand that they, abstracted from observation time, are the *same*.

To use an additional example. Assume the police are told of a crime and given a description of the criminal (20 years of age, male, dark hair). Such a description identifies the criminal *with* a category of persons with whom he *shares* the *same* characteristics.

In order to identify him *as* a *specific* person the police may use his finger prints. On the other hand, if the police had only his fingerprints, i.e., that which *distinguishes* him *as* a specific person (and the police did not previously have the prints in their archives), it would be difficult to identify him without knowing any characteristics he *shares with* others.[24]

We will now try to indicate what the two senses of "to identify something" and their interrelationship implies for being able to use language. In our common-sense language there often exists a relation between a given word or expression and a given action. Every time we use this word or expression we also think of the *same* action. We identify expression *with* action and vice versa. But the *same* word or expression may also be used in a *different* type of action. To be able to relate the *same* word or expression to *different* actions and vice versa, in other words, to be able to shift between "identifying with" and "identifying as", is one way of saying that we know how to use language. An example will be used to elaborate this notion.

When one of my children was a little older than one year and could not yet talk, I repeatedly played a simple game with him, where he would clap his hands. He would do so when I used the word, which in Swedish is "klappa". But the same word also means "to pat". One day we stood beside another child who asked his mother whether he could "klappa" (i.e., pat) a dog. When my son heard the word "klappa", he started to clap his hands.

He had learned to *identify* one word *with* one definite activity. But he had not yet learned to identify the word *with* one activity in one context, and *with* another in a second context. What he had not yet learned was "to *identify* something *as*". I do not know when he learned it. Probably *when he had learned to use language.*

Thus, to be able to use language means to be able to *identify with* and to *identify as*. This is a condition of using language, i.e., the *condition of identification.* It implies knowledge of the context of words and actions, and the expressions we use when identifying *situations* (i.e., the context of words and actions). These words are: "the same", "common to", "different", "specific", etc. Their correct use implies that we fulfil the *condition of identification,* one necessary condition for using language.[25]

2.4.6.3 Are the two meanings of "to identify" exhaustive?

A question now arises. Does the analysis of "to identify with" and "to identify as" refer to basic problems concerning the knowledge of how to speak a language. Or, does it only point to certain aspects of situations we may find ourselves as beings who use language?

One may argue that the word "to identify" is used in other contexts. For example, I may say that "I identified him by (or through) his walk". I think this example does not indicate a specific use, but is a case of "identify as". Assume I say, "yesterday I met one of two *identical* twins (observe that "identical" here is used in both senses). They are so *alike* that one easily identifies *one* with the other and it is difficult to identify one *as* the person he really is. But I succeeded in identifying him *through* his walk". In other words: I identified him *as* twin t_1 by observing his walk.

In psychoanalytical contexts the word "identification" plays an important role. A boy, e.g., is said "to identify himself with his father". I think this means that the boy wants to be the *same* as the father, even in extreme cases at the expense of his individuality. But I don't see that the use of "identification" in this context adds something to the two basic aspects which we have analyzed so far.

2.4.6.4 On identity and the meaning of individuality

The third ambiguity in the use of the word "to identify" has to do with problems of temporal identity or genidentity, with individuality, and problems in the use of words like "substance" and "property". We will try to approach this problem within the framework of our analysis and disregard other attempted solutions (see, e.g., M. Munitz 1972)·

When we talk about "identifying *something*", we often presuppose that the "thing" we talk about must either have *properties*, *substance*, a collection of properties, or an organized structure of properties, etc. In this case, "identity" may either refer to "substance", or "properties", or both, when we oscillate in our use of language between the two possibilities.

We will now attempt to analyze what we may *identify* if the thing we identify is a person.

If two persons are professors of sociology, they have an identical property in common. But "naturally" they are different. Why do we say "naturally"? Because they have their own "individuality". But what is that? Is it a "substance"? And if so, what kind of substance? If we say that something has substance, are we really saying more than that it is identical with itself?

Thus it seems we can choose between two alternatives. First, we could formulate the statement as saying: "something is identical with itself means that it has a substance of its own". In this case, we have formulated a tautology and the solution is trivial.

The second alternative is to say: "Everything has many properties. If two things have the same properties (for example two cars of the same model), then they are identical. But in this case we cannot say that "identical" means "identical with itself". Only one thing can be identical with itself.

Hence, we either accept the idea of a mystical substance and call it "individuality" (or something else) and, by that, save the notion of "being identical with itself". This probably implies that we imprison our thought in a tautology.

Or else, we can abandon the idea of a substance and talk about properties. But in this case, we have to abandon the trivial sense of something being identical with itself. Having the same properties as something else is a relation (often an extrinsic relation) *between* at least two things and not something *within* one thing. If it were such, we would be back to our notions of "individuality" and of "substance".

In addition to the two alternatives mentioned, there is a third, the discussion of which is our next step.

We use expressions as "though he has become 20 years older, he still is the same jolly old fellow". Or we say, "in spite of the fact that he has been appointed professor, he has not changed his behaviour". These expressions are examples of temporal identity. We talk about a person as being the *same and different.* We do this by introducing a time dimension. What does "same" and "different" here refer to? To substance or properties? Or to something else? Let us analyze it through a concrete example. We ask: Is Ludwig Wittgenstein (LW), the author of "Tractatus" (WT) and of "Philosophical Investigations" (WP) really the same person, or are there two different Wittgensteins? The answer must be: It is the *same* person, though there *are* two *different*

Wittgensteins. "Tractatus" and "Philosophical Investigations" are so different, that if written simultaneously there would have had to have been two different authors. But as is well known they were written by the same person at different periods in his life.

We have here a case of temporal identity. When we describe such cases we use both the expression "to identify *with*" and to "identify *as*" and furthermore, we relate them to each other. This can be demonstrated in the following way. We identify LW *as* the author of WT. Then, we identify LW *as* the author of WP. Thereafter, we identify LW *with* WT *and with* WP. Hence we carry out two operations:

$$LW\dashrightarrow \quad as \begin{matrix} WT \\ \updownarrow \\ WP \end{matrix} \quad with \quad \dashleftarrow LW.$$ The two meanings of "to

identify" (*as* and *with*) are both necessary and presuppose each other. We cannot identify WT *with* WP if we have not identified them both *as* different, or specific. And, we cannot identify something *as* specific (WT and WP), if we have not identified them with LW. We could start at either end, as the arrow in our diagram indicates. *The important thing is that we need both operations and that both presuppose each other.* Furthermore, this holds for all identifications. Temporal identity is only a special case of "identity in general", where the time dimension stands out as most important, whereas it is less transparent in, e.g., numerical identity.

However, given the acceptance of both interrelated operations, *what do we identify?* We are identifying *actions* and the *result of actions*. LW has written (action) "Tractatus" (result of action). LW discussed with his students (acting by relating to others or interacting). The *result* became "Philosophical Investigations".

Thus, if we identify something *as*, and this something is a person, we can do it by referring to *previous*, *present*, *intended future actions*, and the *results* of these actions. We can abandon the mentioning of properties.

How do we identify something *with*, when it is a person? How do we know that the LW who wrote WT is the *same* as the LW of the WP? Are we not, at least in this case, forced to introduce in one way or other the notion of substance? No, we are not. We can say that the LW who is the author of both WT and WP once worked as a primary school teacher, or was trained as an architect, or lived at a certain time in a hut in the Norwegian mountains, or was born in Austria. In all these cases, we refer to previous actions, i.e., historical facts, which determined his life, and which he actively initiated. (In the case of birth we refer to a unique event). We need not invoke the notion of substance in order to establish that which characterizes Ludwig Wittgenstein. Nor, that which endows him with what we can call his *individuality*, i.e., that which makes him different from other persons, and establishes his own *identity*.

The fact that we emphasize previous events, actions, and the results of actions, establishes a link between "individuality" and "historicity" in a way we could not, if we talked about properties, e.g., his weight, which may have changed, his facial expresssions, which also change. It is this reference to previous actions which differentiates the identification of a person from the identification of a thing.

Finally, to say that a person has *individuality* means that he has a concrete history, and that this may affect his present actions. Thus, the concrete situations which we produce, or into which we are placed, closely relate to our history, and, consequently, to what we can call "individuality".

G.H. von Wright has indicated that if we want to give an account of actions, we first must give an account of change. Change is a transformation of a state of affairs into another state. Thus, the notion of "process" presupposes the notion of "states of affairs". States of affairs can be *generic* or *individual*. An individual state of affairs, "e.g., that the sun is shining in a certain place at a certain time, obtains only once in the history of the world. Generically the same state of affairs, e.g., that the sun is shining, can obtain repeatedly and in different places". (1968 p. 39–40).

If we view historical facts as past individual states of affairs, we abstract from an ongoing process. Thus if we say, "he lived in the mountains in Norway, from where he moved to England", we describe two states of affairs connected by a change. But, if we would look more closely at "living in the mountains of Norway", we could transform this state of affairs into an ongoing series of actions, interactions, and the results of these processes (e.g., notes written down).

We can identify a person's *individuality* in terms of previous actions, events, states of affairs, results of actions. We can say that Wittgenstein was the *person* who did all the previously mentioned things. But this creates a new problem, namely, what do we mean when we talk about a "person"? Since we are going to discuss this important question in the next chapter (see page 160), we can restrict ourselves here to stating that the notion of "person" is basic to all our attempts in basing our epistemology on language.

In summary, then, we can state that the identification of a person's *individuality* does not necessarily imply the notion of substance, or of properties in the restricted sense of "psychological traits".[26] It presupposes the notion of person.

2.4.6.5   *Some conclusions to be drawn*

In the previous pages we have discussed the meaning of the expression "to identify the individuality of a person". We did not discuss the meaning of another expression "to identify a thing that is not the individuality of a person", i.e., the more general problem. But this we have, in fact, analyzed through our distinction between "to identify something with" and "to identify something as" and their interrelation. The identification of "individuality", as indicated, becomes only a special case of "general identity".

When we discuss "identity" in its most restricted sense, namely, as the reflexive relation "identical with itself", one sometimes answers the question of what this means through implictly assuming the notion of substance. What makes something identical with itself is its substance. But, to use the word "substance" in this context is superfluous. It does not add anything to the tautology. "Identical with itself" and "substance" in this context express the same sense.

To avoid this discussion of substance and, etc., it has been suggested to formulate the law of identity as a *semantical* rule: "x is identical with x" then may stand for "if a proposition is true, it is true". The law of contradiction, which is derived from the law of identity, has for example been formulated in the following way: "In a given descriptive context a precise meaning cannot be both attributed and not attributed to a word in that context". (K.H. Jacobsen 1972, p. 35).

Does the recourse to semantical rules solve the problem? Do we not get entangled in ontological difficulties, when transforming the laws of identity and contradiction into semantical rules? The problem is not solved, because we have to ask ourselves why we should follow these rules. One simple answer would be because such is the way we use language. But if we do not want to reintroduce a separation between knowledge of language and knowledge about reality, i.e., the dualism we have tried to overcome, we must say that these semantical rules are not understandable as abstract rules. They are understandable only if we place them in a concrete spatial and temporal context, i.e., apply them to our daily societal praxis.

Basic to our use of language is a general logic of common-sense language, which tells us how we cannot use language. One of the rules of this basic logic we called the "condition for identification" (see p. 102). Frege would not have been able to distinguish between *same* reference and *different* sense, if he had not used language according to the condition for identification. Thus, in order to speak about "*same* reference" and "*different* sense", one has to use and respect the basic logic of our language. How else could we grasp what Frege says? How else could he say it?

Let me take up one problem indicating the importance of the condition for identification. We can give innumerable descriptions of the world. We can describe the same situation in alternative ways and none of these descriptions can claim to be more true than others. Bertalanffy (1955, p. 253) has tried to exemplify this: "The same table is to the physicist an aggregate of electrons, protons and neutrons, to the chemist a composition of certain organic compounds, to the biologist a complex of wood cells, to the art historian a baroque object, to the economist a utility of a certain money value, and none can claim more absolute value than others".

Thus, we can relate ourselves in many ways to the world, describing it according to our specific way of relating. These descriptions supplement each other, and each one adds new aspects. *To what?* we must ask. Let us once again look at the quotation above. It starts: "The *same* table is ...". Thus in order to identify the table *as* the physicist's or *as* the chemist's table, i.e., in different ways, we must already know that it is the *same* table, i.e., we have identified the *specific* table, *with* the table of our daily experience.

A *relational* approach, i.e., an approach which accepts that we can describe the world in many ways depending on how we relate ourselves to it, would be transformed into a *relativistic* approach, if there did not exist the condition of identification. Thus, to use language means to be able to say: "the *same* table". If we were not able to do this, how could we compare the descriptions of a physicist or a chemist, and an art historian? How could we know they were not talking about *different* worlds? And how could we know they were not *living* in *different* worlds? We would even be unable to pose these questions, because they presuppose that we know what "different", and, hence, "different worlds" means. The use of these words presupposes the use of the word "same". Their use is formulated by the rule of condition of identification. Without the condition of identification we could not use language, and there could be no society.

Another consequence of our analysis is the following. We have previously described a *dialectical relation* in the following way (see p. 98): The relata form a totality, are *different* and *identical*, interdependent and opposing each other.

"Different" and "identical" here means that the relata have something which is specific to them, and something which they have in common. This seems to solve the apparent logical contradiction which has been ascribed to the formulation of "dialectical relations".

But there is another important step. The expressions "to identify with" and "to identify as" also *form a relation* which has all the properties ascribed to a dialectical relation. They are interrelated and form a totality. They are interdependent such that they cannot be used independently of each other. They are different ("with" and "as") and have something in common ("to identify"). In their interrelation they are opposed to each other in a complimentary way (by referring to genus and species).

Thus, the condition for identification is not only basic to the use of common-sense language. It joins the use of language and dialectics: The rule is basic to the *language of dialectics* and to the *dialectics of language*. It can be analyzed itself in terms of a dialectical relation as indicated above.

If that is the case, the *rules describing dialectical relations* belong to those rules which form the basic logic of our language. In this sense we may talk about a "dialectical logic".

For that reason especially, we ought to formulate what we have called the condition of identification: "*The word 'to identify' means 'to identify something with something' and 'to identify something as something'. We cannot in our daily language use the expression in one sense without presupposing the other. In other words, we cannot use the words 'same', 'common to' without knowing what it means to use words like 'different', 'specific'—The reversed also holds true*".

If we did not know what these words mean we could only—like the little boy who had not yet learned to use language—clap our hands. This monkeys can also do. But we could not communicate with each other. We could not ask our children whether we should read the *same* story for them, or read a *different* one. We could not sit in a restaurant and ask for *another* beer, meaning the *same* size and sort, we just have drunk. *Social* praxis in all its forms would not be possible.

How about logic? It must be the same. We can use the *law of identity* correctly only if we already have learned the distinction between "to identify with" and "to identify as". However, one can object that using the law of identity forces one to choose "to identify with", and to exclude "to identify as".

How could I formulate the law of identity as a semantical rule: "A word in a descriptive context must have the *same* meaning wherever it occurs in that context", if I did not know that a word could have *different* meanings? Thus it seems to me, the law of identity is not basic in the sense that it does not presuppose anything. It presupposes the distinction between "to identify with" and "to identify as". We cannot use the law of identity without having learned to use language. Neither can we use language without having learned the law of identity (even if we do not know its name and never have heard of its existence).

What kind of conclusion ought we to draw from this assertion? The laws of identity, of contradiction and the excluded third, are not basic in the sense that they form laws of "thinking" or "speaking". They are part of a network of rules making up the basic logic of our language. To say they are part of a network means that in this logic of language, there does not exist more or less basic rules. All these rules form a network and therefore are equally basic.

To formulate the law of identity as a tautology ("x is identical with itself"), seems to be a way of formalizing a rule by deliberately neglecting one of the relata of the condition for identification. The law of identity, as formulated in a tautological way, only takes into consideration "to identify with". It can only do that by abstracting from temporal and spatial relations. If we do not do it, as in the case of numerical identity, then the law of identity, and the condition for identification may be thought of as different formulations of the same rule. If these remarks are valid, we have been able to get a hint of what a general logic of our language looks like. Furthermore, we may be able to understand that this logic well could be called a "dialectical logic" which is not, as Hegel thought,[27] opposed to Aristotelian logic. Instead, it conceives this logic as a more specific formulation of a broader way of formulating rules of the logic of language.

2.4.7   *On dialectical relations*

We will now try to analyze what we mean by a dialectical relation. At the same time we hope that we will abe able to demonstrate the usefulness of the analysis of the words "to identify".

Let us start with an example. In the beginning of Vol. I of "Captial", Marx discusses the value of commodities, starting with a simple exchange relation between two commodities: 20 yards of linen = one coat. The two commodities have different roles in this simple exchange relation: "The linen expresses its value in the coat; the coat serves as the material in which the value is expressed. The former commodity plays an *active* role, the latter, a *passive* role. The value of linen is represented as *relative value*, or appears in relative form. The coat officiates as equivalent or appears in equivalent form" (1965, p. 63).

Thus, a *simple exchange relation* connects the *relative value* with the *equivalent*. Marx then continues to describe the characteristics of the relata, making up the relation and forming a unity: "They are two intimately, mutually dependent and inseparable elements of the expression of value; but at the same time, they are mutually exclusive or opposite extremes—i.e., poles of the same expression" (ibid).

Let us analyze this description. *First*, relative value and the equivalent make up a whole. *Second*, they are different and separate. *Third*, they are mutually exclusive or, in this sense, opposite (entgegengesetzt), because only one of the elements—the linen—has its value expressed by being related to its opposite, the equivalent. The same commodity cannot, in this value expression, simultaneously assume both forms. "The very polarity of these forms makes them mutually exclusive" (op. cit., p. 63).

Fourth, the elements are mutually dependent on each other. Without an equivalent one cannot express a relative value and without a relative value it does not make sense to speak of an "equivalent". *Fifth*, in spite of the fact that they are different and mutually exclusive, they have something in common (they can be identified *with* each other): They are both the products of human labour. To summarize: a dialectical relation can be characterized as one in which (1) elements form a whole, (2) these elements are separate and different, (3) they are opposite and mutually exclusive, (4) they are mutually dependent and (5) they have something in common.

This explication, however, is not sufficient. Two points have to be further elaborated. *First* of all, the notion of "opposite" refers to various relations. *Second*, by choosing the example presented above, we had to describe a dialectical relation as something static. When we, however, want to analyze dialectics as a process, the description has to be supplemented by a dynamic analysis.

Let us start with an elaboration of the term "opposite". A relation being characterized as opposite, can be *contradictory* in the sense of being *mutually exclusive and exhaustive*, i.e., a third possibility does not exist.[28] Life and death, for example, refer to states which are mutually exclusive and exhaustive. So does the relation between workers and capitalists, between labour and capital, between the social nature of the process of production and the private appropriation of the surplus value. When Mao Tse-tung (1966, p. 79 ff.) speaks about "antagonistic contradictions" he most probably has this relation in mind.

A *second* use of the term "opposite" refers to a *contradictory* relation, which is *mutually* exclusive, but *not* exhaustive, i.e., other possibilities exist. Thus, a military dictatorship and a parliamentary democracy are mutually exclusive. But evidently, there exist other types of political systems. "Good-bad" or "neither one" are other examples of this type of relation. Again, we think this corresponds to Mao's notion of "non-antagonistic contradictions".[29]

Finally, there is a third relation of "oppositeness", in which relata are complimentary, but converse. Take for example, "to buy" and "to sell". If x buys something from y, then y necessarily sells something to x. If x is the husband of y, then y necessarily is x's wife. We can now make our distinction between *intrinsic* and *dialectical* relations more precise. All intrinsic relations are characterized by the fact that the relata are interdependent. Dialectical relations are characterized such that the interdependence of the relata is one of opposition in the three ways in which we have analyzed the term: (1) contradiction which is mutually exclusive and exhaustive (2) contradiction which is mutually exclusive but not exhaustive (3) "oppositeness" as complimentary. In this third relation, the relata negate each other only in the sense of being each other's contrast. This may be called: *contrasting negation* (as, e.g., buying is the negation of selling and vice versa).

In the two other dialectical relations, the relata negate each other not only in terms of contrast. In addition, there is an *interacting negation*. Workers are the contrasted negation of capitalists. In their interaction with capitalists, however, they negate the goals of capitalists if they pursue their own contradictory—both in the sense of exclusive and exhaustive—goals. The same holds for capitalists. Contrasting negation does not presuppose interactive negation, but interactive negation presupposes contrasting negation (see also the discussion in Ch. Taylor 1975, p. 235 ff.).

We can now explicate the meaning of the statement that elements in a dialectical relations are identical and contradictory.

The relata, first of all, make up a whole or totality. Second, they are different, i.e., each of them can be *identified as* something specific. Third, they are interdependent in a contradictory way (in the three senses explicated). Fourth, they are, however, not interrelated arbitrarily, i.e., one to *an unspecified* other, but they are related to *its definite* other. This is because they have something in common, which means that they, with regard to that, can be *identified with* each other. As things they are products of human praxis, and as human beings they have praxis and its various forms in common.

The following quotation from the works of Mao Tse-tung, which without the distinction between "to identify with" and "to identify as" seems unclear, now becomes understandable without difficulty: "In given conditions, all contradictory aspects possess the character of non-identity and hence are described as being in contradiction. But they also possess the character of identity and hence are interconnected (1967, Vol I, p. 338).

Thus, Mao uses four characteristics of dialectical relations and shows how they are related. In addition to being a whole or totality, he speaks about (1) non-identity or, as we have called it, difference, (2) contradiction, (3) identity, i.e., some common characteristics and (4) interdependence.

Mao then combines contradiction with non-identity and identity with interdependence. But, if one combines non-identity with identity (as we have done in our condition of identity), then contradiction and interdependence can be paired. Thus we receive a new aspect of the interplay within dialectical relations.[30]

In addition to the distinction between the two contradictions—antagonistic and non-antagonistic—Mao (1966, p. 23 ff.) distinguishes between the *universality* and the *particularity* of contradictions. The first refers to an ontological principle that contradictions exist within the development of any whole or totality from the first moment of its existence. But, each contradiction also has particular characteristics which differentiate it from other contradictions. One example given by Mao is the particularity of the contradiction between the proletariat and the bourgeoisie, as compared to the contradiction between the great masses of the people and the feudal landlord (1967, Vol. I, p. 321).

Furthermore, since in any social process there exists many contradictions, one can be understood as the *principal* contradiction, which in turn influences other contradictions. In capitalist society the principle contradiction is the one existing between the proletariat and the bourgeoisie.

Finally, in each contradiction there is a *principal aspect*. This means that the relata in a dialectical relation need not carry equal weight. One may be more important than the other. But this is not a static situation: "the principal and the non-principal aspects of a contradiction transform themselves into each other and the nature of the things change accordingly" (op cit., p. 54).

This is a principle of great importance, since it points to dialectics as a process, and the specific process of inversion (see p. 120). Dialectics as a process "is not concerned about how things just *are* but about how things may be *produced, superseded* and *further developed* by man. Dialectics is not mere knowledge, a 'methodology', but a critique of both knowledge and reality" (M. Marković 1974, p. 25-6).

In dialectics, nothing is viewed as given once for all. To be understood as produced, means to be grasped as something integrated in an ongoing process.

M. Marković (undated) adds another point of view for understanding the role of dialectics. It should not be comprehended as a series of dogmas, *"but as the theoretical infrastructure of all critical thought which has as its final goal man's self-realization in history"* (p. 33).

Note that Marković does not talk about critical thought in general, but such critical thought that is concerned with man and his self-realization, seen as a historical process.

The reference to man's self-realization has a definite polemical twist. It makes a great difference whether critical thought takes its point of departure in man and his social situation, or approaches the world from the standpoint of some "superhuman value—whether 'God', 'logos', 'world spirit', 'party' or 'world revolution'" (ibid). We may add "science" as an ultimate value, and the attempt to purge "science from all its so called ideological aberrations".

2.5 ON PROCESSES

Dialectics is concerned with processes. This implies at least two problems. One is concerned with processes in terms of human actions, by which the world is produced and changed. In this context we have to analyze praxis as a basic category.

The second problem concerns what we could call a "process-metaphysics", i.e., an ontology based upon the notion that "everything is process". We will, rather briefly, discuss the second problem and devote our main interest to problems of praxis.

2.5.1 *Is everything process?*

What do we mean when we talk about "processes"? Process is change in two senses. First, in the sense of "movement in a time-space dimension". Second, in the sense of "transformation of the given". Movement, considered as evolution, is transformation of the given into higher or more complex structures. Speaking of "structures" implies that "process" and "structure" are complementary concepts. Speaking of "higher" or "more complex structures" presupposes either values or certain organizational principles, according to which higher levels or complexity can be judged.

The assertion that the notion of process as a contrasting negation presupposes the notion of structure or order, can be formulated in three different ways:

(1) We have an order or structure made up of elements and their relations. The notion of process can mean that elements are exchanged for new elements of the same type so that the structure is maintained. One example is the exchange of cells in biological processes.

(2) The elements are not only replaced, but they are also changed and new ones produced, but the structure at large is maintained. If we look at the process of production with changing techniques, but still within the structure of the capitalist system, we have an example of this type of process.

(3) Not only are elements exchanged, but also their relation to each other, such that the structure or order, partially or in its totality, is transformed. This is process as negation and transcendence.

The problem one faces is this: Should processes be viewed as properties of the structure, or should the structure be viewed as a property pertaining to processes? Traditionally, the first mentioned conception has been predominant. Structure is viewed as basic and process as secondary. Attempts to introduce "a process-metaphysics" try to reverse the picture. Though they may view process and structure as complementary, they emphasize process, and view structure as *pertaining to process*. One idea in this approach is that "things, objects, entities are abstractions of what is relatively constant from a process of movement and transformation. They are like the shapes that children like to see in the clouds (e.g., horses, mountains, buildings). Actually, the clouds are an aspect of a movement of the air, the condensation of water vapour and such. The forms that we see in them have only a certain relative stability". (D. Bohm 1969, p. 42).

An important point in this process view is that "the emphasis is not on static structures of complexity, like the parts of a watch but on a *flow* hierarchy, like the system of vortices, say, below a waterfall, that is on structures that are self-maintaining or self-repeating with a certain invariance, even though matter, energy, and information are continually flowing through them" (P. Platt 1970, p. 3).

Hierarchies are understood as interrelated patterns of various degrees of endurance and stability. Stability here means a certain endurance over time, or a slowing down of a process so that we interpret it as a steady state, and that we are able to abstract from movements going on.

Under certain configurations of time and space, we may either have the perspective of processes or of static states. When one asserts, "everything is process" one attempts to abandon abstractions related to a certain perspective in favour of another.[31]

Take for example a river. If we sit at is bank and look closely at the water, we predominantly see flow, i.e., process. If we step back we may be able to observe both flow and structure. If we fly in an airplane above the river we only observe structure.

Thus, in traditional views one, so to say, chooses the airplane perspective of concentrating on structure.

The dialectical position we tried to outline here does not deny the complementary or contrasting negation of process and structure. It only maintains that structure is a property of process. This thing is basic and not the other way round. This also holds for totality and elements. There is no totality without elements. But in dialectical thinking elements are parts in a totality which is the basic concept of the two. Exactly the same holds for intrinsic and extrinsic relations, as well as for relatedness and things (see p. 133).

The same notion is to be found in Mao's idea of the universality of contradiction, as well as in his notion of the principal aspect of a dialectical relation.

In other contexts we find similar problems. In sociological theory we find a conflict and a consensus approach. Conflict and consensus complement each other. The important difference in sociological theories, then, is which one is to be viewed as *basic* and which one as secondary (see Israel 1972a).

2.5.2   On praxis

The presentation so far has been abstract, i.e., isolated from the
main context of concern namely, the dialectics of the producing
and the produced. Therefore, the presentation has not been
dialectical, but mainly analytical. The central processes within the
field of social science are human actions viewed as processes of
production and the outcome of human actions, seen in their social
framework as praxis.

Marx, in analyzing "bourgeois society" in a general manner,
says about these processes, that if we look at them "society itself
stands out as ultimate result of the societal process of production,
i.e., man himself in his societal relations. Everything which has
solid form, e.g., products, etc., appear only as a moment, a
vanishing moment in this movement. The conditions and objecti-
fications of this process are themselves at the same time moments
of it and as the subjects of this process appear only the
invidividuals, but individuals being in relation with each other,
relations which they produce in the same way as well as in a new
way. It is their own continuous moving process (Bewegungsprozess)
in which they renew themselves as well as they produce the world
of richnesses" (1953, p. 600).

In this quotation we find important aspects of praxis as a form
of human activity. Before we discuss what praxis is, we will very
briefly mention how we will not use the term. We will not use it in
a context in which the word is opposed to "theory". In other words,
we will not use it to oppose the terms "practical activity" vs
"(unrealistic) theorizing".

We will also exclude the context of "practice", in the sense of
training or of custom ("legal practice"), or in the sense of
"practising a profession". For that reason and to emphasize the
distinctions, we will talk about "*praxis*". We will use the concept in
an ontological was well as an epistemological context.

In an ontological context, according to K. Kosik (op. cit., p. 218
ff.), praxis as a concept reveals the answer to such questions as
"Who is man?" and "what is the human-societal world"? This
should not, however, be understood such that the answers given are
viewed as general or transcendental preconditions stating "*the*"
nature of man and society: Praxis itself is a product of historically
specific conditions produced by praxis. Thus, the answers to the

above mentioned questions, viewed through the concept of praxis, indicate more often what man is not or not yet than what he is. Here again the principle of negativity can be invoked.

Praxis, to attempt an explication, is the essence of human existence in terms of producing, forming, and transforming the world. At the same time, praxis as collective productive and transforming activity, makes it possible to comprehend the social world as produced and being transformed, in contrast to viewing it as given.

But in any historical period, the world is the product of previous praxis. The actual form which praxis itself takes is influenced by the world as it exists. However, transcendence of the given is what differentiates *revolutionary praxis* from all other praxis.

Praxis reveals man as a creative, productive being, who, through his process of producing, learns to comprehend the social and the non-social world in its totality, i.e., in its interrelations. In addition, he learns his own role through a process of *becoming* conscious. Consciousness is not something one has, but something which is developing (Marx, using the German word "Bewusstsein", stated that it is "bewusstes Sein", an untranslatable play of words which identifies consciousness as "becoming aware in one's being and acting in accordance with it").

In an epistemological context, praxis can be viewed as a basic category. It is through praxis the world of objects are produced. In this process man emerges as a subject. He himself is produced as the result of his own activities. He becomes a subject in two senses: (1) as a producer (2) in the process of production and the effect the products of his production have on him. Through both he becomes increasingly aware: This awareness extends to knowledge of himself as an active, knowing and knowledge-producing being, as well as to the intentions and goals of his actions. That, in turn, increases his awareness of his possibilities, and especially of his possibilities of transcending the given social world. Revolutionary praxis thus (at least partly) is the result of the increasing knowledge that this world, is produced by man, and especially the growing knowledge of its produced deficiencies.

Revolutionary praxis, attempting to transcend the given, presupposes the coming into existence of an awareness common to and shared by many, e.g., through the development of "class consciousness". This, again, is the result of the *participation* in the "material" process of production, and the experience that gives rise to, *as well as* the *interaction* of those who are the producers in this process. The vehicle of interaction is language.

Thus, work and language, being closely interrelated, manifest themselves as the expressions of praxis and, at the same time as the means by which praxis is transformed. As a third expression we have morals. These are produced by praxis in the sense that praxis sets the goals for society, and the norms by which we are enjoined "to bring about what already is" (Ch. Taylor 1975, p. 376). Through the experience of with what alreeady is, its deficiencies are revealed, thus revolutionary praxis means the setting of new goals (e.g., the creation of a society in which the exploitation of man by man has come to an end and, where as a consequence a class-less society has come into existence). The setting of new goals also demands awareness of the way these goals can be reached (e.g., through class-struggle). There is one last point to be made. When man produces the world, he objectifies himself.[32] This means that he transforms his ideas and his capabilities, existing and potential, into objects (in the world of objects) and into institutions (in the social world). Thus, both worlds are humanized worlds, in the sense of expressing human potentialities. At the same time man is produced by the objective and social world, and this in this specific sense, becomes the objectified subject. Thus, praxis is the unity of the dialectics of the producer and the produced, of subject and object, of man and his world. Praxis constitutes dialectics and is constituted by it. Therefore, praxis itself is historically limited in its forms as well as it is the transcendence of these forms.

2.5.3   *The process of inversion (Verdrehung und Verkehrung)*

Whereas in the previous analysis we have underlined *the active role of the producer*, we now also want to emphasize his *passive role as the object of processes* viewed as a historical necessity, i.e., the conditions which pre-exist and/or are created in the continuous on-going process. We will attempt to describe how things are *turned around*, and how this turning around is a consequence of the internal logic of this process. In order to avoid being abstract, I will try to exemplify by means of two examples. One is the master-servant relation as analyzed by Hegel. The second is the process of reification as analyzed by Marx.

Without accepting Hegel's own assumptions or the context in which the master-slave relation is placed, we use it for purposes of demonstration and clarification. The point of departure in Hegel's analysis is the dialectics of self-consciousness. Self-consciousness is achieved by the recognition of one-self by others. (This idea can be found also in G.H. Mead's theory of the development of the self (1967). But here the similarity between Hegel and Mead stops.) Hegel assumes that the operation of recognition is reciprocal. The other, who recognizes me, must himself be recognized by me as my equal. Only if I can appreciate him as my equal does his recognition of myself have any relevance for me. I would not care to be recognized by someone who I consider inferior and therefore disregard. It must neither be one who I consider superior because he may change his recognition into contempt.

Contradictions, however, arise according to Hegel, at an earlier stage of historical development, where the reciprocity of recognizing has not yet been understood. In such a stage, one person may try to force another into recognizing him, because he has not understood the necessity of reciprocity. This could, in modern terms, be explained through the existence of class-differences and class-contradictions—an explanation which obviously is alien to Hegel.

The situation where one person tries to force another into recognizing him leads to armed struggle in which one side may risk death. Hegel explains that risking of one's life is an integrated part of the demand to be recognized (a duel is the prototype of a situation where one risks one's life in order to have the other recognize one's person, one's honour. Perhaps Hegel thought of duelling when he elaborated this idea).

However, the death of the other does not lead to my desired goal of being recognized by him. In fact, his death prevents his recognition. As an alternative to death one of the combatants may give in and accept enslavement. He prefers a life of enslavement to death. Thus he becomes, so to say, the living, and always present, negation of the other. Both, however, are now related to each other in such a way that they are interdependent, antagonistically opposing each other—a classical case of a dialectical relation.

Hegel explains this master-slave relation with the help of the concept of "Dingheit", i.e., that which characterizes the world of objects. The master's relation to the slave is mediated by this "material" world, through his command over the means of production. Engels made this clear when he wrote that the subordination of man to serfdom already presupposes that the master has at his disposition a means of production, through which the slave can function as a slave for him (1959). The reverse also holds true. Only by producing for his master is serfdom maintained for the slave, since it becomes the precondition of his survival.

The master in this relation becomes one-sidedly a consumer, whereas, the slave becomes the producer, the one who transforms the world. Through this role, the slave becomes more and more aware of himself. He understands his position, but as a producer and transformer of the world, he also recognizes his possibilities for changing the world, and abolishing his serfdom.

The master, on the other hand does not receive the desired recognition. He receives the products of the slave's labour, but at the same time deteriorates into a consumer. He becomes the *slave* of his own continuously changing desires, because satisfaction of one desire changes the desire toward other goals.

The slave, on the other hand, experiences himself more and more as the *master* of his capacities, through conquering "nature", which tries to resist him in the process of production. Thus, an *inversion* has occurred. Through his praxis the slave becomes aware of himself and his potentialities, whereas the master, through the form his praxis has taken, deteriorates to a slave.

The slave through his active participation in the process of production, in other words through his work, has been able to transform himself into a human being. One understands why Marx wrote: "The great thing in Hegel's *Phenomenology* and its final result—the dialectics of negativity as the moving and producing principle—is once and for all that Hegel grasps the self-creation of man as a process ... that he grasps the essence of *work* and comprehends practical (gegenständlichen) man, authentic because real man as the product of his *own work*" (Mega I.3, p. 156).

In summary, then, inversion in a dialectical process can be understood as reciprocal negation of negation, through which, so to say, the relata in a relation are both negated. The negation of this negation has as its outcome that both have shifted place and that the process is now conducted on a higher level of historical development.

2.5.4   *The Marxian use of the process of inversion*

Marx (1953 p. 715, ff.), contrasts living labour as carried out by the worker, with dead or objectified labour as carried out by machines, themselves the result of living labour. As the productive forces develop or are developed, the relation between living and objectified labour is displaced such that objectified labour gains at the expense of living labour. Though Marx adds, this is a tautological statement, since increased productivity of labour means that more can be produced with less human labour power. Societal wealth thus comes into being less and less through human living labour, and more and more through the conditions created (previously) by human labour. Objectified labour becomes more and more powerful.

Seen from the standpoint of capital, Marx declares, "the objective conditions of labour assume an ever more colossal independence, represented by its very extent, opposed to living labour, and that societal wealth confronts labour in increasingly powerful portions as an alien and dominant power" (op. cit., p. 715–16).

The process of objectification, i.e., the process of production in which living human labour is transformed into dead objects, which as new means of production are used in this process, is undergoing an *inversion*. Workers, as the subject of this process, become more and more dominated by the objectified conditions of work. Something they have created, but do not control or dispense. Therefore, they become reified, i.e., transformed into a thing, into labour power. Marx describes this process as one of alienation by which the worker disposes of his living labour (Veräusserung), which, as a consequence, becomes something external to him (Entäusserung).

Capital on the other hand, which starts as the object of the process of production becomes more and more powerful, because objectified labour is transformed into capital. "Within the framework of capitalist production this ability of objectified labour to transform itself into capital, i.e., to transform the means of production into means of controlling and exploiting living labour appears as something utterly appropriate to them. ... In fact the rule of the capitalist over the workers is only the rule of the *conditions of labour*, being rendered over the worker ... (K. Marx 1970, p. 16–17).

The dead objectified means of production created by the worker's living labour submit the worker to the commands of capital. "The capitalist functions only as *personified* capital, the capital as person, just as the worker is no more than personified *labour*" (ibid.). Thus an inversion has occurred. The worker who at the outset was the *subject*, the actively producing agent in the process of production becomes an object only, namely personified labour. Capital on the other hand which started as an *object*, becomes the dominating subject in the same process as personified capital.

"Hence the rule of the capitalist over the worker therefore is the rule of things over man, of dead labour over the living, of the product over the producer ..." (ibid., p. 17–18). The result is the inversion "of subject into object and vice versa. Viewed *historically* this inversion is an indispensable transition to enforce the creation of wealth as such, i.e., the relentless productive forces of societal labour, which alone can form the material basis of a free human society, and to do it at the expense of the majority" (ibid., p. 18).

We will try to illustrate the process of inversion by the following diagram:

Process of production

		living		personified
Subject:	worker ————	labour ————	domination ————	dead labour
	↕	↕ ↗	↕	↑
Object:	capital ————	objectified ——	alienation ————	reification, i.e.
		labour		man becomes
				a thing

In capitalist society the process starts with man as worker being the *subject* and capital being the *object*, of the production process. Between subject and object exists a dialectical relation of an antagonistic kind, as indicated by the double arrow. The subjects using or being living labour, create an increasing amount of dead, objectified labour (e.g., means of production). This is indicated by the arrow. When objectified labour has reached a certain threshold it becomes a means of domination (see arrow), and, therefore, the *subject* in this process of production. Through this domination (see arrow), the worker becomes alienated and ends up as an *object*, whereas, the objectified means of production appears as the *subject* of this process. Still, the same antagonistic dialectical relations exist. Through inversion, however, subject and object, so to say, have been reversed. Marx adds that this process of twisting and inversion (Verdrehung und Umkehrung) "is real, not only a supposed one, existing merely, in the imagination of the workers and capitalists. But obviously this process of inversion is a merely *historical* necessity, a necessity for the development of the productive forces solely from a specific historic point of departure or basis, but in no way an *absolute* necessity of production" (ibid).

This basis can be transcended and thus destroyed, since it has been created by man: "The worker's propertylessness and the ownership of living labour by objectified labour or the appropriation of alien labour by capital—both merely expressions of the same relation—are fundamental conditions of the bourgeois mode of production, in no way irrelevant accidents" (ibid).

But they are only moments in a historical process, it is man who makes his own history. The process of inversion, presented as an *integrated* part of dialectical processes, is analyzed in terms of subject-object relations. In the Hegelian master-slave relation, the slave as an object, through his own work succeeds in self-creation. He transforms himself into a *subject*, whereas the master is transformed into an object. In capitalist production, the worker, starts as a subject but is, through the internal logic of the capitalist process of production, transformed into an object. He is reified. Marx makes it clear that this process is "natural". It is, in his opinion, the transition to the creation of a free human society, in which man again becomes the subject of his own destiny.[33]

We now move to the analysis of the fourth precondition of dialectical reasoning: to relatedness, or relations of relations.

2.6 RELATEDNESS

In our analysis of reality we usually make a distinction between the physical world, the world of objects, and the social world. This corresponds to the division of science into the natural and the social sciences. This distinction, however, is not clearcut. Human beings, i.e., persons, can be treated as objects, e.g., biological and physiological things, as bodies, and they can be treated as social beings. Therefore human beings, i.e., persons, belong to both worlds. The distinction we make between the world of objects and the social world is a manifestation of our thinking and our way of using language. Behind this distinction are hidden ontological assumptions: We can either see the two worlds as separate and introduce a dualistic frame. Or, we can look at the two worlds as a totality, in which they are separate, interdependent, and identical, in the sense of having something in common. What they have in common is the notion that both worlds are a product of human praxis, being produced materially and cognitively, the same as we are the products of our own creations.

The *world of objects* consists of chairs, tables, books, typewriters, sausages, etc. The *social world* consists of social institutions. How can we exemplify that both worlds can be identified *as* different and, at the same time, *with* each other?

Take a common phenomenon, an election. If we want to describe to someone who has never heard about elections, we could do it in two ways which presuppose and supplement each other. We could start by saying that one *goes* to a certain *building*, takes a *pencil* and *writes* on a *slip* of paper. Then one *puts* the *slip* in a *box*. So far we have described elections in terms of *actions* or *possibilities of action related* to *things*. In other words, we talk about relations, and the relata are possibilities of action and things. Thus, when we talk about *the world of objects*, we have to use expressions like "things" or "material objects", and relate them to possibilities of actions. This seems to be a rule: we cannot describe things and possibilities of action separately (see P. Zinkernagel 1962 and p. 169 where we will treat this problem in a different context).

The description of elections which we have presented so far is insufficient. Only a diehard behaviourist would feel satisfied. We should tell our visitor that marking a slip *meant* voting for a certain party. We could tell him that political parties consist of persons, e.g., candidates. But we have to add, that we did not (or not mainly) vote for a candidate, but for that which he stands. Thus, we may have voted for "socialism" and against "private enterprise". Neither socialism nor private enterprise are *things*. These words refer to compex relations: relations of ownership, of production, of exchange and distribution— in general, to societal relations and to the relations, in the sense of connections, between these relations. Societal relations are relations between men, but men not in the individual but in the generic sense, men as classes of man for example.

We could go to a factory and point out to our guest some people and say: "they are workers", to others and say: "they are capitalists". But he would not understand what "workers" and "capitalists" are, if we could not make clear that to be a worker is a relation, and to be a capitalist is another relation. That in a society called "capitalistic", these two relations are interdependent and contradictory. It would not make any sense to talk about the relation of being a capitalist without talking about the relation of being a worker.

Let us summarize what we have tried to say so far. When in our daily common-sense language we speak about the world of objects as related to man, the relata are *possibilities of human* action and *things* and *objects*. The relationship is intrinsic, in the sense that possibilities of human action and things as objects (in the epistemological sense of the word) stands in a complimentary relation to each other. (We can talk about two objects two chairs, e.g., standing side by side. In this case we talk about an extrinsic relation between *things* only).

When we speak about the social world, however, we speak about relations in *which the relata themselves are relations*. We speak about relations *of relations*. Sometimes we seem to forget this and speak about social phenomena as if they were things.

Lenin once defined communism as "electrification and soviet power" (the word "soviet" means "councils"—workers' councils, e.g.). His successors believed that electrification meant building dams and turbines, i.e., things, and forgot soviet power totally, probably because human beings were transformed into things. But "electrification" should mean changing existing relations of production by developing new productive forces, and soviet power should mean developing new productive forces by changing relations of production (e.g., in regard to decision-making processes). Thus not only do we deal with relations when using Lenin's definition, but also with how these relations are related to each other.

2.6.1 *Relations of relations*

We now want to clarify the notion of relations of relations.

Traditional social science is atomistic and constricts its field in terms of extrinsic relations. We have previously quoted Kaplan (see p. 82) who explicitly states that concepts in social science should be formulated with the purpose of isolating well delimited factors (the atomistic aspect) which allow for correlations (the idea of extrinsic relations).

How should a dialectical social science which rejects atomism proceed in favour of a concrete totality? Such a social science must view relations between societal phenomena as intrinsic relations and, last but not least, has to understand these intrinsic relations as a continuously ongoing process of transformation.

First of all, the phenomena it relates should be intrinsically related and understood as a process, being conceptualized in terms of negation, transcendence and inversion, as explicated previously.

Second, that which is intrinsically related, i.e., the relata in a dialectical relation are conceived of not as things, but as relations themselves. This notion of relata, being relations themselves in a continuously ongoing process of transformation, will be called *relatedness*, and understood as the fourth presupposition of dialectics.

J. Piaget (1967), has tried to express the idea of relatedness by maintaining that a totality is a system of relations, in which *each relation by the very fact of being a relation, produces transformations of those relations through which it is related to other relations* (p. 29).[34]

Let us exemplify that. In a capitalistic society we have the dialectical relation between "capital" and "wage-labour". But both terms do not refer to isolated factors which can be intercorrelated (i.e., extrinsically related). They themselves are relations. For example, the notion of "capital" contains in itself the relation between "variable" and "constant capital". These notions are in turn related to the relation between "living" and "objectified" or "dead labour". These, again, are related to "wage-labour". Also, the relation between "abstract" and "concrete" labour is a relation related to "wage-labour". We could go on and show how "commodity" is related to the relation we started with, and how "commodity" is related to "value" and to the relation between "exchange" and "use value", and so on.[35]

Each of these categories contains relations, and these relations are dialectically related to each other. This is so, because the point of departure is a concrete totality, i.e., a totality of many-sided relations which all are necessary in grasping the functioning and transformation of this totality. They represent one-sided, abstracted aspects of it. When we start with one relation, e.g., "capital-wage-labour", we analyze the totality from one certain perspective. Then we can switch to another perspective and, eventually, end up with our first relation again.

We discussed in the previous section the process of inversion. We could there analyze how the relation "capital-wage-labour", in its capacity of being a determining societal relation, produces the transformation of the relation between living and objectified labour, by which it is related to other relations like that of alienated labour and of personified products. This is exactly the meaning of Piaget's explication of a "processing relation", i.e., a relation which is not being transformed, but transforms those relations through which it is related to other relations.

"The relation is the irreducible minimum for all units in Marx's conception of social reality. This is really the nub of our difficulty in understanding Marxism, whose subject-matter is not simply society, but society conceived 'relationally'. Capital, labour, value commodity, etc., are all grasped as relations, containing in themselves as integral elements of what they are, those parts with which we tend to see them externally tied. ... This view does not rule out the existence of a core notion for each factor, but treats this core notion itself as a cluster of relations" (B. Ollman 1971, p. 15).

2.6.2   *An exemplification of relatedness*

Let us repeat: We assume that the relata themselves in dialectical relations are relations, not things. This we call "relatedness". We will now try to demonstrate how this conceptualization works by referring to Marx, who asks: What is a commodity? Following his analysis (Zur Kritik 1972, p. 35 ff.), we can distinguish the following steps:

1. A commodity is a totality or unity, composed of two

elements, being separate, interrelated and opposed to each other, as well as having something in common, namely, use-value and exchange-value. Neither use-value nor exchange-value are conceived as things or characteristics, but as relations. A commodity may in one context be understood as "thing-like", but in another it may be defined in terms of relations, when it is analyzed concretely, i.e., within the context of a totality.

2. The commodity *is* the relation use-value, but only for a person other than the owner of the commodity. Thus, labour-power is use-value in relation to capital, since it satisfies capital's need to produce surplus-value (use-value is always use-value in relation to a *need* or a *social function* as is, e.g., the utilization and realization of capital. See also J. Israel 1971, 1974).

3. The commodity is at the same time not-use-value (or negated use-value) for the owner. For if it were use-value for him, it would function for the immediate satisfaction of his own needs. Therefore, it would not be a commodity. It would not be exchanged. Bread eaten by the baker is use-value to him.

4. For the owner of a commodity, for example, for the worker as the owner of labour-power, the commodity as "not-use-value", is merely the materialized carrier of exchange-value: "as active carrier of exchange-value for the use-value is transformed into means of exchange" (Zur Kritik, p. 38). Therefore, to the owner of a commodity, its use-value is nothing but exchange-value.

5. For the non-owner, in our case, capital, the commodity labour-power has to come into existence as use-value in the process of exchange with other commodities, being the carrier of exchange-value. In order to be transformed into use-value, a commodity has to be related to a specific need, or to a certain function which can be fulfilled.

6. Potential use-values, hence, are transformed into real use-values, through reciprocal or universal exchange, from being means of exchange to means of use.

7. Thus, commodities have *processual* (Marx's term is "prozessierende") relations with each other.[36] In this process the form of the commodity does not change, labour-power, e.g., is labour power. The change in this process of becoming use-value is the transformation from non-use-value for the owner (in this case the worker) to use-value for the non-owner (the capitalist).

8. In this processual relation a commodity comes into existence

as use-value through being exchanged. But this presupposes that it is an exchange-value. Commodities, in order to realize themselves as use-values, have to realize themselves as exchange-values.

9. A commodity viewed as a use-value looks totally *independent*. Viewed as exchange-value, it is from the beginning interdependently related to all commodities with which it can be exchanged. This relation is only potential and theoretical, however, and has to be realized in the process of exchange.

10. A commodity is exchange-value to the extent that it contains a certain amount of labour-power. Thus, a commodity is objectified labour-power, i.e., labour-time transformed into objects, which have a *specific* content. Therefore, the commodity is not immediately exchangeable.

11. In order to be universally exchangeable, the exchange-value must come into existence through being based upon *general* characteristics. Here we are faced with a contradiction. A commodity is a potential-exchange-value as long as it contains *specific* labour-time. In order to be exchangeable in *general*, it must be *objectified general* labour-time. But objectified *general* labour-time is by definition socially useful time, in the sense of being the means for producing use-values. Thus, we have potential use-values, which can realize themselves only by becoming exchange-values. On the other hand, exchange-values can realize themselves only by becoming use-values.

12. As use-values commodities satisfy needs. Needs, however, cannot serve as basis for exchange in a capitalistic market economy, where buyer and seller do not know each other, and where the seller has the predominant goal of making profits. Therefore, an owner of a commodity can exchange a commodity, which for him is merely exchange-value, but for the buyer use-value. The buyer, in turn, can only exchange the commodity which is use-value for him, by offering another, which is exchange-value for him, but use-value for the other.

Since the exchange cannot be based upon needs, another measure must be utilized. This measure is the amount of (socially necessary) labour-time contained in a commodity.

Hence, two conclusions can be derived. In capitalistic market exchange, the needs of the people as buyers, i.e., consumers, play only a subordinate role. More usually use-value is mediated by exchange-value. Second, specific concrete labour, for example, labour depending on the worker's skills, does not play a predominant role for exchange, either, since only general abstract labour is the measure of exchange-value. Therefore, concrete labour becomes subordinated to abstract. People related to each other through the market become indifferent to one another. What they sell (labour-power as well as other commodities) is not primarily use-value to them. Sellers, therefore, are primarily interested in realizing exchange-value, and are indifferent to the needs of the buyers who gain satisfaction through use-values.

This, in concentrated form is the methodological approach of Marx characterized by his attempt to utilize concepts grasped as relations of relations in an analysis of societal processes.

The type of analysis we attempted to demonstrate is difficult to understand, and may even create an impression of strangeness, or seem unnecessarily complicated, unless one understands the assumptions on which is based. For instance that dialectics is founded on the categories of totality, of intrinsic relations, of process and of relatedness. The latter makes it possible to substitute "thing-like" categories by relations, and relations of relations.

The position of relatedness presupposes all the three other categories. Relatedness cannot be fully understood without understanding intrinsic relations. Marx, for example, indicates that production and consumption are not two extrinsically related factors, production can be viewed as consumption, e.g., of raw material, and consumption as production, e.g., of labour power.

A worker and his role can be viewed under various aspects, as, e.g., "labour-power", "abstract labour", "variable capital", etc.—all defining characteristics of the concept. But characteristics, which themselves are relations, intrinsically related to each other and other relations.

If relatedness and intrinsic relations presuppose each other, neither can be understood without presupposing the category of totality. Finally, in order to understand relatedness we have to understand process. Hence, also the presuppositions themselves, which underlie dialectics *form a totality of four intrinsically related categories and of that which they are about.* In other words, a dialectical totality is itself conceptualized through the dialectical interrelations of the four basic categories, totality, intrinsic relations, process, and relatedness.

2.6.3   *Things and relations*

For Marx, the conceptualization of societal processes in terms of relatedness has ontological as well as methodological purposes. On the ontological level, our explication has tried to show how the four categories of totality, intrinsic relations, process and relatedness all are necessary categories, presupposing each other in the establishment of a dialectically functioning framework for dialectical reasoning. They, so to speak, form the ontological basis for "the dialectics of dialectics".

Marx also had methodological purposes. He witnessed as do we, the ongoing process of reification in which market-relations play a predominant role in society. This means that man is to an increasing degree transformed from a subject into an object: into labour-power and into buying-power in the consumers' society. At the same time, products in this process of inversion appear as having social attributes. These two tendencies Marx called the "fetishism of commodities". Thus, in underlining the relational aspects when analyzing societal processes, Marx, purposively or not, tried to counteract the reifying tendencies inherent in "positivistic social science". It treats men as objects only, in the name of "scientific objectivity", but does not treat them as subjects.

There is, however, another aspect to the issue of treating the elements in societal processes as things, *or* as relations which function as relations. This problem can be phrased as follows: What are the basic elements or relata in these relations? This question is concerned with the problem of "individuation". Assume we start with society, then divide it into individuals, individuals into cells, cells into atoms, etc. The question then is how far should, or could, we go in subdividing. Do there exist primary units which cannot be further subdivided? There are two answers to this question:

(1) subdivision in terms of things leads to an infinite regression—a rather unsatisfying solution;

(2) we must find another basic unit than things. R.N. Whitehead, for example, who tried to develop a systematic process view based upon the notion of totality, suggests as a primary unit "event" (op. cit., p. 105).[35]

I do not think, however, that social scientists trying to develop a dialectical *social* science really have to worry about the problem of individuation. What they have to worry about is the unit of their analysis. I think that the basic unit of social science is man himself. Thus Marx, in his Feuerbach-theses, proposed that we should view man as "the ensemble of societal relations". I will try to interpret this expression in the next section, because there is another problem to be discussed first.

When we try to conceptualize the *social world*, I agree that we should systematically use relations, not things and, in consequence, their connections (relations) to other relations as the basic unit of analysis.

What about the *world of objects?* I think here a serious epistemological problem is involved. Let us first, once again, state our position. We have attempted to base our epistemological approach on language and the use of language, instead of using sense-data and perception. One of the reasons for this attempt is our wish to ensure intersubjectivity of understanding as a precondition, and thus to take the "social" as constituting the individual, and not vice versa.

But our attempt has to face the problem of common-sense language, i.e., the language we speak daily. This language is partly the very basis of our analysis because it is the basis of social interaction. In part it is itself an expression of existing social praxis which we cannot neglect or disregard.

Finally, as a third reason, we think of common-sense language as the basis of all scientific languages, including the language in which we conceptualize the social world.

The basic concept of our epistemological approach is praxis as the dialectical unity of subject and object, of producer and product. We can, however, analyze this relation on different levels. When we analyze societal processes, we can, e.g., analyze objects in terms of commodities, where commodities are not things but relations. As our previous demonstration indicated, we can analyze commodities in terms of use-value and exchange-value, and their transformation. We can say that bread the baker bakes is exchange-value when he sells it, and use-value when he eats it himself.

But we cannot meaningfully say that he eats use-values. When we analyze what he eats we have changed the level of analysis. We no longer analyze generic problems but rather individual problems, i.e., the actions of a specific individual. This cannot be done without talking about objects in the sense of "thing". Otherwise, we would violate the rules of common-sense language. (This situation is the same as the one discussed in connection with attempts to analyze human action in terms of brain-processes, see p. 11.)

To summarize. Our problem now is no longer the *ontological* problem concerning individuation. It is the *epistemological* problem of how we describe reality. As we have discussed previously, the word "real" is used in various senses depending on the context in which we use it (see p. 93). In addition, our analysis can be carried out on different levels.

When we describe the daily world of objects, and this is exactly one of the things we do when we interact in our daily praxis and communicate with others, we cannot avoid talking about "material things", in the sense of three-dimensional, solid, relatively enduring objects (e.g., I am now sitting at my *typewriter*, writing this *manuscript*, saying to my son that he should bring me the *book* over there on the *table*.

From an ontological point of view, things can be viewed as events in the sense Whitehead uses the word. In daily interaction, however, viewed as an epistemological problem, they are not viewed as events. They are "things" in the sense that we can do something with them. Furthermore, as we will see later on, the notion of a *person* cannot be used without accepting the notion of a body, i.e., a thing.

Earlier in this chapter we discussed different ways of describing social phenomena, e.g., an election. We tried to indicate that such descriptions have to be done on various levels, using different expressions. We now want to show that there is a relation between different levels. Take the following example (see I. Johansson 1976, p. 30). We ask: "What does a capitalist do?", and present three answers:

1. he maximizes profits
2. he decreases production costs
3. he buys new machines.

If we start with the third answer we are, to use Marx's terms on the level of empirical concreteness, in the world of objects. But the answer is unsatisfactory since it does not *explain* what a capitalist does. Therefore, we may ask *why* he buys machines. The answer could be the one presented as number two. Again, we could ask "why", and can then use answer number one. (We could also have started with answer number one in our example, and by asking "how" arrived at answer number three.)

The different answers represent different levels of description. In Marx's methodological terminology, answer number three represents the level of empirical concreteness. At the same time, we talk on an individual level, about what a capitalist does. Answers two and one represent various degrees of abstraction, but still on an individual level.

In order to understand why a capitalist, as a person, wants to maximize profits, we must ascend to the level of thought concreteness, and attempt a theoretical explanation in generic terms. Thus, to use Marx's model (see our discussion at page 64), when we have *reached the level of thought concreteness and are able to analyze generic events, and, at the same time have attempted to get at the essence, then we can and ought to use relations of relations as our unit of analysis.*

As long as we are on the level of empirical concreteness or the level of abstraction, we analyze individual events and, therefore, only appearances or manifestations, but not essential relations. On this level we may and perhaps must use things as units of analysis. This is the difference between the mode of inquiry and the mode of presentation (see p. 65).

In this connection, it may be worthwhile to point out that the production of what is called "false consciousness" is accomplished—among other things—through avoiding analysis on the level of thought-concreteness, implying generic relations. Instead, in daily political discourse there is a tendency to restrict discussion to the level of empirical concreteness and abstraction. As a consequence, this discourse deals predominantly with (1) individual actions, but not with praxis as a generic category (2) with social phenomena as things (the capitalist buys machines), but not as relations of relations, (machines are capital for the production of surplus-value).

Hence, "false consciousness" is the result of a discourse on the individual level of action, where societal phenomena are viewed as things. "False consciousness" in this context is also the outcome of reification, i.e., the transformation of man into things, at the same time, producing and maintaining reification.

Let us return to our previous analysis and face a serious

theoretical problem. We said that when we analyze societal phenomena we can do it in terms of relations of relations. When we use common-sense language in our daily discourse we must talk about things, since the baker eats bread and not use-values.

Does that imply we can use dialectical thinking only with regard to societal phenomena, since dialectics assumes relatedness, as one of its necessary preconditions? Does not our reasoning concerning different levels, associated with different languages, or ways of expressing ourselves, imply that dialectical language can only be applied on certain levels, whereas on other levels, there must be applied "a language of things".

If this were so, we would violate another, probably the most basic of preconditions for dialectics, namely, the notion of totality. Thus, it seems that we when thinking dialectically either have to abandon the language of things—and as a consequence common-sense language—or alternatively that we must show that the language of things also fulfils the preconditions of dialectics. This I think it does. We will devote large parts of the next chapter to this problem. Here, let me just give a hint of our reasoning. When we analyze our common-sense language and concepts like "things", we will find that the basic units of this language are not words or concepts. Nor are they single, isolated, or basic sentences, the atoms of our language as the Wittgenstein of the "Tractatus" believed. We will find that the basic units of our language are *relations*, interrelations between concepts, and relations of relations. Thus, for example, the word *thing* can never be used in our common-sense language, but only in relation to words which are about *possibilities of actions* (see P. Zinkernagel 1962). Therefore, in the sense we have just spoken, the word "thing" is *a relational term*. We, therefore, do not, as has been suggested by B. Ollman (1971) in his otherwise outstanding book, have to eliminate the "thing-language" and to substitute it by a "relational language". We cannot abandon common-sense language. But we can try to present a proof, that the word "thing" implies relations. Therefore, the preconditions of dialectics do exist on all levels, and for any language which we choose regardless of level.

Furthermore, if we return for a moment to our discussion of "to identify with" and "to identify as" (see p. 101), we could with great validity assume that the rule for identification as a rule of the basic logic of our common-sense language and the basic logic of dialectical relations coincide. In other words, central aspects of the basic logic of our common-sense language satisfy the preconditions of dialectics.

2.6.4   *The relational approach to man and society*

"The society does not consist of individuals, but is an expression of the sum of connections, relations (Beziehungen, Verhältnisse)[38] in which the individuals stand to each other" Marx says (1953, p. 176) and adds, the notions of "to be slave" and "to be a citizen" express certain societal relations. "Man is not slave, as such. He is slave within and through society" (ibid.).

At another, previously quoted occasion, Marx calls the ultimate result of the societal process of production "society itself, i.e., man himself in his societal relations" (op. cit., p. 600).

These quotations affirm the assertion that Marx, when talking about society and societal processes, used relations and their relations. Thus, society is the sum or, which would be a more adequate expression, the complex interrelations of relations in which men stand to each other. The analysis of societal processes cannot deal with individual X as working in factory F, but with individuals as wage-labourers in the capitalistic system, where the notion of wage-labourer itself is made up of societal relations.

Therefore, we should distinguish man as an individual with a life-history, and man as a generic category, defined in terms of relations of relations. Doing that we will be able to view society from two complementary perspectives: as ongoing processes and as the result of these processes. If we view society as the result, we view it, at the same time, as the frame within which society as a process is carried out. A process through which this very frame is transformed. But to understand this double role of processes and results, of producing and product, the analysis ought to be carried out in terms of relations of relations.

So far for the determination of society. Marx also tried to determine man as an individual in terms of relations. In the sixth of his Feuerbach-theses he argues against Feuerbach, who had defined the nature or essence of man in terms of abstract characteristics. The essence of man for Marx, however, was in its "reality the ensemble of societal relations".

We can start with what Marx did *not* intend to say. He did not say that man in his essence is the *product* of societal relations. This is a banality, a sociologistic mistake, in which man is reduced to a product only, instead of a producer and the product of what he has produced.

Second, I do not think that Marx tried to state that man's nature is *identical with* the ensemble of societal relations, as if he wishes to present a simple definition, a definition which would be unsatisfying.

I think what he really intended was to set up a *methodological* rule of the following kind: If you want to grasp the essence of man don't look for abstract anthropological or ontological properties. Look for societal relations in any given historical period. If you do that, you may get at what is essential to man in the generic sense.

Furthermore, I do not think he wanted to state a rule which sometimes is given as the content of the *position of relatedness*, (as defined in the previous presentation) but which it is not. This rule says that when analyzing social psychological aspects of individuals, one should not do it in terms of properties, traits, substances, but in terms of relating one individual to another.

Though this rule is important and will be defended later on, it misses a point. In German, the word which is used when talking about "social" is "*gesellschaftlich*". It has two different, though interrelated meanings, namely, "societal" and "social". *Societal relations* are generic relations as "capital-wage-labour". *Social relations*, in this sense, are relations between individuals e.g., social interactions within a group. Marx was mainly concerned with societal relations, whereas, social psychology as we know it, mostly is concerned with social relations.

There is, however, a connection (or relation) between *societal* and *social* relations. The social relations, e.g., between workers in a factory and management, are manifestations of, or influenced by, societal relations. Why, for example, do managers give orders to workers and not workers to managers? Because their social relations or interactions are determined by the "capital-wage-labour relation", where ownership of means of production also implies authority and power, i.e., all that Marx called "relations of production".

These societal relations are reproduced, and eventually changed in the daily social relations which not only affect "consciousness", but also the "material" conditions within which social relations or interaction occurs.

I think the task of a dialectical social psychology is to analyze the interrelations between societal relations and social relations. Marxists usually have disregarded social relations, whereas social psychologists usually disregard societal relations.

Here, as a final point, let us discuss *the relational rule*. When analyzing individuals on a psychological level, we should prefer doing it in terms of actions and interactions, instead of in terms of properties, traits, inherited and/or acquired characteristics or substances. This rule in general states: If we observe that x is aggressive, we do not ascribe his behaviour to an expression of something which is *inside* x, the property of aggressiveness, for example. Let us look at his behaviour as something *between* him and other persons in a given situation. Thus, we can say that x behaves in a way which we, in daily language, describe as "aggressiveness" in *relation to y in situation s*. Thus, if we want to grasp what x does and why he does it, we should look for other persons to whom he does it (and who do something to him), and to the context in terms of situations. In so doing we may be able to develop the dialectics of interaction (see on this point K.F. Riegel, undated).[39]

One objection which is usually made against this relational position is that persons repeat their actions. One person, e.g., may be married, get a divorce, remarry, and act the same way. Is this not an indication that he has "something inside", certain properties and traits? Not necessarily. It could be that he defines *different situations* as *similar* or the *same*, and therefore repeats his actions. Such a point of view, again, points at the analysis of "situation" and its dialectics.

Finally, another objection usually made is that the relational position brings us directly into the arms of behaviourism. This position suggests that we should concentrate on a person's *actions* in relation to others in situations. Does this imply die-hard behaviourism? I do not think so.

Assume, we observe a man crossing the street on a red light, risking his life to enter a tobacco shop a minute before closing-time. We observe his actions and, *at the same* time, ask ourselves why he did it. We usually answer in terms of intentions (he wanted to reach the tobacco shop before closing-time) and purposes (because he is a smoker without cigarettes). It does not matter whether the explanation is correct or not, what matters is that we talk and think in categories of "intentions" and "purposes".

Assume, however, that a policeman has watched our man and gives him a ticket for crossing the street against the red light. If our man tries to explain his intentions and purposes, the policeman may object that he does not care, because he only is interested in factual behaviour. His task is to maintain law and order.

To assume a relational position, thus, does not mean to accept the law and order psychology of behaviourism. Let the behaviourists be "policemen" if they wish. A dialectical social psychology demands more of its practitioners.

NOTES

1. G. Lukács in his last work (1972), discussing a Marxian ontology, underlines this point. Thus he writes, concerning the dialectical relation of continuity and change, that the "preserving is grasped as the continuous maintenance, renewal, unfolding in the real complexes of reality, in that the continuity as internal form of the movement of the complex transforms the abstract preservation into a concrete preservation within becoming" (p. 83).

2. P. Connerton (op. cit.) in his analysis of the last two mentioned types of criticism, ascribes the criticism of obstacles to the Hegelian tradition in German philosophy and reconstruction to the Kantian. Both types have been further developed by the Frankfurt-school (p. 17).

3. The importance of the category of totality has been brought out in G. Lukács' famous dictum: "it is not the predominance of economic motives in the interpretation of society which is the decisive difference between Marxism and bourgeois science, but rather the *point of view of totality* ... is the essence of the method which Marx took over from Hegel and, in an original manner, *transformed* into the basis of an entirely new science" (1971).

4. A consequent reductionist position could maintain that social phenomena should be explained in terms of psychology and psychological laws, psychological phenomena should be explained in terms of physiological laws, physiological phenomena should be explained in terms of the laws of chemistry which in turn can be reduced to laws of physics. This was perhaps the ideal of an atomistic orientation propagating "unified science".

There is, however, one important argument against the possibility of a systematic reductionism: "Reduction is something which takes place, if at all, between two theories" (L. Addis 1968, p. 323). This means that, *given certain conditions*, one theory of, e.g., chemistry can be substituted by another theory of physics. But what are these conditions?

Assume that we have a container of gas. The container is locked and we therefore have a closed chemical system. When such a system is closed, all variables which are of importance can be identified, their characteristics described and quantified. With regard to our example the system can be described by its volume, pressure and temperature. Assume that there are no more variables of importance. We therefore do not only have a *closed*, but also a *complete* system. Under conditions of closure and completeness "the values of *any one* variable at any time can be computed by means of laws from the values of *all* the other at any time" (M. Brodbeck 1968, p. 290). Laws of that type are *reversible* with regard to time. That means that any two states in a closed and complete system can be inferred from each other, regardless of which of the states comes first in time.

Assume now that at least one variable in a closed, complete system, varies. Assume further that in our example this variable is temperature and that this variation is parallelled by the variation in velocity of particles. *Velocity*, however, is a variable used in a different theoretical frame, namely, in a physical theory. If the temperature of the gas can be explained with the help of the velocity of its particles, the variable temperature can be substituted by velocity. In that case, a reduction has occurred from a chemical to a physical theory. "Reduction" as the term is used here, is possible only if the theory is concerned *with closed and complete systems*. The systems with which social science deals—man and society—however, are *open* and *incomplete* in the sense that we cannot specify and quantify all relevant variables.

If closeness and completeness are necessary preconditions for reduction then we can, within the social sciences, remove from the agenda the discussion about reduction.

5. It seems that monism does not presuppose intrinsic relations. If this is correct we have one argument for the impossibility of dialectics to include monism.

6. Take as an example that I am looking through my window and see a landscape, the roofs of some houses, trees, a fence, and just in front of my window a bush. What I *concretely* see is a whole: "In normal vision ... I direct my gaze upon a sector of the landscape, which comes to life and is disclosed, while the other objects recede into the periphery and become dormant, while, however, not ceasing to be there. Now with them I have at my disposal their horizons, in which there is implied, as a marginal view, the object on which my eyes at present fall" (M. Merleau-Ponty 1962, p. 68). The whole sector upon which I gaze is a precondition for being able to isolate the bush and concentrate my look upon it.

7. Basic concepts and categories such as "abstract" and "concrete", "appearance", and "essence", have usually more than one meaning in Hegel's language. Furthermore, two meanings of the same word, used in different expression seem, when related to each other, to form epistemological hypotheses. I think that Hegel—and to a certain extent Marx—being aware of the various meanings of the same word, used this

variation in order to indicate that concepts and categories themselves are not stable, unequivocal and well delimited, but part of a process of change (see also p. 86).

8. Take as an example the analysis of empirical data by means of statistical correlations. The use of correlations presupposes that the variables to be correlated, are independent and that their relation is extrinsic. Thus, the use of a certain statistical method implies already the acceptance of a certain ontological position, something which rarely is clarified in textbooks about "the scientific method".

9. It should be made clear that the categorical notion of "essence" does not have any metaphysical connotations in the sense of referring to "ultimate causes" or to the "ultimate nature of reality", thus offering some "absolute truth". It refers to the *essential* theoretical aspects by which we may explain what we study.

The word "essential", in addition, has two related meanings. One meaning of "essential" is "indispensable". Thus, in the capitalist production man as labour-power, i.e., as an object, is indispensable and in this sense "essential" for capitalistic production. "Essential" here is that which is specially necessary and therefore abstracted from all other characteristics. Thus, man as labour-power is stripped of his many human characteristics. This is an *essential* aspect of the theory of reification (see J. Israel 1971).

In the last sentence we have used "essential" in a second sense. "Essential" here refers to that which enables us to give a coherent explanation of complex social relations and processes.

The two meanings of "essential" can be related. By abstracting, i.e., singling out that which is *essential* in the sense of indispensable, we disregard the multitude and manysidedness of that which makes up the essential nature of the social process. Thus, essential in the sense of "indispensable" and essential in the sense of "basic aspect of a complex structure" complement each other in the indicated theoretical framework.

In general, the category of "essence" in Marxian theory is used in at least three senses. On the *ontological* level essence refers to "the totality of the social process as it is organized in a particular historical epoch" (H. Marcuse 1968, p. 70). For example, one could equate "essence" with "mode of production", if the latter expression is taken in a broad sense.

On the *methodological* level, "essence" refers in the Marxian theoretical context to processes which are more basic than others and therefore can be called "essential processes", e.g., the process of material production.

On the *epistemological* level, finally, "essence" is opposed to "appearance". Things as they appear to man are thought of as manifestation of a structured process forming the essence.

10. As an example of Marx's position we can quote an analysis of a problem to which he returns quite often, namely, what the difference is between human and animal productive activity. In "Capital" (1965, p. 192 ff.), in the chapter on the labour process he states that both man and animals carry out work. But human labour is different from the activity animals engage in. A spider carries out operations similar to a weaver's

work. A bee sometimes is superior in its constructing activity, to the work of a building contractor. However, in one aspect the worst building contractor is superior to the most excellent bee. The "cells" he builds have been previously designed in his head before he builds them. Therefore, at the end of the labour process the result is that which existed in the builder's head as an idea from the beginning. The result is the "objectivation", i.e., the transformations of human ideas and capabilities into objects. But this transformation is at the same time a realization of *purpose* and *intentions*. In addition, the efforts made by the purposive will (der zweckmässige Wille) is a necessary condition for human labour. "The most simple aspects of the labour process are the purposive activity of labour itself, its object and its means" (ibid., p. 193).

11. Althusser (1965, and in the later work "Lire le capital") interprets Marx's distinction between empirical concreteness and thought concreteness as if Marx here introduces a totally antidialectical dualism between what he calls a "real object" and the "object of knowledge". Thus, he introduces an epistemological dualism which goes beyond Hegel and reminds us of Kant (though it can even be interpreted as a position going beyond Kant). Marx makes it clear that the theoretical reconstruction of reality in thought concreteness is not a result, but has been the point of departure, though not grasped as such. What has changed is the way one relates oneself to reality, through a process of abstraction and reconstruction, by which the dialectically essential features of reality are grasped. The change is from mere understanding to grasping, from appearance to the essential.

In Althusser's version there is a dualism between the real world and the world of knowledge. Both are separated. Through a process of reorganization and transformation the "object of knowledge" is changed in order to bring it nearer the "real object". Althusser's ideas suffer (1) from introducing a dualism which cannot be reconciled with the presuppositions of dialectics; (2) the dualism assumes the existence of a world being *independent* as well as *extrinsic* (see p. 37 and 236). By this, he violates a second precondition of dialectics, namely, that of "intrinsic relations", (3) by doing this he comes into difficulties when he wants to explain how the object of knowledge changes to reach a better agreement with the real object. He has to reject the idea that change concerns not only our knowledge, but that which it is about. How can one uphold the idea of *one* process of change, where the social world is changed and, therefore, our knowledge, if one at the same time asserts that our knowledge, more and more, approximates "reality". Thus, he violates the third presupposition of dialectics, the notion of an indivisable totality where there is only one process of change, whether we understand and grasp it, or not. Finally, Althusser takes Marx's views about science as an indication of his anti-empiricism. But Marx was not at all negative to empirical research. He was against an empiricism based upon a sense-data epistemology as, e.g., presented in Anglo-Saxon phenomenalism. This is quite a different problem (see also A. Schaff 1974 where a different criticism is launched against Althusser on the same subject).

12. J.P. Sartre uses "totalization" in somewhat a different sense. He distinguishes "totality" and "totalization". The former he considers as a regulating principle for the totalizing activity (1960, p. 138 ff.).

13. The development of modern physics seems to have led to a similar ontological position. Thus, the physicist D. Bohm (1972) writes concerning the introduction of "the quantum of action" that it implies "that the world is thought of as more like an unbroken network of indivisible links than like an interacting system of separately existing objects" (p. 257).

14. Such laws are called "composition laws" (L. Addis, op. cit.). They are of limited value. Their basic idea is that it should be possible to compute values of variables in a more complex situation from the values of the variables in a less complex situation. However, since there may be limits to the degree of complexity which can be included we may never reach the complex level of the social context. This is one reason why social psychological textbooks usually only *talk* about the social context but do not *include* it.

15. This approach is a type of "sociologism", an inverted reductionism, since man is eliminated as an active and acting subject. The opposite to sociologism is "psychologism", where societal conditions are reduced to psychological, e.g., "the women's liberation movement is due to the sexual frustration of some women" which is as absurd as saying that the "labour-movement is due to the sexual frustration of some workers" (see also Israel 1972a).

Furthermore, it is interesting to note the similarity between this type of interpretation of Marxism and other mechanical theories like behaviouristic psychology. The latter also assumes a sharp division between subject and object. It postulates that the organism, in receiving stimuli stemming from the world of objects is onesidedly influenced. Stimuli impinge on the organism, which emits responses. This amounts, as in the mechanical interpretation of Marxism, to the elimination of the subject as an agent, as actively and productively involved in the process of producing knowledge.

Both approaches are implicitly based upon the assumption that "reality is the more real, the more the subject in a consequent way is eliminated from it" (K. Kosik 1967, p. 19).

16. A methodological rule, when analyzing social systems and their sub-systems, is to view them as open systems. An open system is defined by Bertalanffy (1969, p. 70) as follows: "a system is closed if no material enters or leaves it; it is open if there is import and export and, therefore change of components". Human beings and social systems are open. Therefore, change occurs. A closed system is e.g., a container filled with gas. Closed systems have a tendency to lose structure and to reach a state of entropy. When they have reached a maximum of entropy, closed systems reach a state of equilibrium.

Open systems, on the other hand, can reach a state of quasi equilibrium or balance. But this is accidental. Open systems are not only characterized by *ongoing change*, but also by *contradicting* tendencies among those elements, which make up the whole. Contradictions can be viewed as "driving forces" for transformations within and of the whole. Why do open systems, which are of concern for the social sciences have inherent contradictions? The answer roughly is that they have purposes or goals. Having purposes and goals presupposes choices, both as regards to the goals themselves as to the means of reaching them. Choices presupposes alternatives. Certain alternatives in complex systems are mutually exclusive and exhaustive, others are mutually exclusive. Some may be compatible. As a consequence of the existence of incompatible goals and purposes, conflicts and contradictions arise. Thus, contradictions are constituting characteristics of *complex*, open systems.

One of the basic weaknesses of those sociological and economic theories which are based upon notions of "equilibrium", "balance", "harmony", "consensus" is that they either take the social system as a closed system, or if they accept it to be open, this assumption is logically opposed to the above mentioned notions (see J. Israel 1972a, concerning contradictions in open systems).

17. The process of dialectical movement has often been described as thesis, antitheseis and synthesis. This does not do justice to Hegel's thought, but tends to transform his ideas into superficial generalities. Hegel never used these terms, though Fichte and Schelling did.

18. Kaplan, however, is not unaware of the problem, as the following quotation indicates "concept formation and theory formation in science go hand in hand ... every conceptualization involves us in an inductive risk. The concepts in terms of which we pose our scientific questions limit the range of admissible answers" (op. cit., p. 52–3).

19. The idea of an intrinsic relation is predominant in ancient Chinese thought: "It binds man to the universe; 'nature forms a single order' ... The Chinese do not oppose the subject to the object as the West has done. Subject and object are linked in a unitary fashion. The problems of epistemology which characterize Western intellectual history are not found among the Chinese" (C.W. Mills 1963, p. 498). See also M. Granet (1934) and Chang Tung-Sun (1970).

20. The presentation does not do justice to Hegel. For him it was not only an epistemological, but also an ontological problem. The fact that we have knowledge about the material world is for Hegel not only an expression of human abilities, but a manifestation of the Spirit. Why should we talk about a Spirit at all, if there were no ways in which he could manifest himself? We can talk about him as a consequence of his manifestations. The problem is how we know that the world is a manifestation of the Spirit. If we assume that the Spirit is absolute he must be embodied. Otherwise, the world would not be part of the Spirit.

21. See also W. Kaufmann 1966.

22. See also B. Ollman 1971.

23. Another difficulty is connected with the ambiguity in the word "to be". God *is*, means "God exists", Margarete *is* the Queen of Denmark means "Margarete is identical with 'Queen of Denmark'". The chair *is* brown, either means it "has the quality" or "belongs to the class of objects having brownness", whatever that is.

"Few people are aware that they use so common and important a word as 'is' in half a dozen different senses" (S. Langer 1953, p. 55). A comprehensive discussion of this problem is in H. Gipper (1969).

24. Professor Johan Asplund has pointed out to me that the distinction between "identifying with" and "identifying as", in fact, corresponds to the relation between "genus proximum" and "differentia specifica". To identify two events *with* each other is to refer them to the *same* genus. To identify one event *as* something is to find differentia specifica. Furthermore, genus and species presuppose each other. If the introduction of the distinction I have made here does not amount to anything else, it is well known and trivial.

However, if one, as I am going to do, tries to indicate that this distinction, and the relation between genus and species is at the basis of our language and part of a general logic of our common-sense language and, furthermore, also the basis for talking about "dialectical relations", we have established a relation between the general logic of our common-sense language and can, at the same time, speak about "dialectical logic" in a meaningful way.

25. Similar problems as the one I have exemplified here, concerning the behaviour of my son, is treated, in fact, in the first 15 paragraphs of Wittgenstein's "Philosophical Investigations", He did not, however, discuss the interrelationship between words and actions within the context of the meaning of "to identify". Instead, he uses them to explicate what he means by "language games". Since my son's name is Samuel, I will call the mistake he made "Samuel's mistake".

26. We often identify things in terms of substances. This is due to traditional habits. Speaking about the social sciences and their borrowed ideals, Kaplan says: "The older categories of matter and energy have not yet been integrated in much of our thinking with the new category of information, so that order does not seem to us as real somehow as the materials which exhibit the order, and the message seems more ethereal than the channel by which it is transmitted" (Kaplan 1964, p. 323).

27. Hegel understood well, however, that "identity" is used in the two ways we have analyzed it. In his "Encyclopedia" he says: "When understanding sets itself to study Identity, it has already passed beyond it and is looking at Difference in the shape of bare Variety. If we follow the so-called law of Identity, and say—The sea is the sea, The air is the air, The moon is the moon, these objects pass for having no bearing on one another. What we have before us therefore is not Identity by Difference. We do not stop at this point however, or *regard things merely as different. We compare them one with another, and thus discover the features of likeness and unlikeness. ...* "

Likeness is an Identity of those things which are not the same, not identical with each other: and Unlikeness is a relation of things unlike.

The two therefore do not fall on different aspects or points of views in the thing, without mutual affinity: "*but one throws light into the other*" (my ith.).

Also, F.H. Bradley has analyzed identity in a similar vain.

28. The word "contradiction", as well as its German translation

"Wiederspruch", has a double meaning. Partly, it refers to *language* (two sentences are contradictory when one denies what the other affirms). Partly, it refers to factual, in our context, social relations, being of an "antagonistic" kind. When we *talk* about social reality, being antagonistic we must talk in a non-contradictory way. Only one of the two contradictory statements can be true: "There exist antagonistic contradictions between workers and capitalists" and "There does not exist antagonistic contradictions between workers and capitalists". For a classification of "linguistic oppositions", see Lyons, 1969.

29. Logically the two relations of contradiction can be described as follows: Take "male–female". The denial of the one implies the assertion of the other and the assertion of the one implies the negation of the other. If x = female and y-male, then $\sim x \supset y$ and $y \supset \sim x$, as well as $\sim y \supset x$, and $x \supset \sim y$. For the second relation, however, only the second in the two pairs of implication holds. If x = long and y = short, then $y \supset \sim x$ and $x \supset \sim y$. If somebody is short then he is not long. But if he is *not* short then he is *not* necessarily long, because he could be of medium size.

30. In fact, one could make a system in order to grasp the complexity of dialectics. If we use the four characteristics, (1) non-identity or difference, (2) contradiction or opposition, (3) identity or sameness and (4) interdependence, we get the following relations between pairs of characteristics, if one characteristic appears only once in any combination:

$$1 \,\&\, 2 \,-----------------\, 3 \,\&\, 4$$
$$1 \,\&\, 3 \,-----------------\, 2 \,\&\, 4$$
$$1 \,\&\, 4 \,-----------------\, 2 \,\&\, 3$$

All three pairs of relation make sense: If a dialectical relation possesses the characteristics of non-identity and contradiction it also has identity and interdependence. If, on the other hand, identity and non-identity are the most predominant features, it also must have contradictions and interdependence. Finally, if non-identity and interdependence are emphasized, it also must have identity and contradiction.

31. It is interesting to point out that traditional Chinese metaphysics was based upon a "process-view" (see e.g., J. Needham 1956).

The "process view" seems to be connected with the particularities of the Chinese language, e.g., its extremely simple syntax. Also, the fact should be mentioned that the same word can be used as a noun and a verb. Therefore, the distinction between thing and action is not as sharp in Chinese language as in ours.

The notion of order has been analyzed by a nuclear physicist (D. Bohm, op. cit.). Take a wall of bricks. It consists of bricks being *similar* in size and shape but *different* in position and orientation. One can therefore talk about "*similar differences*" or "*constituting differences*" as the first aspect of "order". Take another brick wall being made of the similar bricks, but being lower and standing in another direction than the first. A comparison between the two walls shows that they are *similar*, but at the same time *different*. In other words, when making comparisons between two orders one can talk about "*different similarities*" or "*distinctive differences*", by which one order can be distinguished from another. If we combine orders into higher orders (bricks constitute a wall, walls a room, rooms a house, etc.), we get a structure. What has been illustrated here in terms of *spatial* orders and structures, also applies to *temporal* orders and structures, (e.g., take music with themes, which are repeated transformed and together with new themes make up a structure). Thus, starting with constitutive differences and adding distinctive differences we can proceed to hierarchically ordered configurations. Evolution, then, can be defined as "a set of changes within a given order of process" or as "coming into being of a new and higher order of process" (op. cit., p. 26).

There are some problems involved in this kind of reasoning. "What is needed is to develop a new mathematics of order and structure. ... The main difficulty seems to be to develop a new structure of mathematical symbolism that takes into account the hierarchical potentialities of order and that does not tacitly commit one to view that the world is composed of separate 'elements', whose orders and relationships are *external* to what these elements are. In addition, it is necessary that the symbolism explicitly differentiates between constitutive differences and distinctive differences so that it will permit the expression of how these two kinds of differences are related in a vast set of cross-references of one aspect of structure to another" (D. Bohm 1969, p. 24, our ith. See also Y. Barel 1973 and M. Polany 1962).

Bohm and Polany both show that the term "randomness" is complementary to the term "order". Randomness ought to be conceived of as an order with infinite dimensions. However, it is usually conceived of as absence of order. When we talk about random events, we mean that they occur by chance. "Chance" means that we cannot predict any ordered occurrence of events. The notion of "order" and that of "randomness", however, are necessarily related to each other. The conception of order implies the conception of randomness and this in turn presupposes order.

Assume, that we find a pattern or any ordered set of events. Take as an example three dice all showing six. We can ask how this order has been brought about. The immediate answer is that this order is due to chance. We can then, with the help of the calculus of probablity, predict how often three dice will show the orderly pattern of three dice showing six.

Constructing a calculus of probability can, paradoxically, be equated with an attempt to set up a system of rules by which one can state the frequence of ordered events occurring randomly (i.e., unordered). Turning it around, one can maintain that the "conception of events governed by chance implies a reference to orderly patterns which such events can simulate by coincidence" (M. Polany 1962, p. 36).

In fact, we are dealing with two types of orders: (1) A set of events forming an ordered pattern like three dice, all showing a six; (2) the order of frequency at which an ordered set of events occurs, i.e., its probability.

32. In German, there are several words like "Gegenständlichkeit", being that characteristic which can be ascribed to objects or things. The activity of creating things in terms of human capacities is "Vergegenständlichung"—objectification, which has to be distinguished from "reification", being the alienated form of Vergegenständlichung within the

capitalist society (see about "reification" J. Israel 1972, 1976). One can also talk about a "gegenständliche" activity which means a practical, sensory constructive activity within the context of epistemology.

33. Louis Althusser (op. cit.), introduced a distinction between the young and the mature Marx, between the ideologist and the scientist. An expression of the "ideological Marx" is, according to Althusser, the theory of alienation in the early "Economic-Philosophical Manuscripts", which Marx, according to Althusser, abandoned in the "German Ideology", and to which he never returned. But this is not correct at all. In the "Grundrisse", as our quotation indicates, not only does the notion appear again (which it does several times, as well as in Capital), but without it one of the central processes of dialectics, namely, inversion, cannot be grasped, and, therefore, not dialectics in its essence, either.

Mao Tse-tung, thinking dialectically, treated the process of inversion when he speaks about the principal aspect of a contradiction (see p. 114). He says that the principal and the non-principal aspect of a contradiction transform themselves into each other and continues: "Some people think that this is not true of certain contradictions. For instance, in the contradiction between the productive forces and the relations of production, the productive forces are the principal aspect; ... and there is no change in their position. This is the mechanical materialist conception, not the dialectical materialist conception. True, the productive forces, practice, and the economic base generally, play the principal and decisive role; ... but it must also be admitted that in certain conditions, such aspects as the relations of production, theory and superstructure in turn manifest themselves in the principal and decisive role" (1968, p. 58).

34. Piaget discusses various notions of totality comparing Durkheim with Marx. He characterizes Marx's view of totality as different from Durkheim's, as processing relations. "Le tout social n'est ni une réunion d'éléments anterieur, ni une entité nouvelle, mais une système de rapports donc chacun engendre, en tant que rapport même, une transformation des termes qu'il relie" (op. cit., p. 29).

35. Bertell Ollman in his book "Alienation" (1971) is one of the few modern interpreters of Marx who has grasped this basic dialectical condition and analyzed Marx's work within this framework. Therefore, his work should be specially mentioned. Also J. Asplund in his book published in Swedish, "Inledning till strukturalismen" (Introduction to structuralism, 1973) presents the problem of transformation of relations in an extraordinary way by analyzing the structure of Ibsen's plays.

36. Marx describes the process in Hegelian terms: "Only through this universal disposal and externalization (Entäusserung) the labour contained in commodities becomes useful labour" (Zur Kritik, p. 38).

37. Whitehead's proposal for this primary unit is the event. Each event is characterized by a certain pattern or form. These patterns are affected by "eternal objects" as colours, sounds, scents, geometrical characters, etc. The activity of each event is characterized by its infusion into other several events, under aspects of these eternal objects, qualifying these other events. Therefore, each event corresponds to two patterns, an intrinsic and an

extrinsic: "the patterns of aspects of other events which it grasps into its own unity, and the patterns of its aspects, which other events severally grasp into their unities" (Whitehead, op. cit., p. 105). This is an attempt to construct a *process* metaphysics, in which "things" are replaced by "relations" as basic units. An "event" *is a relation* in a very definite sense. It has no definite "borders" and "delimitations", but is "overlapping" into other events: it "grasps" the patterns of other events into their unity.

38. Marx uses in his analysis words such as "Beziehung" and "Verhältniss" which makes the explication of his work somewhat difficult. "Beziehung", in English can mean (1) connection, (2) relation, (3) relationship. "Verhältniss", in addition to the three senses which "Beziehung" has, can also mean (4) conditions, (5) state of affairs (6) comparison (im Verhältniss zu ...).

The most usual senses in which Marx talks about "Verhältniss" is "relation" and "condition". These two senses are interrelated, such that societal *conditions* should be grasped as *relations* and *relations*, therefore, are the *conditions* of social processes.

39. There seems to be a parallel to the relational rule in quantum mechanics, as the following quotation indicates. "Contrary to Aristotelian physics of qualities and in contrast to the Newtonian physics of primary properties, the language of quantum mechanics is a language of *interactions* and not of *attributes: processes* and not *properties* are the elements of its syntax. Every attempt, for example, to describe in terms of attributes (or their mixtures) the spins in an unpolarized beam of electrons is doomed to failure...

Much of the present dispute on the foundations of quantum mechanics seem to derive from the reluctance to renounce the attribution of primary qualities to elementary particles" (M. Jammer 1966, p. 381).

3: Persons, Actions and Interactions: Overcoming Dualism

> To wear out one's spirit in order to unify things without knowing that they already are in agreement—this is called "Three in the morning". What is meant by this? A keeper of monkeys said with regard to their ratios of nuts that each monkey was to have three in the morning and four at night. But at this the monkeys were very angry. Then the keeper said they might have four in the morning but three at night, and with that arrangement they were all well pleased. His two proposals were substantially the same, but one made the creatures angry and the others pleased. Thus the sages harmonize the affirmation "it is" and "it is not" and rest in the natural equilisation of Heaven. This is called "following two courses at once".
>
> Chuang Tzu

3.1 SUMMARY

In this chapter we are going to pursue two interrelated tasks. We try, first of all, to show how dualistic notions like body-mind, language-reality, can be abandoned and by that the road paved for one presupposition of dialectics, namely, the notion of totality. Second, by indicating how dualism can be overcome we are led into basic problems of the dialectics of language, the discussion of which will be the main and central theme of this chapter.

The chapter begins with a short analysis by G. Ryle of Descartes' dualism, which he criticizes in terms of a "category mistake". Then, the question is raised whether the problem of body-mind dualism can be solved by means of an empirical study. An experiment carried out by the brain-surgeon W. Penfield is used to demonstrate that interpretations of the results of his experiment presupposes clarification of the conceptual issue at stake, and that the experiment, as such, cannot contribute anything to this clarification.

Central parts of the following sections are dedicated to the analysis of the concept "person" as performed by Strawson. He indicates, by means of a conceptual analysis, that the person concept is a logically primitive concept in the sense of being presupposed when we speak about body and mind or "states of consciousness", as Strawson calls it. In short, he says that we cannot talk about "person" without talking about "body". Furthermore, we cannot talk about "states of consciousness" without talking about "body". There are no states of consciousness which are not embodied, and there are, in consequence, no persons without having bodies and states of consciousness.

Thus Strawson is able to overcome the mind-body dualism. At the same time, he formulates what Zinkernagel calls "conditions for descriptions". These are ways of talking about our world, such that if we deny their being so, we contradict ourselves. These conditions for description are characterized by the fact that they interrelate certain expressions. Thus, Zinkernagel, for example, shows that we cannot talk about things independently of possibilities of action. These conditions make up the basic logic of our language.

Conditions for description are such that they form the basis for any analysis of language, and that they themselves cannot be further explained. Any explanation of these conditions has to be made in terms of new conditions for description and, therefore, leads to an infinite regression. Conditions for description have ontological implications because they do not state anything about language alone, but at the same time also something about reality.

Thus, Zinkernagel, through his conceptual analysis is able to overcome the language-reality dualism. He also rejects the *theory* of analytic and synthetic propositions, though he accepts the distinction, as such.

Using the analysis by Strawson and Zinkernagel we attempt in the following pages to formulate conditions for description of society. Our analysis starts with a description of what we mean by "action". Hereby, we base our analysis to some extent on von Wright's deontic logic.

We then try to show that the concept "possibility of action" is a central one. Possibilities of action are dependent on the state of the physical world, and on the state of the social world. Both impose limitations to our actions. The limitations of the social world are of a normative kind. Next, we argue that it is logically impossible to talk about "society" without talking about "rules". Furthermore, we try to show, that we cannot characterize man as user of language independently of assuming the reciprocity of action. This means interaction such that persons involved are interchangeably subjects and objects.

As a next step, we try to show that reciprocity of action presupposes the notions of "freedom" and "equality". In this context we can draw heavily from an analysis by Karl Marx.

Finally, we attempt to show that intersubjectivity of meaning is not something which can be established through interaction, but that it is presupposed to interaction. Furthermore, it is indicated that intersubjectivity of meaning is not in contradiction to different and opposing uses of language, e.g., as consequences of antagonistic contradictions in a class-society.

This analysis of intersubjectivity also give some hints about what can be meant by the expression "false consciousness", which is analyzed briefly.

The chapter ends with a summarizing overview of our position on the dialectics of language. It makes clear that any linguistic analysis must begin in the concrete social situation historically determined, of the speaker, and that language cannot be contrasted to reality. Language is a part of reality.

This chapter, hence, discusses and tries to elaborate basic principles of the dialectics of language and, also, comes to the conclusion that language cannot totally be described in terms of a game.

There exists conditions for descriptions or rules of the basic logic of language which differ from the rules of a game in the following way: If you change the rules of a game you still play a game, though a different one. If you change the rules of the basic logic of language you are no longer playing *any* language game at all. What you in this case try to say does not make sense.

3.2   OVERCOMING DUALISM

In chapter 1 (p. 9) we briefly discussed the position of dualism and tried to place it in an historical context. Our main argument against dualism is that its presuppositions are incompatible with the preconditions of dialectical thinking.

Within the social sciences, psychology especially has been affected by various dualistic notions and the problems which they create. Also, certain notions within Marxist theorizing, for example, the notion of knowledge as a mirror, are based upon implicit dualistic notions and are, therefore, incompatible with a dialectical Marxist theory.

Dualism, as developed by Descartes—though he was not the first philosopher to assume this position—is based upon the idea of two basically different substances: *res extensa*, i.e., a substance which is extended in space; and *res cogitans*, a thinking substance. Both are mutually exclusive, and represent two modes of existence. Based also upon a dualistic position is the notion of an outer and an inner world, and, related to this, a body-mind dualism. In most dualistic distinctions, the two different substances, or whatever they may be, are related to each other through extrinsic relations. Traditionally, the notion of an outer world includes physical objects as well as the human body. In this view, the inner world of human consciousness is accessible only to oneself and is, therefore, private. Knowledge of this private, inner world can be obtained only, for example, through introspection. There is no direct access to the experiences of others or to their consciousness.

Language, in this dualism is understood to be about reality (as well as about language itself). But it is not understood as being a part of reality itself. Rather it is a system of signs denoting objects. This relationship between signs and denoted objects is thought of as extrinsic and arbitrary.

Since the outer world of physical objects is extrinsically related to our inner world of experience and consciousness, there develops a series of problems. First, how it is possible to have a correct or veridical perception of this "outer" world. Since subject and object are sharply separated, perception becomes an effect of external causes which impinge on our sense organs. The dilemma arises that we never can approach this world directly, since it is external to us. The only knowledge we have about this outer world depends on the phenomena believed to be an effect of stimuli, located in this outer world.

Now, how can we prove that phenomena represent a veridical or true representation of this unknown world? We cannot. In fact, veridicality is implicitly assumed to exist between "objective things" and "things perceived", in order to prove that such a veridicality is the case.[1]

In other words, one moves in a circle where what has to be proved is silently and implicitly presupposed.

This state of affairs is aggravated by the notion that knowledge has to be based upon sense experience, upon perception. Furthermore, the subject is viewed as a passive being who does not participate in the cognitive construction of his world. Instead, he is viewed as relatively passive, a receiver of sense-data, or whatever it may be, that reflect the world of objects.

3.2.1 *On body-mind dualism*

We now shift, after this short introduction, to an equally brief discussion of the body-mind dualism. This can be formulated in a "strong" and in a "weak" version. The strong version maintains that the body and the mind are not only two different and separated substances which do not depend on each other. In fact, they are completely unrelated and cannot, therefore, influence each other. Since the main function of the body is to act and the main function of the mind to think, we have a double person: one who thinks without acting, and one who acts without thinking. This strong version is rarely accepted today.

The weaker version assumes that the mind, being in some way lodged in the body, interacts with the body. This interaction can occur in two ways. One version assumes that all mental events are *caused* by physiological or chemical states or processes going on in the body. It is very difficult to understand how, for example, the thoughts I am writing down here could have been caused—in a meaningful sense of that word—by neurophysiological or glandular processes. This does not mean that such processes do not go on simultaneous to my thinking, but that they should be the cause of these specific thoughts is difficult to understand.

The other version has to do with a preoccupation with problems of the will, the determining of human actions, and possibilities of a free will that causes us to act. It is, in other words, bound to problems of rationality and freedom. "And it is in fact when we focus on pure thought, on the selective activity of the mind when it is pondering some problem in science or mathematics, when it is deliberating on some principle of morals, that the mind seems freest from external control—in a way it does not appear to be, for instance, in our emotional life. It is in this realm that the thesis of dualism seems to be most plausible" (Ch. Taylor 1975, p. 82).

Thus, one consequence of such a dualistic position is to assume that the will, located in the mind, being mind, or an important aspect of it, determines the actions of the body.

A detailed criticism of the idea that mind directs the actions of the body through will was formulated by G. Ryle (1963). He called it, "with deliberate abusiveness", the idea of "the ghost in the machine". If we ask, how it is that the mind causes us to will, and therefore to exert a decisive influence on the body and its actions, we can think of at least two answers.

One answer maintains that the expression "the mind wills" is a matter of definition, i.e., purely a semantical problem. To say "to have a mind" is synonymous with saying "willing something". In this case, it does not make sense to say "our mind causes us to will".

The second answer assumes there are really certain mechanisms which determine the mind to will and, in consequence, the body to act. Then we have to ask what are the mechanisms which determine the mechanisms, which determine the mind to will. In other words, if we accept that there is "a ghost in the machine", we must look for another ghost, determining the decisions of the "original ghost", which leads us into infinite regression.

G. Ryle called this idea of the mind determining the actions of the body a "category mistake" using logical arguments.[2] What is a category mistake? Ryle uses several examples to demonstrate this. One example, a person visiting Oxford is shown colleges, libraries, museums, scientific departments, and administrative offices. He asks where the university is and where its members reside and work. In doing this he commits a category mistake. He assumes that "the university" is an additional member of the class of the other units. "He was mistakenly allocating the University to the same category as that to which the other institutions belong" (op. cit., p. 18).

One cannot speak of "colleages *and* the University", but only of "colleges *of* the University".

A similar category mistake is made when one views the mind as a ghost locked up in a machine, the body. The mistake is due to the fact that "mind" and the "actions of the mind" cannot be described in the language of physics, chemistry and physiology, as the body can. Therefore mind must be a complex unit like the body is a complex unit. If this were the case, then we could speak of "body *and* mind". Instead, we should attribute mind or states of mind to the body. In other words, we can speak of "the states of mind *of* a body". In order to be able to speak of a mind or of consciousness and their states, we have to attribute it to an organism, e.g., a body. On the other hand, we can think and talk of organisms without states of consciousness like we can talk about universities without talking about university libraries. If we can discover that we commit a category mistake, i.e., a logical error, in speaking about mind *and* body, we can start to resolve the problem of their bifurcation. As a consequence we take an important step in overcoming dualism.

The attempt at overcoming this dualism has been further pursued by P.F. Strawson in his analysis of what we mean when we talk about a "person" (1964). A person is characterized by mental as well as physical characteristics, by publicly observable states and by private state. But these are all characteristics *of* a person.

To ignore this, says Strawson, is to ignore the structure of our language and of our concepts (op. cit., p. 91).[3] We will discuss Strawson's analysis extensively. Before that, let us look at another problem.

3.2.2   *Can dualism be saved empirically through experiments?*

As we discussed in chapter 1 (p. 11), one solution to the dilemma which dualism leads us is reductionism, as, for example, expressed in the identity thesis. It maintains that every mental state is identical with a physiological state.

As we indicated before, it would be impossible to identify, e.g., complicated choice situations with physiological states.

There is at least one experiment whose results are contrary to the identity thesis. Furthermore, this experiment seems strongly to support dualism. For that reason we want to discuss it and its consequences. To make sure that we have understood the intentions of the author, we will quote his description.

The experiment was carried out by W. Penfield, a well-known brain-surgeon. During one of his surgeries he applied electrodes to the motor area of the cerebral cortex, which made the patient move his hand opposite to the area stimulated. If the patient is asked why he moved his hand, he cannot explain it. He does not experience the light electric shock applied to his cortex, being insensitive to such stimulation in terms of pain. Penfield describes his experiment in the following way: "Once when I warned such a patient of my intention to stimulate the motor areas of the cortex, and challenged him to keep his hand from moving when the electrode was applied, he seized it with the other hand, and struggled to hold it still. Thus one hand, under the control of the right hemisphere driven by an electrode, and the other hand, which he controlled through the left hemisphere were caused to struggle against each other. *Behind* the 'brain action' of one hemisphere was the patient's *mind.* Behind the action of the other hemisphere was the electrode" (W. Penfield, quoted in Koestler 1970, p. 235, our ith).

One part of the experiment—planting electrodes in the brain, electric stimulation and involuntary movements—can be described in the language of neurophysiology. The patient's struggle to control his hand is described by Penfield as "the action of the mind" in a "mentalistic" language, understood as a counterpart to the former.

What does this experiment indicate? That we must uphold the mind–body dualism? Does Penfield try to convince us that the experiment indicates there are two subjects? One subject having corporeal characteristics, e.g., a brain which can be stimulated through electric shocks, leading to movements which cannot be controlled through "will". And another subject—a mind or a consciousness—to whom we can talk, give orders and who, by his will or his own efforts tries to follow orders and control what the "mind" cannot control. Is this idea of *a person* composed of *two subjects*—which essentially is the basic idea of dualism—not a strange idea? How strange this idea is becomes clear when we try to translate it into our common-sense language. We can attribute body as well as consciousness to *a person*, for example, by saying "the consciousness of a person" and "the body of a person". But we cannot attribute person to consciousness and body. It does not make sense to say "the person of a consciousness" and "the person of a body". Hence, the concept of person must be more basic than the concept of consciousness and of body. But, if this is so the dualistic notion which assumes two subjects—mind or consciousness and body—make up, or are basic to a person, cannot be upheld. Then we must accept that the concept of a person is basic in the explanation of body, as well as of consciousness. It is the great merit of P.F. Strawson (op. cit.) to have analyzed this. We will shortly present his analysis. Before that I would like to make two final remarks in connection with the analysis of the experiment carried out by Penfield.

I think it should cause the representatives of a "raw empiricism" within the social sciences some second thoughts. Experimental, and other empirical observations do not solve any basic epistemological and methodological problems. They may be interpreted in various ways, as our example indicates. But if we make a thorough conceptual analysis, and by this I mean that we try to find out what we can say and what we cannot say, then at least we should be able to exclude some explanations as not tenable. We may not be able to present one valid explanation, but we will be able to exclude those that seem convincing, but do not make sense when further scrutinized.

Finally, the experiment suggests that we abandon dualism. But that, in turn, demands another conceptual strategy. One which "seems to point towards ... a dissolution of the alternative materialism–idealism; it invites us to examine a non-dualistic conception of man which is nevertheless not linked with a reductionist notion of the science of man. This would, of course, involve an ontology with more than one level; in other words, it would mean that although some principles govern the behaviour of all things, others apply only to some; and yet the latter cannot be shown as a special case of the former" (Ch. Taylor 1972, p. 465).

3.2.3   The concept "person"

In order to overcome the body–mind dualism, it is necessary to find a concept that neither presupposes the concept "body" nor those attributes which we employ when talking about "body". Neither should it presuppose the concept of mind or consciousness (we will from now on substitute the ambiguous word "mind" by the no less ambiguous word "consciousness"), or all the attributes which we use when talking about it.

This concept should, however, not only be such, that it neither presupposes "body" nor "consciousness", but that these two concepts, in turn, presuppose the more basic concept. Strawson (op.

cit.), analyzes the concept "person" and shows convincingly that it fulfills these two conditions. Furthermore, accepting his point of view leads to a series of consequences of utmost importance.

Let us try to recapitulate some important points in Strawson's analysis. When we talk about ourselves we use attributes as weight, size, height, colour, etc., i.e., *physical* or *corporeal* attributes, which we also employ when talking about things.

We also attribute to ourselves *location* ("I am here in the room") and *bodily postures* ("I am lying down"). In addition, however, we ascribe to ourselves *thoughts* and *feelings* ("I think", "I am angry"), as well as *perceptions* and *memories* ("I see", "I remember").

When we start reflecting about how we describe ourselves, we may find it strange that we ascribe to ourselves states of consciousness as intended actions, thoughts, perceptions, etc. Assume we do not take it for granted or self-evident that we make these kinds of ascriptions. We can then pose to ourselves two questions: "Why are one's states of consciousness ascribed to anything at all?" and "Why are they ascribed to the very same thing as certain corporeal characteristics, a certain physical situation, etc?" (P.F. Strawson, op. cit., p. 90).

When we answer these questions, we will find that they are not unrelated. First of all, the answer to the second question is that we do it because we have the concept of "person" and we employ it all the time in our daily common-sense language. In fact, to be able to speak a language, or to have knowledge of language implies, among other things, that we know the concept "person" and its meaning; a single individual, i.e., an entity such that we ascribe to him states of consciousness, as well as, corporeal attributes. (Whereas when we apply Cartesian dualistic notions we have to assume the existence of two separate subjects, one having corporeal attributes, the other states of consciousness.)

The concept of "person", therefore, according to Strawson, is logically primitive. It neither presupposes the concept of "an individual consciousness" nor of a "body". Quite to the contrary, these both presuppose the notion of person. We cannot talk about a person without a body, and we cannot talk about states of consciousness without attributing them to a person with a body. (We can, however talk about a body without attributing states of consciousness to it. Take as an example, the victim of a traffic-accident who for a long time is in a state of coma. This example indicates that a human body without any states of consciousness is no longer to be considered as "really living", but merely being "kept at life". We also talk about "brain-death".)

This discussion also indicates the type of relation existing between our two previously posed questions: It is a necessary condition for ascribing states of consciousness to anything at all that they be ascribed to something that has corporeal attributes.

This can also be expressed in a different way. If we take particular things with corporeal attributes—i.e., bodies—and particular states of consciousness—e.g., the perception of a red spot—we can only identify the state of consciousness by attributing it to a person: he or I perceive a red spot, where "he" or "I" refers to a person. *Material* particulars in the sense of three-dimensional, solid and relatively enduring things, including bodies, are basic particulars. They can be identified and re-identified directly. Whereas non-material particulars like thoughts or single perceptions, have to be identified with reference to basic particulars (these ideas were mentioned in chapter 1, p. 15, as an example of how one can talk about "materialism").

There is another point to be made. We must be able to identify others as persons, i.e., as particulars, in order to be able to identify ourselves as persons. How could we identify ourselves as individual persons, if we were not able to differentiate between other persons and ourselves. This seems obvious. However, a consequence is not so obvious. The fact that we know the concept "person", as a user of language, logically implies that we also know the concept "consciousness". When I have learned the meaning of the concept "person" so that I can use it correctly, I also have learned the meaning of the concept "consciousness", since both are logically interrelated, as discussed above.

If we have learned what the concept "consciousness" means, and can attribute it to others, we are able to apply it to ourselves. This means knowledge of the fact that we can attribute consciousness to others is a necessary precondition for saying that we ourselves have consciousness. Or, to say it differently: in order to talk about "my consciousness", I must have the concept "consciousness". But this concept presupposes knowledge of the concept "person".

Let me summarize the arguments. We could not ascribe states of consciousness or experience to ourselves, unless we were ready and able to ascribe them also "to other individual entities of the same logical type as that thing to which one ascribes one's own states of consciousness" (op. cit., p. 104). A necessary condition for this is that we can *identify different* subjects of the *same* type, i.e., different subjects having these attributes.

A condition for this, in turn, is that each individual, including myself, is such that we can ascribe to him both states of consciousness, and corporeal attributes. In other words, we can talk about others as persons.

3.2.4   *Epistemological consequences of this analysis*

1. We can now relate our condition for identification (see p. 110) with the concept of "person". By that, we can perhaps show its basic role in the logic of our common-sense language.

We can say we have acquired knowledge about the concept "person", if we can identify *different* subjects as belonging to the *same* logical type (as having bodies and states of consciousness). This means we are able to *identify* them as specific and, therefore, different from each other. Also that we can *identify* them *with* each other, i.e., as belonging to the same type. But we could not identify anything *with* something else (as belonging, e.g., to the same genus) as long as we have not been able to identify it *as* specific (as, e.g., being a species). We cannot in reverse, identify something *as* specific, without simultaneously knowing that it is identifiable *with* something else. These two types of operations, therefore, have to be characterized as interrelated, which again—as we will see later—characterizes basic conditions of elements in the logic of common-sense language.

An attempt to identify something only *with* something else for example, as done in classical conditioning experiments, amounts to committing Samuel's mistake (see p. 147) when applied to the problem of what it means to possess language. This mistake partially accounts for the inability of a strict behaviouristic explanation to account for what it means to have a language.

It seems to me, however, that learning the condition for identification is genetically prior to learning the concept of "person", since the condition of identification not only applies to persons but also to such things as toys, nipples, and bottles.[2]

In any case, it seems justifiable to say that the concepts of "to identify with" and "to identify as" *and* the words which are logically related to them, for example "same", "common", "different", "specific", *and* the concept of "person" are all interrelated. We cannot use them independently of each other.

This points to a very important epistemological principle. The basic epistemological units of our language are not concepts, but *relations between concepts.* Thus, concepts such as "persons", "body" and "consciousness", as well as "identify with" and "identify as", are logically interrelated. This holds for other concepts also (as our discussion later on p. 206 indicates). From an epistemological point of view, our language basically consists of a *network of interrelated concepts* (and the words which are logically related to them). If this is correct, we must reject atomistic notions of language (as for example those expressed in "Tractatus"). Furthermore, we can apply one of the four basic presuppositions of dialectics, namely, relatedness, to language. *The basic units of linguistic analysis thus seem to be relations and relations of relations.*

2. Strawson's analysis of the concept "person" fits very well into ours concerning dialectical relations. Corporeal characteristics are different from, and opposed to, states of consciousness. At the same time, however, they closely relate *one* to *its* other and form a totality, namely, that of a person. But here we must make very clear one point to be observed. Strawson maintains—I think correctly—that the concept "person" is basic. Thus, when we say it is composed of body and states of consciousness we mean to apply the dialectical principle "*one divides into two*", i.e., "person " is more fundamental than "body" and "states of consciousness". When we say, as we did above, that body and states of consciousness form a totality, namely, that of a person, we do *not* imply that "two unites into one". We can grasp only that something is fundamental when we can "divide it into two". But, in order to understand that it is fundamental, we must know the two into which "it can be divided".

We now can better understand the basis of what G. Ryle called a "category mistake" (see p. 157). In our terminology, the essential feature of a category mistake is that two things are identified *as* belonging to the same category, i.e., they are identified *with* each other, when they do not. For example, if one speaks of "university *and* colleges" (to use Ryle's example), or "bodies *and* states of mind", instead of "colleges *of* a university", or "states of mind *of* a body" (of a person respectively).

Furthermore, in speaking about "bodies and minds" one could make another category mistake, namely identifying the two things *as* completely different. That is, as if they belonged to two separate categories which have nothing whatsoever in common (which cannot be *identified with* each other), when in fact, they ought to be identified *as* different and at the same identified *with* each other. Body and states of consciousness are *different*. They have, however, the characteristic in *common* that they both are attributes of a person.

This second category mistake, where two things are only *identified as* different (and not, at the same time with each other) seems to be the opposite of "Samuel's mistake", i.e., the mistake made by the little boy who could only clap his hands. He could only *identify with* and not, at the same time, *as* (see p. 102).

The interesting point here is that Strawson's analysis, carried out in the tradition of analytical philosophy, and as intepreted here, comes to results which illustrate the dialectics of language as formulated in the condition for identification (see p. 110). At the same time, this condition, also, is basic to the language of dialectics. As we have seen previously (p. 112), a dialectical relation can be defined as characterized by the relata forming a whole or unity (e.g., person). That they are different (can be identified *as*, e.g., body and states of consciousness). That they are interdependent (we cannot speak about a state of consciousness without attributing it to a body). And that they are identical (they can be identified *with* each other, e.g., as body and states of consciousness, being both parts of a person).

We once again want to repeat, the condition for identification is basic to the language of dialectics as well as to the dialectics of our common-sense language. At the same time, this condition links together the language of dialectics and the dialectics of language. It is, as we will see later on (p. 169), a condition for description, i.e., one of the basic rules of language, which cannot be further explained, but which is nevertheless, one of the rules which explain how we use language.

3. The third point we want to make is the following. In traditional epistemology, perception, as the basis of analysis, sense-data or other phenomena of the same type, are often made

into basic particulars. A consequence is that epistemological analysis is then based upon "private experiences", and has great difficulties avoiding ending up in solipsism. Strawson rejects the idea of "private experiences" as basic particulars, saying "on the present criteria, they are the most obvious inadmissible" (op. cit., p. 41). Instead, he introduces "material particulars" as basic, and convincingly demonstrates that "private particulars" can only be indirectly identified, i.e., only with the help of "material particulars".

Without introducing a traditional ontological materialism, which also presupposes dualism, he introduces—in a very restricted sense of the word a "materialistic epistemology": which not only avoids dualism, but transcends it. Furthermore, this makes impossible the use of perception as the basis of epistemological analysis. It must be substituted by language: thus avoiding the pitfalls of a strict phenomenalistic position and making it possible to argue for the intersubjectivity of knowledge.

4. Strawson makes clear that in order to have a notion of "my consciousness", it is necessary to know what it means "to have consciousness", and to attribute it to others. This is opposed to the more traditional notion where I conclude from my own experience, analyzed, e.g., through introspection, that others ought to have the same experience. In fact, from such a position we can only make guesses about the experiences of others. In this respect there is some similarity between Strawson and the position advocated by G.H. Mead (1967). Mead maintains that social interaction precedes the formation of an ego and not the opposite. If we assume that the word "ego" can be exchanged with "own states of consciousness", the similarity between the two positions stands out clearly. But Strawson goes one step further.

He argues that a person cannot infer from ones own experiences how to ascribe states of consciousness to others, "for unless he already knows how to do this, he has no conception of *his own case*, or any *case*, i.e., any subject of experience" (op. cit., p. 106). One not only must accept such a position in order to avoid scepticism about the possibilities of attributing states of consciousness. One must accept it "in order to explain the existence of a conceptual scheme in terms of which the *sceptical problem is stated*" (ibid). Thus, we would not even be able to express our scepticism about the possibility of attributing states of consciousness, if we did not know what it means to attribute such states, i.e., talk about them.

5. Strawson also asks the classical question how the ascription of states of consciousness is done to others as well as to myself. With regard to others we can observe their behaviour. But, must I observe my own behaviour in order to ascribe states of consciousness to myself? Do I really observe myself in order to inform myself about my own states. I may tell others that I am tired in order to inform them. But I have no need to inform myself, since *I feel* that I am tired. However, is there not a difference in saying "I am tired" in the first person and "you/he is tired"? Strawson says dictionaries do not give two sets of meanings, for saying the expression in the first-person or in the second/third. But still, we can ask if there aren't differences. When I say "I am tired", *I feel it without observing it.* When I say "he is tired", *I observe without feeling it."*

Traditional psychological and philosophical assumptions differentiate between observations of another's behaviour and observation of one's own behaviour through introspection. They either assume that observation of another's behaviour is in an analogous way transferred to the understanding of one's own behaviour. Or, they alternatively assume that the knowledge I have through introspection is, by analogy, transferred to the behaviour of others. In the first case one has no private experiences at all. In the second one has only private experiences ("we oscillate between philosophical scepticism and philosophical behaviourism"), as Strawson expresses it (op. cit., p. 109).

The solution Strawson proposes is that certain predicates we use, when describing states of consciousness, are such that when I talk about myself *I feel it without observing it,* and when I talk about others, *I observe it without feeling it.* Take the concept of "depression": "X's depression *is* something, one and the same thing, which is felt, but not observed by X and observed, but not felt, by others than X" (op. cit., p. 109). I do not think this is the whole problem. To *feel* a depression and to *observe* a depression are different things, and we use different words for them. At the same time, they are identical. Again, we can explain this by the interrelationship of *identifying* something *as* specific (as observation or as feeling), and by *identifying* something *with* another (my feeling and his observation, my observation and his feelings).

Thus, we can say the problem of philosophical scepticism and its alternative, philosophical behaviourism, can be overcome through an analysis in terms of dialectics.

3.3   THE ANALYSIS OF COMMON-SENSE LANGUAGE AS A MEANS OF OVERCOMING DUALISM

In the previous sections we tried to indicate through reference to the analysis carried out by Strawson how the body–mind dualism can be overcome. It is overcome when one grasps that the concept "person" implies with the strength of logical necessity the relation between body *and* mind (or consciousness) and at the same time their unity.

We can now also understand why Descartes' scepticism, which formed the basis for his dualism, does not hold for logical argumentation.

Descartes' sceptical attitude in epistemological matters is formulated in terms of the thesis that we cannot be sure of the existence of any material object, including our own body. We can always bring forward arguments to support our doubts. But there is one thing about which we cannot throw any doubt: the very fact that we are able to express doubts. This indicates that we at least can think. We cannot doubt our cognition. Therefore, he concluded that "*cogito ergo sum*"—I think therefore I exist.

But to maintain that thinking implies existence, and at the same time to make the assertion that we can doubt whether we have a body or not, seems remarkable. It adds up to saying: I exist though I do not know whether I exist with our without a body. Hence in other words, as a consequence it would be possible that there exist human beings who are capable to think, but who do not have a body.

Strawson convincingly argues that the notion of thinking as a state of consciousness presupposes the notion of a body, and that both notions presuppose the notion of person as a primary and logically necessary concept.[4]

Zinkernagel (1961) also discusses the same problem. He asks himself why it does not make sense to speak about cognition and at the same time to doubt the existence of a body. His answer, which was formulated prior to and independently of Strawson's, is in short this. When we speak about ourselves and of our immediate environment we are able to make correct statements. Their correctness can be logically proved by trying to deny these statements or descriptions. For example, we can correctly maintain "persons are able to use language". To deny this statement does not make sense. At the same time it is not a tautological statement.

Thus, when we ask "what does it mean to have a language", Zinkernagel answers that we can make some correct descriptions, since we immediately know that their denial is meaningless.[5]

But this ability to distinguish between basic correct and false statements presupposes that we possess intersubjectively the concept "correctness" in a logically primitive sense. It cannot be explained, since all explanations presuppose that we already possess the very concept of "correctness". This in turn enables us to develop decision procedures, according to which we can decide whether such statements, whose denial is not absurd, are correct or false. The majority of propositions in all sciences are of this kind. Thus, any theory of truth presupposes a primitive notion of "correctness" (see also p. 228).

3.3.1   Conditions for description

Zinkernagel develops the idea that there exist certain rules of language which he calls "conditions for description". It should be underlined that "rules of language" are not "rules for language" alone, implying that language could or must be opposed to reality. It is exactly this dualism Zinkernagel wants to overcome. Conditions for description are such, because the world is such. Zinkernagel's basic idea is that there exist *interrelations* between concepts such that we cannot use one type of concept without using *its* related type. This amounts to saying that the basic units of our language are not atoms, but *relations* (see also p. 171).

We will now present the rules of language as he formulates them.[6] The first states "We must not use designations of things and designations of possibilities of action independently of one another, and we must not use designations of possibilities of action independently of persons".

This rule describes or expresses the interrelationship between three concepts, namely, "persons", "things" (or objects) and "possibilities of action". It is not an attempt at definition. It is an attempt to formulate the rules of how we actually use language or, what we do as users of language. The question then is why we do it that way? Because if we did not, our language would become meaningless. Take the following as an example: "I asked *him* to *bring* the *chair* over here". "To bring a chair" is a possibility of action.

I would not say this to a two-year old child because he has not (yet) this possibility of action. Second, it would not make sense to say "I asked him to bring" without saying what. Third, if I say that I went to fetch the chair, I have changed the situation. I could not say that I went over there and brought the chair back, and at the same time assert that my possibilities of action had not changed. I cannot, e.g., stand on the same space that I placed the chair. Thus, we may conclude that "possibilities of actions" (or more precisely statement about them) and "designations of things" are interrelated. Furthermore, these two concepts are interrelated with the concept of "person", or the pronouns we use when talking about persons (in our case "him"). We can also turn around our reasoning and say that if we follow Strawson's analysis and take "person" as a primary or primitive concept we will find that "person" implies "possibilities of action" and "possibilities of action" implies "things". We will, however, expand on this problem later on and distinguish between "possibility of action" in two senses, namely as "*acting upon*", in relation to things or objects, and "*acting together with*", in relation to other persons.

Now, somebody could argue that we use "possibilities of action" also in other contexts. For example, we may say "heavy rains moved the rails of this railroad". But I do not think that we are here talking about "possibilities of action". What we are saying is as a consequence of heavy rains, rails were moved. We describe the consequences of a natural phenomena. To call them "possibilities of actions" is to use language in an inadequate way.

Zinkernagel's second rule is the following: "We must not use designations of states of consciousness and of persons independently of one another". This rule, after our lengthy discussion of Strawson's analysis should be grasped immediately. Using such expressions as "wishing", "desiring", etc., without reference to persons does not make sense.

The third rule has the following wording: "We must not use designations of persons independently of designations of bodies and we must not use designations of bodies independently of designations of things."[7] Again, we can easily understand this rule if we relate it to Strawson's analysis. We cannot talk about persons without a body, and we cannot use the word "body" without talking about an object. We draw the following conclusions: *First*, the three conditions for description are *necessary* though not sufficient for describing how we use language. *Second*, they are themselves interrelated. For example, we can easily see how rule one and rule three supplement each other. Thus, we can correctly say that (1) one condition of description expresses relations between concepts and (2) all three conditions for description are interrelated, and, hence, are *relations of relations* in the very sense of the term used in the previous chapter (see page 125). *Third*, they not only fulfill the dialectical condition of relations of relation, they also fulfill the condition of holism. They are opposed to "an erroneous notion about the relation between language and reality, namely the notion that we would be able to penetrate into the essential nature of things and in an atomistic manner point at elements which correspond to fundamental concepts. To the contrary it is per definition such that we always talk about the essential nature of things when we talk correctly. Therefore it is self-contradictory wanting to explain why something is correct. It would imply that we could talk correctly without having the fundamental concept of 'correctness' ".[8]

Naturally, this only holds for statements which are *general*, i.e., whose denial would be meaningless and *fundamental* and that are presupposed in any characterization and, therefore, that cannot be used in characterizing something.

Thus, as *fourth* and derived conclusion, conditions for descriptions are logically compelling, not only because language is such, but because language is the way by which we inform ourselves about what there is.

But if conditions for description are of a logically compelling kind, what about the rules of formal logic, for example the law of identity? Zinkernagel also includes the law of identity among conditions for description, in addition to the three mentioned.

3.3.2 *Formal logic and conditions for description*

Logical principles, for example, the law of identity, are usually thought of as principles which can only be meaningfully used in the context of a formalized and axiomatic system. But—and this is Zinkernagel's point of view—we can also use them in a meaningful way in a non-formalized context—namely, as conditions for everyday common-sense language. In other words, we are not concerned with rules of formal logic as applied in an axiomatic system, but rather with principles of logic used in daily common-sense language. *But what does that exactly mean?* How can we make this distinction clear such that we grasp its profound meaning?

Formal logic presupposes atomism. It can be used to the extent that we deal with propositions of an atomistic kind: Their truth value is independent of other propositions. Such is the case of propositions formulated as tautologies (for example, A is identical with itself). It is usually added that these propositions are formal and have no content. Only if applied to reality do they have content.

If we accept this we also have to accept the bifurcation of language and reality. In daily common-sense language, however, if our analysis so far has been valid, we cannot accept this bifurcation and the logical atomism on which it is based. As mentioned before, we reject the dualistic notion that basic concepts correspond to basic elements in reality, since accepting this means accepting a category mistake.

We have stated that the three conditions for description are themselves characterized by two conditions: they express interrelations between concepts, interrelations which are such that the concepts involved cannot be used by themselves without rendering our language meaningless; these relations should not be tautological, i.e., they should not be analytic propositions.

The law of identity does not fulfill these two conditions. It expresses a reflexive relation if any at all (see p. 99), (e.g., A is identical with itself), but this relation is a tautology.

We seem to face the following dilemma: We cannot accept the law of identity based upon tautological propositions and presupposing logical atomism. But we can neither dismiss the principle which the law of identity expresses as a condition for description: a word in a given context has identical meaning whenever it occurs in this context. Otherwise, we could not communicate with each other. To quote Peter Zinkernagel, "the only way in which the existence of such conditions can be contested is by showing that it is possible to speak in a clear and well defined manner without paying attention to them" (op. cit., p. 32).

I think we can give reasons why in a given context we must use a word with the *same* meaning. What does it mean to say that in a given context a word has the *same* meaning? It means that we can *identify* clearly and unambiguously the meaning of this word *with* the meaning of this word at a second time in the given context.

Our previous analysis has brought the comprehension that we cannot identify anything *with* anything, without simultaneously identifying it *as* something specific and to relate these two operations. If we separate them we either commit "Samuel's mistake" (clapping the hands) or the second version of the category mistake (see p. 165).

If we, on the other hand, accept that there exists a *necessary interrelation* between the concept "to identify with" (as expressed in the law of identity) and the concept "to identify as", such that they presuppose each other and that we cannot use them independently of each other, we have attained the following:

(1) We do not need the tautological, atomistic law of identity as a condition for description;

(2) We need not and, really, cannot abandon it. Instead, we can use it as *one relatum* in a relation, where its other relatum (and I emphasize, "*its*") is "x is identical as something specific";

(3) We now fulfill the essential characteristics of conditions for descriptions: they should designate necessary interrelations between concepts; and they should not be tautological statements;

(4) since the law of contradiction is derived from the law of identity, it can now be rephrased in order to express a relationship. That can be done in the following way: We cannot in one context, use one expression in two different ways because, when we have *identified it as* something specific, we must in all further usages in the same context, *identify* the expression *with* the way it has been specifically identified.

The condition of identification, as formulated previously (see p. 110), seems to indicate that the traditional law of identity, based upon atomistic presuppositions, is one link or one relatum in a more general principle of identity. If we have difficulties seeing this, it may be because we have been blinded by Aristotelian logic. We want to underline once again that we do not reject the law of identity. We only see it as a special case of a broader principle of identity.

First, when we accept the principle of identity as a condition for description, we can understand and explain the role such words as "same" and "different" play in our language. Without this communication would be impossible (see p. 108). Furthermore, as also pointed out earlier, without this principle the definition of a dialectical relation appears to be self-contradictory (see p. 109).

From now on for semantical reasons, we will not use the expression "condition for description" or "condition for identification". Instead, we will talk about rules which make up the basic logic of common-sense language. Formalized and axiomatic logical systems may be viewed as being based upon this basic logic, since we cannot formulate any specific rules of a formalized logic without using common-sense language. This also applies to the rules which govern the use of common-sense language.

3.3.3 *Some consequences of this analysis*

In the previous section we tried to clarify the distinction between the law of identity, as used in the context of formal logic, and a condition for description, comprising the law of identity in the context of common-sense language.

Conditions for description are logically compelling. To deny what they state implies that we do not use language in a meaningful way. However, they themselves are not propositions in a system of formalized logic. Their logically compelling character is a consequence of the fact that these conditions do not merely state principles concerning the use of language and have nothing or little to do with reality: "If there are any such general conditions for the description of reality we cannot characterize the knowledge of such conditions as *knowledge about language* as opposed to reality" (P. Zinkernagel op. cit. p. 41, our ith.).

Rejection of the language-reality dualism means that Zinkernagel also can reject the *theory* of analytic and synthetic propositions. He does not reject the dichotomous notion concerning a certain class of propositions called "analytic propositions", i.e., which are true by definition since they only express linguistic rules, and another class called "synthetic" which may be either true or false. He rejects rather the theory which claims "that there are no other general conditions for description than those expressed in formal logic. If this assertion cannot be maintained, the theory of analytic and synthetic propositions must be abandoned" (op. cit., p. 41). With it, logical atomism has to be abandoned: The claim that there exist in reality basic elements corresponding to concepts. Hence, the bifurcation between language and reality must be abandoned. We have several times argued for this and we have done it from various perspectives. But now we can understand why and how the theory of conditions for description is a necessary precondition for overcoming a dualistic metaphysics.

In fact, Strawson and Zinkernagel's analyses, taking different points of departure reach similar and sometimes identical conclusions. By overcoming dualism they pave the way for dialectical thinking. In addition, conditions for description as formulated here, seem to be the building blocks of a dialectics of language—a rather neglected aspect of dialectics in general.

A final remark should be made. In the previous chapter (see p. 133), we discussed whether relations or things should be the unit of an analysis. There we maintained that we cannot avoid talking about "things", but that the concept "thing" is relational in the sense that it cannot be used without referring to possibilities of action, and vice versa. Thus, the question whether we should use relations or things as basic units for our analysis becomes obsolete. When we analyze the social world (being the business of social scientists) we should start by analyzing our language. In doing so we will find that the most pressing problem is not the development of concepts, but the development of *relations* between concepts, or statements containing these concepts. How should we otherwise grasp the complexities of the social world?

3.3.4   About statements and concepts

In the previous analysis of conditions for description we tried to characterize these conditions as logical rules which contain interrelations between concepts, and that these interrelations are not formulated as tautological statements. In order to avoid a probable misunderstanding, I want to underline the following. My point of departure is not with concepts looked upon as well delimited atoms and then related to each other. The point of departure is a unity or a whole: statements expressing logical rules, that designate conditions for our way of using language and whose denial would not make sense.

Taking the point of departure in a complex whole follows one of the preconditions of dialectical reasoning. From this follows the principle that we should look at processes in terms of "one divides into two" and not the other way round. We need a totality in order to be able to look for "ingredients". Having identified them we can reverse this process.

Finally let me say a few words about the relation between the rules of basic logic of language and ontological assumptions. These logical rules are such that their denial would render our language meaningless. A denial of what these rules state is something which we cannot assert. The reason why we cannot assert certain things is that the world is as these basic logical rules maintain.

The statements or propositions we talk about are neither analytic, i.e., true by definition (e.g., A is identical with itself), nor synthetic, i.e., true or false. They are true in the sense of being logically compelling but not definitions. As we have repeatedly said, their denial would not make sense. (E.g., We cannot say that we have talked to a person who responded without having a body and without being in any state of consciousness whatsoever.)

What, then, is the relation between these logical rules and ontological assumptions? We cannot describe ontological conditions and processes ("one divides into two") without accepting these logical rules and these logical rules can, on the other hand, only be grasped as something necessary for the description of the world, since they refer to conditions of an ontological kind. This means they are logically compelling because they describe basic human conditions. These rules cannot, however, *be explained* by reference to ontological conditions since any reference presupposes the rules. Thus, there is a complex dialectical relationship between the rules and ontological conditions. This becomes still more complex because as acting and talking beings we formulate rules for our use of language, and use this language in order to formulate the rules. Finally, the fact that we are acting persons in addition means that we are participating in a process through which we change the world and are changed by it.

A sceptical person may still have a last argument. He could say we cannot be sure about all this. Because we can never be sure—far from being able to put forward correct statements—that we are capable of putting forward any statements at all.

To this we can answer the following: The sceptical person has really done what he questions. He has put forward a statement, namely, the statement that we cannot be sure that we are capable of putting forward statements at all.

How do we know that we are capable? Because we cannot deny our capability and at the same time start our argument with a *statement* that questions this capability.

Still he could say: I accept that we have the capability to put forward statements, but we cannot be sure that we can put forward *correct* statements.

Again, if his argument is *false*, we can put forward correct statements.

If his argument is correct, then the content of his statement must be false: Namely, the claim that we could not put forward any correct statements. Because, at least, his own statement is *correct*.

When we have grasped *one correct statement*, we also have grasped the notion of "correctness". This notion then is presupposed in all attempts to explain what "correct" means. Thus, we cannot deny we can put forward certain correct statements, because such a denial can only be made as a correct statement. Hence, we cannot maintain that we do not know what a correct statement is. Neither can we say that we do not know what it means to use language and put forward statements of this or any kind. We have to accept that we are capable of making some correct statements. This is our situation as users of language. If we do not believe it, we can have another person read it and ask whether it makes sense to him (which is another statement). Thus, the capability of making correct statements is basic to all our communication, because only if they are correct will others understand them. This does not imply that we cannot talk nonsense and that others do not understand that it is nonsense.

3.4   ACTING AND INTERACTING

So far, the analysis of the dialectics of language has been restricted to analysis of persons having bodies and possessing states of consciousness, and their possibilities of action in relation to things.

Hence it has had a peculiar onesidedness. It has neglected the analysis of the relation of persons to other persons insofar as these other persons were not bodies, but embodied states of consciousness.[9] Or, to say it in other words: So far, persons have been treated as subjects in relation to objects only. What we have to do now is to extend our analysis to persons as subjects and objects involved in interaction with other persons, others who at the same time are subjects as well as objects. Being a subject means being an acting person. Being a person and an object means being acted upon. Interaction means the dialectical interchange of acting and being acted upon and the transformation of these relations in an ongoing process.

In the last section, we ended our reasoning by saying that we cannot deny that a person is characterized by the fact that he is capable of putting forward statements. Neither can we deny that he can put forward at least some correct statements. This amounts to saying that a person is characterized as a *user of language.*

This assertion in turn presupposes that there are other persons who are also users of language, since it does not make sense to state that one person alone could use language. I cannot speak without speaking to somebody, even if this "somebody" is myself.

The assertion we have presented amounts to saying that in order to characterize a person as a user of language we must attribute to him the characteristics of being a *subject* as well as an *object,* i.e., that he acts and is acted upon in a continuously ongoing process in which he changes positions. In other words, the characterization of a person as a user of language presupposes the notion of interaction. Later on in this chapter, we will argue for the thesis that interaction in which a person is both a subject and an object presupposes freedom and equality (an argument which Marx, among others, has used, see 1953, p. 153).

There are, however, some further problems. The expression "a person is a user of language" is ambiguous. It may mean, (1) to use language, implies action. To be able to use language means to carry out speech-acts or, as we have formulated it; to be able to put forward statements; (2) the expression that "a person is a user of language" does not only imply that he is capable of putting forward statements, but that he can put forward *meaningful* statements or, more generally, that he can act in a meaningful way. A meaningful action, in this context is an action which is understood or grasped by others. (The distinction between understanding and grasping was introduced in the previous chapter see p. 56.) This is a logical consequence of the fact that one person alone cannot be characterized as a user of language.

Only if he could speak in a way that nobody understood could one person alone use language. But how would we know that he uses language? (It is interesting to note that even if a person speaks such that we do not grasp what he says, we understand that what he says has meaning, even if it is nonsense. In this case it has the meaning of being nonsense).

Thus meaningful action presupposes intersubjectivity of understanding and grasping, in the sense that what is done or said is shared by others. Intersubjectivity also is a precondition for interaction. *Intersubjectivity cannot be estasblished through interaction* because interaction is not possible without intersubjectivity. Though interaction can deepen and facilitate intersubjectivy when established.

We now try to summarize: (1) the concept of person as a user of language presupposes the notion of interaction. Interaction means at least two individuals, being subjects as well as objects, are interchangeably engaged in an ongoing process; (2) the concept of interaction presupposes the concept of intersubjectivity of understanding and grasping (or comprehension). Now we have the task of trying to answer the following questions (1) what does it mean to speak about the intersubjectivity of understanding and comprehension? (2) How is intersubjectivity possible? If we can present an acceptable answer to the second question we have also been able to say what "the social" is. We mentioned earlier the strange onesidedness which characterized the analysis of "person" and "possibility of action" by not extending it to interaction. Interestingly enough, interaction and intersubjectivity are implied in Strawson's analysis in at least two instances.

First, when he indicates that the notion of "I myself have a consciousness", presupposes the general notion of "consciousness" and, therefore, the notion of "others having a consciousness". How could I have a notion of another's consciousness without interacting with him, acting upon and being acted upon?

Second, the idea of interaction and of intersubjectivity is implied in Strawson's analysis of the use of first and third person expressions of feeling and emotion. He constitutes a dialectical relation between what I feel, but do not observe, and what others observe, but do not feel. What I observe is the action of others and what they observe are my actions. But neither I nor they only observe. When we observe we always try to understand and/or comprehend the meaning of others' actions. Why is this so? Let us look at Strawson's example. We observe that somebody says he is tired. From this we conclude that there is more to it, more than just the speech-act. We assume that he really has a *feeling* of being tired, or if he does not have a feeling, he has certain *intentions* in saying it, e.g., trying to deceive us. Thus, when we observe another's actions we cannot take them, so to speak, at their face value. We always relate actions to certain states of consciousness: (1) *statements* about feelings and emotions, to *states* of feelings, or alternatively, intentions, why such statements are not related to feelings or emotions. (2) *Statements* of beliefs and convictions. (When a person says that he believes in God, we assume that he *means* it, or if he does not *mean* it, we try to make the statement meaningful by developing hypotheses about the intentions he has for not meaning it.) (3) Actions other than speech actions to which we attribute intention and purpose (willing and goals).

We may ask why we do this? One answer is that: intersubjectivity of understanding and comprehension are basic human conditions presupposed in interaction and in the experience of others as persons. These we try continuously to produce and reproduce *because* we are human beings. One final point ought to be made. What holds for the attribution of states of consciousness to myself, also holds for the understanding of the *meaning* of another's actions. It is not possible to infer from my actions the meaning of another's actions. I must be capable of understanding the meaning of another's actions before I can start to reflect about the meaning of my own action.[10] Knowing what I do is not something I have learned primarily through observing myself. I usually do not infer at all that I am acting. I act. When I begin to reflect on my actions I try to recall what I did and how I did it. I would not reflect about my actions if they were unproblematic in the sense that no one reacted to them. Thus, I would not reflect about my own actions, unless another has reacted and evaluated them. This is a basic thesis in G.H. Mead's analysis of the self. He calls the acting part of the self "I" and the reflecting "me", and elaborates the dialectical interrelation within the self (see J. Asplund 1972 and J. Israel 1976a).

Our problem now is to extend our analysis to interaction. As a first step let us present a short account of "action".

3.4.1 On action

Usually we speak of actions as accomplishments. We intentionally, i.e., wilfully, want to accomplish something. When we talk about accomplishments, we implicitly refer to certain purposes or goals. We may not always refer to certain purposes or goals. We may not always have a clear idea about our intentions, and may not always exactly know our goals or, which is more important, the "unintended consequences of our intentional actions" (as K. Popper 1969 calls it)[1]. But, in general, we always have intentions and purposes, which direct our actions in order to accomplish something. Thus, the first type of action is *accomplishing* or *producing*.

Take, now, the case of a capitalist who produces a certain commodity which he wants to sell with maximum profit. If he does not bring the commodity on the market now, he may get a higher price later on. Thus he *omits action*. But his omission also has intention and purpose and social consequences. Following G.H. von Wright (1968) we distinguish between two types of actions: Producings or accomplishments and omissions or forbearances.

To analyze actions we must make another distinction. Assume we have a certain state of affairs, let us call it "monopoly capitalism" (whatever that may be). A person's action will now depend on whether he wants this state of affairs or he does not want them. If he wants the given state of affairs his action must see to it that a *change* is *prevented*. If he does not want the given state of affairs his action must see to it that a *change* is *produced*.

The same holds for omissions. If he wants the state of affairs unchanged, his omission will *leave something unchanged*. If he wants a change, his omission implies that he *lets things happen* (like the capitalist who does not sell his commodities).

In summary then, we have four types of actions, depending on the existent state of affairs and on our specific ways of relating ourselves to it:

	wanting to change given	do not want to change given
	state of affairs	
Producing	1. Producing change	2. Preventing change
Omission	3. Let it happen	4. Leave it unchanged

We can define action, according to von Wright (1968, p. 38):
"To act is intentionally ('at will') *to bring about* or to *prevent* a *change* in the world (nature). By this definition, to forbear (omit) action is either to *leave* something *unchanged or to let something happen*".[11] As we have previously mentioned (see p. 106), if we define actions in terms of change or the prevention of change "then in order to give an account of action, we must first give an account of change. A logic of action may be said to presuppose a logic of change" (op. cit., p. 39).

What then is change? Change may be defined in various ways as pointed out earlier (p. 115). Let us here assume that we, at any given point in history, are able to identify certain states of affairs, which can be generic or individual. A change, according to von Wright, occurs when one state of affairs ends and a new one starts. When a state of affairs continues to exist, we have no change with regard to the specific state of affairs. Changes are accomplished by *agents*, who can be a person, a group, or a class. (We can say, for example, Mao Tse-tung has changed the state of affairs in China, and we can say that the Chinese masses or the Chinese working class has accomplished it. In all three cases we can use the term "agent".)

Assume we have a state of affairs s, which at time t_1 characterizes the world. At t_2 we have *not-s*. Assume that there is only one agent in this world and that we know that if he had not interfered the transformation from s to *non-s* would not have occurred. From this we can conclude that it was the agent who brought about the change.

According to this analysis three conditions have to be fulfilled in order to talk about action: (1) We must be told the *initial* state of affairs of the world, (2) we must be told the state of affairs when the action ended, i.e., the *end-state* and (3) we must be told the state in which the world would be, had the agent not interfered but remained passive (op. cit., p. 43).

Condition 1 and 3 may be called the *acting situation* or the *opportunity* of action. Condition 2 can be called the *result* of action. *Opportunity* and *result* of action (1, 2, and 3), together, determine the *nature* of action.

Usually the situation is more complicated. We do not have one agent only, but in many situations we have two or more agents. Thus, changes may often be the result of the *interaction* of several agents. Therefore, we must analyze the way two or more agents can bring about change. There are several possibilities of interacting. One is such that all agents involved act together in order to produce a state of affairs or to prevent it, let things as they are or let them happen, respectively. Another situation or opportunity of action is present when some agents want to produce a state of affairs, whereas others want to prevent it, while a third group of agents may stand by and let things as they are or let them happen. Thus, interaction between two or more agents complicates our scheme.

The end state or result of action usually is the goal of the intended action. Goals have to be shared or to be common, in the case of several agents interacting. Common goals can in principle be of two kinds. Let us demonstrate this with the help of a football game. In order to produce victory for one team all the agents or actors of this team have to act in a manner that facilitates the accomplishment of the common goal. Their interaction can be called co-operative. The two teams, however, share the common goal to win. But if the one team accomplishes this goal it prevents the other from doing it. Their interaction can be called competitive.

There is still another problem. So far, we have talked about states of affairs where the way of expressing ourselves implicitly makes us think about objects. Thus, we so far have talked about agents or actors accomplishing something with objects.

In interaction however, there are often two agents who try to accomplish something *with each other*, and not only together. Or, they may act *against* each other. In this case, both agents are subject and object interchangeably, in an ongoing process.

3.4.2   *Possibilities of action*

In our analysis of the concept of "action", it was pointed out that production or accomplishment, as well as omission or forbearance, are ways of changing the world and of preventing such changes. In other words, they are ways of acting. Thus in this sense, "action" becomes as fundamental a concept as "person". We cannot say that there are persons who do not act, in the sense the word has been explicated. We can neither say that there occur actions without a person. We can talk of actions in relation to individuals as well as in relation to groups ("our football team played and won"), to a class ("the whole working class participated in a general strike") and to other collectives, such as, e.g., nations ("the United States fought a war in Vietnam").

All these examples indicate there are actions that imply co-operation as well as competition between several persons. Whereas the mentioned examples only point at *interaction*, in the sense of several people interrelated in producing or preventing something, we find also a more definite type of interaction: An ongoing process between two or more persons, whereby they alternately take the position of being a subject, i.e., acting, and being an object, i.e., being acted upon. The prototype of this interaction is the dialogue.

As we have indicated before (see p. 179), we cannot talk about a "person as a user of language", without implying interaction of the dialogue type. We cannot talk about a person without referring to presupposed social conditions.

There occur in our society situations where persons are treated mainly as objects. In the process of "material" production, for example, workers are often treated as objects in the sense of being "labour-power". This is characterized by a communication situation in which orders are given from higher levels in a hierarchy, and where reciprocal communication is brought to a minimum. But most communication, e.g., among workers them-selves, follows the dialogue model.

There is an additional reason why "action" is such a fun-damental concept. In the previous chapter, we tried to analyze what it means to say that "a person has an individuality" (or alternatively "a personality"). We maintained that the identi-fication of individuality in terms of a mystical substance can be abandoned in favour of an identification in terms of past and present actions and the results of actions. This also points to another fundamental condition. If we want to identify ourselves and other persons as having an individuality, and if we do it with reference to past actions, what we are doing is referring to historical conditions.

It is not possible to assert that we can talk about a person being the same as when we encountered him before, or to identify him as being different from others, without referring to historical and social conditions.

We must go a step further. In the analysis of conditions for description (see p. 169), as well in the attempted explication of the word "action" in the previous section, we not only talked about actions, but also about "possibilities" or "opportunities" of action. This points at the fact that actions always are performed within the context of the physical and social world, and that these contexts have a restricting effect on what we can produce or omit:

1. "Possibilities of action" exist when actions are in accordance with abilities, the only restrictions being the physical make-up of our world. This seems to be a truism. I can move the book on the table, but not through the table. I cannot jump out of a sixth floor apartment without being seriously hurt or killed.

If we analyze these situations, however, what appeared to be a truism disappears.

The point is this. We have *knowledge* of possibilities of action and the restrictions imposed upon them by our physical world. We have this knowledge without necessarily have acquired it through direct empirical tests (in some cases, e.g., jumping out a window, it would not even be possible). We usually need not convince ourselves by doing it, that a glass can be broken by a hammer.

When we have learned to use language, we also have learned many rules of a kind which represent primitive "laws of nature". These can be formulated as conditional sentences, where the antecedent states an action or something to be done and a necessary condition of this action is stated in the second part of the sentence: "If the water is to be boiled, it ought to be put on a hot stove", etc.[12]

In our daily action we respect such rules without being aware of them because the restrictions they formulate are so well known. We follow the rules without being aware of it.

2. Possibilities of action exist in a second sense. It is not only the physical world that sets restrictions on our actions, but also the social world. Possibilities of actions become limited by existing customs, by rules of the "social game", by norms expressing expectations about what ought and ought not to be done, etc.[13]

All these rules and norms are barriers which indicate the types of actions allowed and prohibited. In addition, legal norms stipulate sanctions to be applied in the case of violation. Both legal and moral norms often state much more clearly what is prohibited than what is allowed. This is in agreement with our principle of negativity. Thus, in the social world there are rules and norms which delimit and restrict our possibilities of action. When we have learned language we most often have also learned these rules. It is up to us to follow them unless we are ready to face sanctions.

Societal processes often induce limits to our action. Take, for example, the case of a capitalist who decides to produce without profit. Such a decision will put him out of business quickly. Thus, the societal order and the processes going on delimit and restrict possibilities of action. A capitalist, however, has the freedom of producing without profit if he does not want to continue as a capitalist, but prefers, for example, to be a hippy. Through his isolated action he cannot change the rules of the societal game. But, he can decide to play another role within this game. We may conclude that being able to speak a language implies that we have learned to follow primitive "laws of nature", as well as a number of the rules of the societal game. But playing the societal game means participating in producing the world: being established as an actor, i.e., as a subject, and as being acted upon, i.e., being established as a social object. Knowing a language implies knowing possibilities of action, i.e., how to interfere in things, how to produce things, and how to omit them. It also means knowing how things can obstruct, how we can manipulate them, and how we can bring about intended states of affairs. It means, in short, knowing how to produce and prevent change, as well as how to omit or/and let change happen.

Language does more than teach us how to play the social game. Language itself is a system of rules. This system has one characteristic which differentiates it from all the rules and laws mentioned so far. When using language we cannot, like the capitalist, decide to leave the game, play another role, or try to change together with others the constituting rules. Language has constituting rules which are such that they cannot be changed. These constituting rules are what we have called, "rules of the basic logic of language". In the final section of this chapter we will try again to discuss the nature of these specific rules.

3.4.3   *On language games*

With Wittgenstein we accept the notion of the impossibility of one person alone being a user of language. To characterize a person as a user of language logically implies interaction between at least two persons. To speak a language is to follow rules. Thus, if it is not possible to speak a language alone, it is, in general, impossible to follow a rule alone.

Assume a game of chess. for those playing the chess game, the rules of the game have a normative function. They prescribe which draws are allowed to be made and which not. For those who watch the game, the rules have more than a prescriptive, i.e., normative, character. For them, the rules also *describe* what it means to play chess. Assume that among those who watch a game of chess, there is one person who does not know how to play. He may for example, ask why the tower is not moved along the diagonal. As an answer he may get a description of the rules of chess. Thus, for those who observe rule-following action, the rules themselves have a descriptive character.

This idea has been expressed by I. Winch, 1958 in the following way: "it is only in a situation in which it makes sense to suppose that somebody else could in principle discover the rule which I am following that I can intelligibly be said to follow a rule at all" (p. 30).

We have here an occasion of complimentarity in following a rule, analogous to the one Strawson formulates with regard to talking about observations and feelings (see p. 167): A feeling is something I feel and do not observe and which others observe but do not feel. A similar dialectical relation exists in rule-following. For a player of a game, rules prescribe how to act but do not describe his actions. For the observer of a game, the rules describe the actions of the player but do not precribe anything for him. Thus, descriptive and normative functions of sentences are not sharply separated as some language theories try to indicate, (e.g., descriptive statements can be verified, the others cannot). They seem to be interrelated dialectically in a manner just mentioned.

For the two players in a chess game the situation is a changing one. For the player who is going to draw, the rules are prescriptive. For the other, they describe the move. When the other is the player and the first the observer, the situation is reversed.

Thus, rules of the game are prescriptive as well as descriptive. They prescribe for the actor or subject and describe for the one acted upon or the object. They determinate action. This is another way of saying, that possibilities of interaction are restricted by rules.

Rules, however, can be transgressed and violated. If, for example, one player in a chess game proposes to the other player to move the tower along the diagonals and the other agrees, they are still playing a game, though not chess. The character of the activity is still "playing a game". They are like the capitalist who has chosen to play the hippy game within the frame of the capitalist society.

Does this also hold for the rules of language? Wittgenstein maintained that speaking a language is like playing a game and that we make and change the rules as we go along (1958, §83). But how can we make and change the basic rules of the logic of language, without using language? At least, we must have rules for making and changing the rules, such that they are not themselves made and changed when changing rules of language.

Consequently, Zinkernagel (op. cit.) rejects the game analogy: "The law of contradiction is like a rule in a game, insofar as it states certain things we may do, and others which are not allowed. It is *different from such a rule* in that we cannot modify it in the same way as we can modify the rules of the game" (p. 31, our ith.).

We cannot use language without contradiction and, at the same time, assert that we can change the law of contradiction in order to use language in a contradictory way.

Zinkernagel, therefore, concludes that rules of the chess game can be altered without changing the character of a game. When we alter the rules and continue, we just play another game. If we, however, allow for contradictions in our language game, we have stopped playing a game at all. This holds for all rules which were called "the rules of the basic logic of language".[14]

Let me present another example to demonstrate this point. Berger 1975) in an interesting analysis of basic problems of the philosophy of social science, discusses difficulties for determining rules for linguistic expressions by means of unambiguous definitions. One argument he uses is that language games are not neatly separated from each other, but overlap and even contradict each other. They may undergo change in the course of history, and they may be used in different ways in various social groups and classes. He therefore proposes that the linguistic analysis of meaning ought to be substituted by the determination of those societal action situations (Handlungssituation) in which linguistic expressions occur. This has to be done within the context of the various societal life-styles or life-worlds.

It seems reasonable to analyze the meaning of linguistic expressions within the broader societal context of life-styles, etc. But how can the societal action situations of *linguistic expressions* be determined *without using linguistic expressions?* And how are those linguistic expressions, being the means of determining the societal action situations of linguistic expressions, determined? Thus, one either introduces an infinite regression or a total relativism of a self-defeating kind.

This can be avoided if we introduce rules that need no other determination, than calling attention to the fact that we cannot violate them without contradicting ourselves.

3.4.4   Is it a logical necessity to have rules?

What we have said so far regarding the role of norms and rules in restricting possibilities of action, is in one way or another accepted knowledge in sociology. Society presupposes the existence of rules and norms, according to which persons interact. Possibilities of action are submitted to the constraints of societal norms and the rules of the social game. This has been said from Durkheim and Marx on to modern sociology. Wittgenstein's contribution is his analysis of what it means to follow a rule.

In the previous section we indicated that the analysis of following a rule, and the notion of language-games are not sufficient for avoiding relativism or regression.

We therefore must accept that there exist conditions for using language that form the basis for the very use of language. Some of these conditions have already been presented and discussed (see p. 169). Our position would be still stronger, if we could show that it is logically necessary to interrelate the notions of "society" and of "rules". Thus, if we can indicate that we cannot talk about society without talking about rules and reversed, without involving ourselves in contradictions, we may be able to state another basic condition of the logic of our language.

The expression "to share rules" or "there exist common rules in every society" is ambiguous.

To say that I share a rule with another person can mean: (1) that I understand that the other, in his actions, follows a rule (his rules have a descriptive function for me), and even that I understand the details of the rules he follows. But I do not accept the rule, and therefore, do not follow him. (2) To share a rule with another can also mean, that at least two persons follow the same rule when acting in the same or similar situations or when interacting. This can be done even without being aware that one follows a rule.

If "sharing a rule" exists in the first of the above senses, we could think of a situation where two persons each follow a different rule, but have knowledge of the fact that they do so.

In order to talk about "society", we must show that the second, and stronger, interpretation of following a rule is a necessary condition for our language.

I think we have already given sufficient reasons for the necessity of following some rules. We cannot use language without following basic rules making up a general logic, which are accepted by all. By "acceptance" I do not mean a deliberate choice or decision, because to learn and to use language presupposes acting in accordance with these rules. These rules, in turn, provide for intersubjectivity of meaning, or, what probably is a more precise statement, when we talk about intersubjectivity we *can refer* to rules accepted by all who participate in speech interaction. Thus, we have one necessary set of rules for any society to exist, the basic rules of language. No society can exist without human interaction and no interaction can take place without language.

The basic rules of language, though necessary for society to exist, are not, however, sufficient. Any society, to be maintained, must be daily produced and reproduced. This is done in the process of production, the human life-process, as Marx called it: It is praxis, the human essence in terms of producing and transforming the world. This basic process of producing the world of objects and social institutions, and, in consequence, of man as the socialized being, also must follow certain rules. The reason for this is that the basic process of production and transformation can only be understood as a collective, societal process. Not as the activity of single, isolated, and/or autonomous beings who are competely independent and unrelated to other human beings.

Collective action or interaction must follow rules. These rules are first of all dependent on the goals towards which the processes of production, reproduction, and transformation are directed. It does not make sense to speak about society without talking about common goals, i.e., goals shared by all or, at least, by some who can force others to accept these goals. We can neither talk about specific goals of certain classes (or other categories), if we cannot presuppose and talk about at least some common goals. We cannot reproduce ourselves biologically without at least the goal to maintain and preserve the species in the biological sense. But this cannot be done without a specific family-and kinship-system, which itself must be reproduced. Thus any such system has to be based upon certain rules. This is the meaning of saying that it is institutionalized.

Social institutions, in this sense, are a collection of rules according to which we organize societal relations and social interaction in order to achieve certain goals. Thus, the goal of biological reproduction presupposes social interaction which, by definition, has to be regulated or which follows certain rules. To the extent these rules are repeated and made valid for a larger collective, they become institutionalized. In order to interact and co-operate with regard to biological survival, family-and kinship-systems are organized. These systems are, so to say, the materialized manifestation of rules.

When we want to describe and talk about society we can and must do it in two, dialectically interrelated, ways: (1) we can observe the ongoing relations between individuals, i.e., their social interactions. In this case we are talking about individuals. But these interactions can also be analyzed on a generic level as societal relations (see p. 139 for the distinction between "social" and "societal"). Societal relations are praxis and must be understood in an ongoing process of change and transformation; (2) the

rules which *are an integrated part* of praxis become institutionalized, making up the frame within which societal relations
and social interaction go on. Thus, in this second sense we speak of
society as "institutions".

When we want to talk about society and describe it (e.g., as a
task for the social sciences), and if we want this description done in
a dialectical way, we are forced to talk about rule-governed
relations as well as the institutionalized rules which make up the
frame for these relations. In other words, we have praxis in the
double sense of an ongoing process and the result of previous
praxis, forming the framework of societal relations and social
interaction.

For this reason, we cannot talk about society without taking into
account historical facts in terms of institutionalized praxis, and
cannot talk about society without talking about rule-governed
activity, i.e., structured processes of relations and interactions.
Thus, the basic logic of the language about society must include
concepts like "rules", "relations", "interactions", and the way
these concepts are interrelated. We have chosen to use the concept
of "praxis" to indicate the interrelationship between these concepts.

We have previously argued that we cannot give a total
description of anything. All our descriptions are partial. This holds
especially for descriptions of society since we deal with extremely
complex matters. One of the complexities is the dual perspective
we may and must have of society as an ongoing process of
relations, and as institutionalized praxis. This is one reason why
there exist so many descriptions of society. Now let us once more
return to family and kinship. We cannot have them with only the
biological goal of reproduction. There must be some economical
goals which have to be fulfilled in order to maintain (or to
transform) an existing family-and kinship-structure.

These economic goals in turn presuppose the existence of
common rules. Further, these rules are changed as a consequence
of changes in the economic system, i.e., institutionalized praxis and
its goals. All economic activity presupposes certain types of
ownership of property which again has to be regulated by rules.

"Property signifies originally nothing else than man's way of
relating to natural conditions for production as something
belonging to him, as being his, as being presupposed to his own

existence; relating to these conditions for production as natural preconditions of himself, as conditions which so to speak form his enlarged body. Actually he does not relate himself to his conditions for production, but exists in a double sense: subjectively as he himself, as well as objectively in these natural unorganic conditions for his existence" (K. Marx 1963, p. 391).

In societies with a limited technology the rules of interaction are determined by the natural conditions of existence. The development of these productive forces changes the relations between men (the relations of production) and, therefore, the rules which regulate these relations. Changed relations, in turn, make possible the use and development of productive forces, especially those that are represented by man's own capacities (as e.g., expressed in science), and by his ways of cooperation.

In summary then, we can—to use our terminology of the analysis of action—have a society in which there are *productive* changes and changes by *omission*. But we could not have a society that functioned by omission only or which could be transformed in this way only.

It becomes, therefore, clear why Marx emphasized the role of the process of material production. And why he formulated a methodological rule for the social sciences according to which the study of this process must be placed at the centre of its interests, as well as forming the point of departure for any societal analysis.

Any society in consequence, needs a multitude of rules.[15] The type of rules it needs is, however, dependent on its goals and of the means by which the goals are attained. Reproduction within a capitalistic economical and social system presupposes other goals, and consequently other rules, than, e.g., reproduction of a socialist system.

3.4.5   The dialectics of intention and convention

Our discussion so far has established a relation between possibilities of action and norms and rules, respectively. Does this mean that all our actions are norm directed?

There are situations in which we speak about that we did things we did not want to do, and other situations, where we wanted to do things we did not do.

These two ways of speaking imply that there seems to exist a contradiction between what a person *intends* to do—i.e., his intentions—and the rules and norms he follows doing it. (For the sake of simplicity we will summarize rules and norms under the label of "conventions").

How can the conflict between intentions and conventions be explained? Psychoanalysts assume the existence of basic human drives, which in their nature are asocial. They drive us to do what gives immediate pleasure. Society, they maintain on the other hand, demands we abandon this pleasure principle and accept the realities of social conventions. However, a residual of the pleasure principle remains active when we do what we want to do though we break rules or, in reverse, when we follow conventions but do things we do not want.

The notion of a contradiction between a pleasure principle, and a reality principle that is social seems extremely strange. First of all, it contradicts our previously stated assertion that the social is basic (see p. 179); We become individuals only in and through society (as Marx, among others, stated it). For example, the experience of "my consciousness" presupposes knowledge of the concept "consciousness", and therefore of "the consciousness of others". The social constitutes the individual and not vice versa.

Second, the idea is strange in the sense that when we use words like "asocial"—e.g., a human being being asocial—we can only do it by using a language that is basically social. Thus, only with the help of what is social can we talk about what is not social or asocial. But we cannot do it the other way round. Speaking about the "asocial nature of man" is the activity of *social* man who, in order to grasp what the asocial is, must be social.

Not even the objection that newborn babies are asocial, since they deploy only activity which seeks need-satisfaction and therefore pleasure, carries any force. Again, this is an interpretation of the behaviour of babies by socialized man.[16]

Let us return again to our problem and try another approach. We usually reject responsibility for actions we have been forced to do. This principle, e.g., played an important role in the Nuremberg trials against the German war criminals. They rejected the responsibility for their notions by maintaining that they only followed orders. Furthermore they maintained they could not have acted otherwise, *even* if they had *wanted* to. Thus, even if one wants to do what one is supposed to do, one presupposes the distinction between what one wants (intends), and what one must do if one follows conventions.

One way of solving the problem is to assert that we, as human beings, are exposed to many contradictory rules. Thus, if we act in accordance with some conventions, we are forced to act against others. Those conventions which subjectively are the strongest are supposed to coincide with one's intentions.

The accusation in Nuremberg also followed the line I have sketched. The defenders were accused of blindly obeying orders—e.g., to exterminate people—which contradicted basic moral conventions, and which they therefore ought to have wanted to follow, even at the price of breaking the convention of blind obedience to given order. Thus, there seem to exist different kinds of rules or conventions. Some of them are such that when we follow them we feel that we are free, that we have choices, that we follow our intentions and that we do what we want. Others are such that when we follow them, we feel we do what we do not want to do. The former rules seem to be more basic and more general.

These conventions which are more basic seem to imply that a person is an *acting subject*, and therefore has possibilities of choice, and not only an *object* which more or less passively follows the directions of conventions. In other words, there seem to exist rules of language assuming that we *are* subjects, i.e., are able to choose, to make decisions, and to take responsibility for our decisions.

In order to grasp that I am an acting subject, or a subject, who can take the initiative and the responsibility for actions, I must grasp the general notion of "being a subject", i.e., *that others are subjects.* This means they can make decisions and act, in general, and act upon me, specifically. If I have grasped the idea that there are subjects, then I have not only grasped the idea that others can act upon me. In this case I have only grasped the notion of "being an object". I must also have grasped the idea that I have possibilities of acting upon others. Hence, the notion of being a subject contains, as logically necessary, the idea of reciprocity. For example, as expressed in such words as "each other". (Thus "we can speak *with* each other", "we can talk *to* each other", "we can fight *against* each other", "we can work *for* each other", etc). Previously, we discussed the role of words, like "same" and "different" for their capability in identifying things. It appears now that expressions as "one another", "each other", i.e., expressions which refer to reciprocity, are as basic as the ones previously mentioned. If we have learned them we have learned the notion of reciprocity, in the sense that we are subjects as well as objects in social interaction.

The notion of reciprocity also logically presupposes the notions of equality and freedom. We cannot have an idea of ourselves or anybody as subjects, without having a minimum amount of freedom to take the initiative for action, to choose and make decisions and a minimum amount of equality (i.e., at least in certain areas) with those towards whom we act.

K. Marx (1953, p. 154) has developed these ideas dialectically. Two persons A and B, he says, are *different* with regard to their needs and with regard to their production. This is a precondition for interaction in terms of exchange. If they had the *same* needs, there would be no reason for interaction and exchange. Since they are different, and since they possess different use-values (which they have produced), they interact. But this can only function under conditions of equality. They accept each other as the owners of equivalent objects which, on the basis of equality, are exchanged. "The differences in their needs and their production constitutes the occasion for exchange, and for their social equality within it; the natural difference, therefore, is the precondition for their equality in the act of exchange and in general for the relation through which they interact as producing" (p. 154).

Since both A and B possess things which have use-value for the other, they need and serve each other in order to serve themselves. They need to be aware of the fact that the process of exchange (1) achieves its purpose only as far as it serves the other as means, (2) that being means for the other is transformed into purpose for oneself (Selbstzweck), (3) that reciprocity, according to which everything is means and purpose, only serves the desired result insofar as it becomes a means only as far as it is taken as self-purpose. Thus in order to be something for another, one must be something for oneself (i.e., a subject), and the other, in order to be something for the first, must be something for himself. This, in turn can only be achieved if freedom exists in the sense that each enters the exchange relation voluntarily and without coercion. "As the economic form—the exchange—determines the *equality* of all subjects in all directions, so the content, the stuff-individual as well as material—determines the freedom which propels exchange.

Equality and freedom are not only respected in the exchange, being based on exchange-values, but the exchange of exchange-values is the productive, real basis of all *equality* and *freedom*" (op. cit., p. 156).

If we view interaction in general as a process in which one person tries to satisfy the needs of the other and the reverse, and, if we remember that what for the receiver is use-value, is exchange value for the sender and vice-versa (see p. 130), we can try to generalize the Marxian ideas to include reciprocal interaction in which a person is a subject as well as an object.

Let us, by summarizing, return to the dialectical relation between intentional and conventional actions. These actions exhibit all the characteristics of a dialectical relation. Intentional and conventional actions make up a whole, they are different, inter-dependent, and have something in common, namely being guided by rules while at the same time being opposed to each other. We cannot act intentionally without knowing the limits conventions may enforce upon us. Neither can we act conventionally without being aware that we could have acted otherwise, if we had wanted. We did not act otherwise, because we did not want as we could have wanted.

Assume again the Nuremberg example. The German Nazi-leaders excused themselves by maintaining they only obeyed orders. Using this excuse is equal to saying they were objects only, not choosing subjects. They were submitted to the arbitrary actions of others without being able to initiate actions themselves. But somebody must have given the orders. They, at least, must have acted, i.e., have been subjects. Thus, we cannot think of a society in which everybody is an object only. Slaves are only slaves in relation to a master. Neither can we think of a society where some people are subjects only. In the German case, those who gave the orders were themselves objects, since their possibilities of action were limited by the actions of others (e.g., the Allied forces).

From our analysis we can conclude that—as persons we are always sometimes subjects and other times objects, and further-more that an interaction of reciprocity is necessary for a person to be subject and object, and finally, that reciprocity presuppose a minimum of equality and freedom. Two further conclusions can be drawn: (1) if we opt that freedom and equality should not be granted to all and to the same extent, we opt for a class-divided society and the reverse. A class-divided society is characterized by the fact that some have more opportunities to be subjects than others who, thus, are more often objects; (2) if we independently of differences or, as Marx tries to show, taking differences as the basis we take another option. We opt for maximum equality and freedom. This means that we opt for reciprocity in being an acting, choosing, decision making subject, as well as an object. An object which is exposed to the choices and the decisions of others, and being acted upon. If we do all this, then we opt for socialism.

This option can be expressed as a rule: If we talk about persons we must always assume that they are *different* as well as *alike*. They are alike in regard to being subjects, which implies that they have possibilities of action of choosing and of making decisions and of acting in accordance with them. They are also alike in regard to being objects. This *sameness* in being a person is not a quantitative problem. One cannot be half a person or a partial subject.

Persons, on the other hand, are *different* from each other in regard to their *individuality* (compare the distinction between identifying a person and identifying his individuality, p. 103). Since we have defined individuality in terms of previous actions and the results of previous actions, we can now state that persons are different with regard to their history. Furthermore, their history may affect their present actions. In addition, they may differ with regard to innate capacities, inherited gifts, and even acquired properties due to their history.

The above quotation from Marx's "Grundrisse" indicated that there exists a dialectical relation between a person's equality and difference. Interaction would be impossible if there were no equality and no difference whatsoever between those interacting. Furthermore, *differences* between persons are necessary conditions for establishing interaction. But they are not contradictory to accepting *equality*, i.e., *sameness*. This is a practical application of the condition for identification, which requires sameness as well as difference.

Interaction thus presupposes the dialectical interrelation between *equality* and *difference* of persons. It also, as Marx points out, presupposes the dialectical interrelation of *freedom* (to be a choosing, decision making subject) and the *constraints* which social rules exert (of being an object acted upon and exposed to decisions). The dialectics of freedom and constraint can, and have been formulated here as the dialectics of intention and convention.

Finally, as Marx also points out, there is the third dialectical relation presupposed in interaction. Namely, between self-purpose and means for others: Equal and free interaction presupposes being a means for the other and a self-purpose for the actor. Thus in this context, being a subject means to act according to self-purpose, as a means for the object, and being an object is to accept the other's self-purpose as a means for oneself. The transition from object to subject occurs if one can reciprocally make one's self-purpose into the means for the other.

Having accepted the three preconditions for interaction (a) equality and difference, (b) freedom and constraint, (c) self-purpose and means for others, makes it possible to establish the dialectics between being the acting, choosing subject and being the object of choices of being acted upon.

Then we may correctly ask why we could not arrange our social institutions and, hence, societal relations, such that all persons are treated as persons, i.e., that they, to the same extent, can be subject and object in an ongoing process of interaction. This would lead to a rule which may qualify as the basic ethical rule of social interaction.

Its violation would imply that we either treat some persons more as subjects and less as objects or the reverse, and that we may (or may not) defend this action by reference to existing differences between individuals. But, if it is correct that the identification of something, and therefore of somebody, as being *different*, presupposes his identification as being the *same* and reversed, it seems difficult to imagine why we should violate the mentioned rule and defend it with reference to logic. If we do, we deny the practical applicability of the condition for identification. This condition, however, is not only a theoretical rule for the use of language, it is about reality and therefore has practical consequence. To deny this is to reintroduce a dualism which we have abandoned.

3.4.6   *On intersubjectivity*

Our approach in this chapter has, so far, had the main goal of analyzing those conditions necessary for our use of language, also and especially when we talk about society. We have tried to

present some rules of the basic logic of language and attempted to
show their interrelations. Thus, given these rules, the problem of
intersubjectivity does not arise, since the intersubjective use of
language must be presupposed. If there are rules of the logic of
language, they also establish the intersubjective use of language.
But the problem of intersubjectivity arises also in another context.
Assume we live in a class society characterized by antagonistic
contradictions between classes, such that each class deploys goals
of such a kind that when one class achieves some of its goals, it
prevents the other from doing so. In such a society we would expect
to develop different kinds of praxis in each class. (We prefer the
word "praxis" as explicated before—see p. 118—to words like
"life-style" or "life-world".) This means there also develop
different languages. Take the word "solidarity". It may mean
something specific for, e.g., when workers in a capitalistic society
use it within the context of a strike situation where they appeal for
the support of other workers. The word "solidarity" will have a
different meaning when used by a bourgeois politician with a high
income to exhort workers with low income to show "solidarity"
with society by not going on strike during an economic crisis.[17]

Thus, the praxis of the working class, including a system of
moral norms, and life in an antagonistic society, may endow the
word "solidarity" with a specific meaning, one different from the
use of the word within the bourgeois world.

However, and this is the point to be made, assume that the
bourgeois class wants to fight the working class and, therefore,
wants to acquire more knowledge about it. Thus, they may try to
understand—to continue our example—what workers mean when
they use the word "solidarity". Do they mean the same thing as
when used within the bourgeois class, or something different? The
same can be said about workers' attempts to understand the use of
"solidarity" by the bourgeois class.

In general, as we have seen before, in order to *identify* the use of
the word "solidarity", as used *differently,* one must first have
identified the extent to which it is used in the *same* way. And, in
order to identify "sameness", different uses must be identified. In
order to be able to speak about the *same* use, we must assume, in
spite of the fact that workers and bourgeois have different kinds of
praxis and therefore different languages, they also have some parts
of their language in common. Otherwise, they could not try to

identify each other's different use. If the classes had nothing in common with regard to the word "solidarity", they could not even attempt to find out what the other class means, when speaking about it. It would be equal to speaking a foreign language which the other had not learned. This amounts to saying that there must exist a basic degree of intersubjectivity in order to be able to understand each others' differences.

Thus, we can speak of intersubjectivity of *sameness* and intersubjectivity of *differences*. The latter is established if one understands the other, talking differently.

A first step in understanding another's use of language is the understanding that differences in meaning exist. Sometimes people use the same word differently without knowing it. This is nearly trivial to say.

The second step, is to understand *how* the others use the word differently. If a worker learns the contexts in which bourgeois people use the word "solidarity", he has not only obtained an understanding. He may also *grasp* something of the praxis of the bourgeois world. "Grasping" refers here to the same phenomena as explicated before (see p. 68): to place something within the context of a totality. Three conclusions can be drawn:

(1) If a person grasps the totality of praxis of another group or class, it implies that he can place ways of using language into the context of this totality. It does not, however, imply that he has *total* knowledge of this totality. Furthermore, he may grasp it from "outside", so to speak. To grasp it from "inside", he must have lived and experienced it from within. (This is one reason why Marxist intellectuals often talk *about* the working class, but not from *within* the working class.)[18]

(2) In order to *grasp* the praxis of another group or class, in the sense talked about above, a person has to *understand* the concepts by identifying them as "same" and as "different".

(3) *Understanding* (in the Hegelian sense of "Verstand") means being able to give explanations of the use of an expression. *Grasping* (in the Hegelian sense of "Vernuft") means being able to present *explanations* a well as the *rationale* for the explanation. To present the rationale means being able to *justify the rational use* of the expression. But by having presented an *explanation* and its *rationale*, we have given an *interpretation*. We can now see what it means to establish *intersubjectivity*, in the second, more limited,

sense of the word. It means the capability to give *interpretations* of another's different use of the same language. An interpretation then can be viewed as the dialectical relation of explanation and justification. (It may be pointed out that justification has the double meaning of giving *rational* reasons as well as *moral* reasons, and that we leave it open to include both aspects.)

Thus, in summary, *interpretation* refers to the dialectical unity of grasping, in terms of explaining the actions of others and being able to justify them. Intersubjectivity, in the limited sense of the word, is established if one can interpret another's actions. This we do daily, and usually our interpretations are presented in terms of intentions and purposes of actions.

3.4.7 A short note on false consciousness

Our previous analysis of interpretation used as an example the existence of an antagonistic class society. We can now try to explicate the notion of "false consciousness" by using the same example and applying our analysis of "interpretation".

Assume that somebody asks another person: "Do you know that women in our society doing the same job as men get payed less?" The answer to this question is usually "yes" or "no", because it is formulated as a question about factual conditions. Whether these conditions prevail or not, is in this context not important.

Assume now that the question is phrased differently: "Are you aware of the fact that women in our society ...". In this case the question is, in the first hand, not raised to elucidate whether the listener possesses knowledge about the pretended fact, but it is assumed that he knows it. The question really wants to find out how the listener judges or evaluates a known fact. In other words, what kind of *interpretation* does he want to give.

In German the word "Bewusstsein" means "consciousness" as well as "awareness", When Marxists talk about "false consciousness" they usually refer to "false awareness". What then is false awareness? Assume, that we have two antagonistic classes in a society each with its different praxis. Assume furthermore, that each class interprets the world in such a way that their interpretations facilitate acting in accordance with their own antagonistic short-term and long-term goals. A false awareness then exists, if members of one class interpret the world in such a way that their interpretation make it difficult or impossible to act in order to achieve short-term or long-term goals. A stronger kind of false consciousness exists when members of one class interpret the world such that their actions facilitate the achievement of short-term or long-term goals of the other class, which are contradictory to their own goals.

In our society we do not learn facts about the world in a strictly "factual "manner. We learn to interpret the world in various ways. This is due to several processes. When Marx assumed that it is one's social existence which determines one's awareness (i.e., interpretation of the world), he thought of a class society with such a strict division of labour, and so widely divergent patterns of consumption, that there existed to divergent kinds of social praxis.

In a modern capitalistic society class-*differences* though not class-*contradictions*, have been smoothed out. Further, the contradictions have been mystified through a process of producing awareness: through schooling and education and through mass-media. If it is such, that the educational system and the mass-media produce interpretations of the world favourable for acting in accordance with the achievement of the goals of one class, but detrimental to the achievement of the goals of the other class, then these awareness-producing organizations create false awareness among the members of that class. Their actions, then, become detrimental to their own goals.

3.4.8   Some concluding remarks

In the "German Ideology", Karl Marx pointed out that neither thoughts nor language form an isolated realm. They are the expressions of real life (Mega 1.3).

This will be our point of departure, as it must be for any analysis of the dialectics of language. A person as a user of language, is always in an historically determined concrete social situation. As a subject, he is involved in the ongoing process of production, i.e., of change. At the same time, as an object he is affected by the previously produced and still existing social conditions.

To use language is not a theoretical, but a practical activity. It can be viewed as a process of production. Thus, if the use of language is a practical activity, to follow a rule also is a practical activity. This also, and especially, holds for those logical rules which are called "the basic logic of language". Following a rule is an activity which usually is done without one being aware of it. This is one of the meanings of saying that rule-following is a practical and not a theoretical activity. Usually, we first become aware of the activity of following a rule when a person violates one, i.e., does not follow it. If, for example, a foreigner who does not speak our language well, makes grammatical and syntactical mistakes, we immediately know that he does not follow a rule, even if we do not know which one.

In discussing the dialectics of language, we will quickly go astray if we carry out the analysis in a highly abstract way. Also if we divorce it from the real life of living, acting, producing persons. Persons who are always immersed in a societal context and being themselves produced by the social conditions, existing at any historically given moment. We go astray if our analysis attempts to separate itself from societal praxis.[19] Hence, we speak about basic rules of language as logically necessary conditions for how we use language, these conditions are not the formulations of abstract principles. They are—to use Marx's words again—the expressions of *real* life. With them, we formulate some general, well established, and indisputable statements of knowledge about the totality, which we call "reality"; a totality about which we cannot have total, but only partial knowledge.

Basic rules of language express indisputable knowledge, because denying their content would make our ways of talking unintelligible and self-contradictory.

We have, for example, tried to argue that talking about society necessarily presupposes talking about rules and reversed. To say, I live in a society in which there exist no rules whatever is, as we have shown, self-contradictory.

It is also contradictory to say that yesterday I talked to a person who had no intentions, wishes, and perceptions, whatsoever. It is as contradictory as to say that he did not have a body or, though he was not deaf or dumb, he did not know how to use language, etc.

It is false, to say that we live in a society without talking about freedom and equality. Even in a slave society there exists freedom and equality for the masters. It is because freedom and equality are necessary conditions for a society to exist that we first can raise the question why freedom and equality should be restricted, or unevenly distributed in the class society we know.

Hence, we have some general and indisputable knowledge about man and society. It is indisputable because to deny it would make our ways of talking unintelligible. We talk this way because our language expresses the way we are, and the way we live.

Thus, some general and indisputable knowledge is expressed in the way we use language. Analyzing the use of language makes it possible to formulate basic rules of the logic of language. It is of utmost importance to comprehend that these rules are not understood as abstract constructions, but as expressions of real life. We have formulated them in terms of general and—admittedly—abstract statements (because they could not be formulated otherwise). They are in Marx's words "*Daseinbestimmungen*", i.e., characterizations of our existence.

But we have tried previously to indicate that these abstractly formulated rules have practical consequences (see p. 199).

The basic rules of the logic of language, consequently, have ontological implications in *one definite sense*. Knowledge of these logical rules is, per definition, knowledge about reality, i.e., the world we live in. They have their logically compelling character due to the fact that we must respect them, if we are going to talk about reality in an intelligible way.

But they *do not have ontological implications* in a different sense. The logical correctness of these rules cannot be *explained* by referring to reality and its characteristics. In order to *explain* their character we must use other logical rules, and these again have to be explained with the help of additional rules. Thus, we get an infinite regression.

To *explain* the logically compelling character by reference to reality is without meaning and self-contradictory, unless we can *talk* about reality and its characteristics independently of the rules of the basic logic of language.

We have, however, mentioned before that knowledge about the rules of language, per definition, is knowledge about reality. Thus, somebody may object, if we *define* knowledge of rules of the basic logic of language as knowledge of reality, are we then not talking in a self-contradictory way, because definitions, per definition, are rules of language. How can rules about how to use language be about reality?

Our answer must be that they could not be rules about language alone, unless we are able to separate knowledge of reality and knowledge of language. But then, we either must assume a linguistic reality outside reality, or maintain that language has nothing to do with reality. Thus, to say that knowledge about conditions for description, by definition, is knowledge about reality, is not an analytic proposition in the usual sense. It is another way of saying that there is only one reality, and language is part of it.

When we first have grasped the idea of rules of the basic logic of language, and the fact that we can formulate some correct statements which cannot be further explained, because any explanation presupposes that we know what "correct" means (and that in order to explain the word "correct" we must know what "correct" is), then this comprehension opens many possibilities.[20]

First of all, we can overcome the dualism between language and reality, a precondition for accepting the notion of totality, which is, in turn, a precondition of dialectics.

Second, we have a foundation for linguistic analysis as the basis for epistemology. This eliminates the problem of infinite regression of rules, or alternatively, a total relativism, that is self-contradictory.

Third, these rules of the basic logic of language define intersubjectivity of meaning. Thus, we do not need to explain intersubjectivity, which again would lead us into an infinite regression. Instead, we can postulate the intersubjective use of language as a precondition for social interaction and, in consequence, for the *social*.

Fourth, we have to accept another of the preconditions of dialectics, namely, relatedness. The point of departure for the understanding of language is no longer atomistic concepts, but interrelations between expressions or statements. For example: (a) we cannot talk about persons independently of saying that persons have bodies and states of consciousness, (b) we cannot talk about things independently of possibilities of action, (c) we cannot talk about psychological expressions independently of persons, (d) we cannot talk about possibilities of action independently of primitive "laws of nature" and of social rules, (e) we cannot talk about society independently of rules, (f) we cannot talk about persons as users of language independently of talking about reciprocity of actions or reciprocal interaction, (g) we cannot talk about reciprocal interactions without having learned words like "each-other", "together with" or "against each other" etc., (h) we cannot talk about reciprocal interaction independently of talking about freedom and constraint, about equality and difference, self-purpose and means for others, (i) we cannot talk about society without talking about relations and/or institutions, (j) we cannot talk about persons, societies, things in general, without using words that are logically related to "identify with" and "identify as".

We have been able to present ten rules of the basic logic of language. We could add others, such as the reformulated law of identity, the rule that we cannot use the word "truth" independently of the word "fact", and so on. There seem to be a great number of rules which together make up the network of the basic logic of language.

If we follow the above mentioned rules (and others we have not identified) we talk about persons and society in a way that makes sense. To deny talking in this way would be self-contradictory. This also indicates that when we take our point of departure in the concrete situations of real human beings, i.e., if we take our point of departure in human praxis, then we can do all we just have enumerated. When we do all this we have enumerated, we must take our point of departure for analysis in human praxis.

If we do that, we may be capable of using the language of dialectics, because we have grasped the dialectics of language. If we have grasped the language of dialectics, we also comprehend the dialectics of language. Then we may be capable to lay the foundations for a dialectical social science.

NOTES

1. N. Prætorius (1970) in analyzing Gibson's theory of perception, has brought out its circularity. Her reasoning goes as follows: If one says that the world specifies the stimulus one gets: 1. $S = f(w)$. The stimulus is a function of the world. Furthermore, perception is a function of stimulus s. $P = f(S)$. Therefore, it must hold that 3. $P = f(w)$. In other words, we could say that we perceive the world because such is the world. Further-more, the world can be presented to us only as a percept, since the percept is the final product of processes caused by stimuli. But since we only know the world as a percept, we can deduce that 4. $w = f(P)$. Thus we have 3. and 4. and therefore we must conclude that $P = f(P)$.

2. The notion of category–mistake was, as W. Kaufmann points out, already used by Hegel. Asserting philosophy as the objective science of truth, and that therefore only one philosophy can be true, Hegel argues against those who maintain that even if there are different philosophies they have at least in common that they are philosophy. "Whoever, therefore studied or mastered any philosophy at all would thus master some philosophy. This excuse and argument that merely clings to the difference I have elsewhere compared with a (pedantical) invalid whom his doctor advises to eat fruit and who is offered cherries or plums or grapes, but who will not take any ... because none of these are fruits, but merely cherries or plums or grapes" (quoted after W. Kaufmann 1966, p. 282–3).

3. From a genetical point of view I suggest that small children in their prelinguistic level of learning do not discriminate between persons, toys and other things. Probably what they learn is "a person-who-presents-a -bottle-with-milk-making-some-sounds". For the child, probably, the intonation of the words the adult says are more important than the content. Thus the small baby is presented a complex situation of unordered things, words, sounds, persons. Slowly it learns to differentiate and to relate. Learning a language, thereafter proceeds in a conditioning way. The child learns to establish one-to-one relations between words and things, between words and actions, etc., for example, to clap the hands when hearing the word "clap". Hence, in the beginning of learning a language, identifying *with* seems to proceed genetically identifying *as*. But to possess a language means to be able to carry out both operations and to relate them to each other.

4. Also, Peirce criticized the Cartesian position. He argued that initial scepticism is a "mere self-deception, and not really doubt". He could have added, that in order to express doubt we must at least have sure knowledge about what the word "doubt" implies. Peirce also points out that the Cartesian doubt has the consequence that "the ultimate test of certainty is found in the individual consciousness". Therefore, he formulates and criticizes at the same time a Cartesian criterion of truth: "Whatever I am clearly convinced of is true". Truth becomes a private not a social matter. Using language as the basis for our knowledge transforms truth into a social matter (Peirce is here quoted after J. Buchler 1939).

5. Again we want to make a reference to Peirce, who speaks about "common-sense" as "those ideas and beliefs that man's situation absolutely forces upon himself". He also tried to show his version of pragmatics entails the demand "to accept common-sense as the fundamental basis of knowledge" (J. Buchler op. cit., p. 93).

6. We do not present the original, but the reformulated versions as they were published by K.H. Jakobsen (1972) with the oral consent of P. Zinkernagel.

7. The wording of the last rule corresponds to Zinkernagel's own original formulation (see 1962, p. 51), except that he speaks of "personal pronouns" when we use the word "person".

8. The quotation is from a letter which Peter Zinkernagel wrote to me.

9. Strawson devotes a short section to problems of interaction and the

social, but does not elaborate it with the same stringency as he deals with the concept "person". In fact, his individualistic bias becomes quite open when he discusses actions, such that we only can talk about them as *"we have done"* (*we* have conquered another country or *we* have won a football match) without using the singular form. Strawson comments: "When we think of such cases, we see that we ourselves, over a part of our social lives—*not happily, a very large part*—do work with a set of ideas from which that of the individual person is excluded, in which its place is taken by the group" (op. cit., p. 114, my ith.).

10. A. Schutz (1971) distinguishes between the "in-order-to-motive" and the "because-motive". The first motive refers to intentions, whereas the second refers to the reasons for or the goals of intentions.

11. I have once pointed out (1972a) that traditional social science under the pretext of being value-free and non-political, has argued that it cannot be the task of social scientists to accomplish or to contribute to changes in society. This, it is maintained, is the task of politicians, whereas social scientists through their results can (under most favourable conditions) offer means to reach the goals which politicians want to achieve. This standpoint is the standpoint of action as omission or forbearance. It demands of the social scientist that he either acts such that he *leaves things as they are* (thereby indirectly and involuntarily supporting conservative political forces) or *lets things happen* (thereby renouncing all responsibility and moral obligations).

I cannot see that taking the standpoint of action in terms of omission should be less a political standpoint than the standpoint which demands a social scientist participate in producing actions, either in the sense of preventing or of accomplishing change. But I do maintain, from a moral point of view that the ideal of action as omission, guiding social scientists, is inferior to the standpoint demanding productive action. In the case of action as omission, one demands in the name of "value-free science" that the social scientist should be systematically irresponsible.

12. G.H. von Wright calls the proposition which we are talking about "anankastic propositions", i.e., a proposition in which is stated a necessary condition for achieving a certain goal (1963, p. 10).

13. An extensive discussion of various kinds of norms and rules and the implications of their use if found in G.H. von Wright's book about norms and actions (1963).

In the continuation of our analysis we will use the word "rule" and not the word "norm" (though at times we may use them interchangingly). The preference for the word "rule", without here going into a detailed analysis of the use of the term, can be explained in the following way: (1) "rules" make possible the reference to descriptive as well as to prescriptive aspects of action. Hence, by using the word "rule" we try to smooth out a traditional sharp distinction between descriptive and normative statements. Instead, we attempt to show the conceptual interrelation between descriptive and normative aspects of statements. (2) The word "rules" brings forward associations to games, i.e., to processes of interaction. Hence, society can be viewed as a social game having some rules which cannot be changed and others—being a majority—which can and are changed all the time. (3) The word "rules" finally brings forward associations to the verb "to rule". Thus we can say that we "are ruled by rules" and we "rule by using rules".

14. E. Gellner (1968) has from a different point of view an interesting criticism of the notion of language games.

15. The logical contradiction in demanding the complete absence of any social norms and rules is quite easily demonstrated.

Assume an anarchist who declares: let us create a society or social organizations (like the scientific establishment) in which there do not exist any norms at all, because "everything goes". In such a case, there must at least exist one single norm, namely the norm that everything goes. Furthermore, it is necessary that all persons involved in such a society or social organization *strictly* follow this norm and uphold it. In fact, if there were only one rule in a society, no room for violation of this single rule could be allowed, leading to strict enforcement procedures.

Hence, we can formulate the rule that in order to have a completely anarchistic society, everybody must accept the norm of not having any norms, and it must be ensured that this norm is followed strictly.

16. An additional criticism against the psychoanalytic approach is the use of words like "drive", "instinct", etc., in explaining human actions.

17. A similar example is used by R. Norman (1971) in a discussion of a comparable problem, though within a different conceptual framework.

18. A similar problem consists in whether we can understand what it means to undergo psychoanalytical treatment. I think it is fully possible to do it without oneself having experienced it. But by undergoing such an experience one may add another dimension of depth to one's understanding. One may *grasp* what it is all about.

19. Reading the "German Ideology" or "Grundrisse", to mention two of Marx's most important works, gives a vivid impression how well Marx understood the function of language.

20. We want to remind the reader about our argument that we cannot doubt that we can make correct statements. Because if we say "we cannot be sure that we can make correct statements" then what is this very statement? If it is correct, then we have at least one example that we can make correct statements. If the statement is false, then we can make correct statements (see p. 176 in this chapter).

4: Some Epistemological Problems

When I talk about language (words, sentences, etc.) I must speak the language of every day. Is this language somehow too coarse and material for what we want to say? *Then how is another one to be constructed?* And how strange that we should be able to do anything at all with the one we have!

L. Wittgenstein

4.1 SUMMARY

The main content of this book is concerned with problems of epistemology and knowledge. This chapter, being dedicated to epistemological problems, attempts to take up for discussion some issues which were touched upon before but not analyzed sufficiently.

In section 4.2 we begin with an analysis of the concept "knowledge". The English language does not make a distinction which is made in other languages such as French and German. In German, one distinguishes between "wissen", i.e., know, and "erkennen", i.e., cognitize. Hence it is easier to conceptualize the process of knowledge, as a process of *producing* knowledge.

We distinguish between four meanings of knowledge, and try to relate them to each other in terms of epistemological hypotheses. The first concept is "knowledge as acquaintance", i.e., something we have and which we do not reflect about, but use in our daily life. In this context, one can make a distinction between "be able to do a thing" and "knowing what one is doing". The second concept we call "cognizance". It refers to a state where our acquainted knowledge has become problematical, or where we meet problems which we cannot solve with our "acquainted knowledge". The third concept is "knowledge as transcendence". It designates attempts to overcome the limits of knowledge which we have at our disposal. By using a concrete example—the creation of a sculpture—we try to conceptualize this process of production of knowledge in terms of transcendence and negation of a negation. We postulate that these are central mechanisms in the production of knowledge. The fourth concept, finally, is "insight" and refers to the new product of the knowledge producing process. Slowly, insight is transformed into "knowledge as acquaintance".

The process of transcendence is, thereafter, treated in terms of psychological mechanisms, as distinct from the earlier analytical treatment. It is shown that psychological processes correspond to the analytical concept of transcendence, which, among others, refers to the distinction between focal and subsidiary awareness and shifts between them.

Thereafter we once again take up the problem of language and relate it to "knowledge as acquaintance". We maintain that having a language is as much the ability to produce correct statements, as being able to recognize when rules are violated, without necessarily knowing the rules.

The second aspect refers to our principle of negativity, mentioned in the first chapter. This principle and different uses of "negative", "negative fact", "negation" are explicated in the following section in order to make more precise their use.

In the last two parts of section 4.2, we try to analyze the use of the word "correct", when we say we can produce correct statements. We distinguish between "correct", in the sense of stating logical meaningful relations (often related to the basic logic of our language), and "correct" in the sense of "valid". In the second sense, the word is used when we try to develop procedures, for deciding whether a statement presented is valid or not. We try to show that the use of "correct" in the sense of "valid", presupposes "correct" in the first sense: We cannot develop any decision procedures without assuming that certain statements we make are correct.

In section 4.3 we deal with some problems of a Marxist epistemology. First, we try to show that the concept "praxis" is basic to such an epistemology, and that the concepts "subject" and "object" presuppose the concept of "praxis". We then discuss what a dialectical, relational realism implies and conclude that it is central for a Marxist epistemology. Therefore, we strongly reject the mirror-image thesis, which maintains that knowledge is the mirroring of "objective reality" in consciousness. We use epistemological arguments first. Then, we show that such a thesis not only makes impossible dialectical reasoning. It is also contradictory to a central thesis in Marxist theory, namely, that social existence determines consciousness. Finally, we use the psychological analysis of images as an argument against the mirror-thesis.

In the last section, we once again take up the process of producing knowledge, this time from a genetic point of view. We try to present some of the problems of Piaget's genetic epistemology and to interpret them within the framework developed in this book. Piaget's theory emphasizes the production or construction of knowledge as a process of transformation. In early childhood, Piaget maintains, the subject as well as the object are produced in this process of ongoing transformation.

In a final appraisal of Piaget's theory, we try to show that it is based upon some of the presuppositions which we found basic to the language of dialectics. We also show that the development of pre-linguistic knowledge in the small child, and its mechanisms, cannot be conceptualized without using what we have called "the condition for identification". Hence, we postulate that the production of pre-lingustic knowledge as analyzed by Piaget, is not basically different from the production of linguistic knowledge. In any case, its description presupposes the basic rules of the logic of language.

4.2   ABOUT KNOWLEDGE AND KNOWING

4.2.1   *Knowing and producing knowledge*

In the first chapter, we maintained that a distinction must be made between two problems. The *first* is: what does it mean to have a language. The *second* is: how do we acquire language. We also tried to indicate that we cannot answer the first question by referring to processes of the acquisition of language. Conceptualization of the problem how we acquire language, presupposes that we possess language and can use it according to the basic rules of the logic of language. In other words, we cannot *talk* about how we acquire language without *possessing* language.

A variation of this problem is the distinction between what it means to have knowledge, and how we acquire knowledge. In this chapter, we will deal with the problem of acquisition of knowledge, conceptualized as a process of production.

This second problem, namely, the process of production of

knowledge, in our analysis will be related to the basic notion of dialectics: the negation of a negation.

In German, "epistemology" or "theory of knowledge" is "Erkenntnistheorie". Hence, in German as in many other languages, one distinguishes between "wissen", i.e., to know something, and "erkennen", i.e., to cognitize in the sense of producing knowledge. The distinction is between something already established, which I therefore possess and am able to use, and something which I actively produce by transcending the existing limits of what I possess and make use of.

In the English language, the German "wissen" and "erkennen" are translated into "to know" and the noun, "knowledge". The distinction easily made in German, between that which is possessed and that which is produced, is, therefore, not immediately available. We believe that this lack of distinction renders difficult, or impedes, the analysis and understanding of the meaning of such phrases as "to possess knowledge of something", on the one hand, and phrases referring to "erkennen", i.e., the process of producing what I eventually may possess. Including the way it is acquired and integrated.[1]

We will start with an attempt at a semantical analysis and try to distinguish different meanings of the vague concept of "knowledge". We then attempt to relate these different meanings to each other, in order to establish epistemological hypotheses.

In a *first* sense, "knowledge" means that one is *acquainted with something*. This could be things or events, or actions through which we do certain things without necessarily reflecting about it or why we can do it. Hence, we are acquainted with a multitude of *things* in our daily, immediate environment. It means we can identify and re-identify them. This amounts to saying we know how to use these things (e.g., what we can do with a chair). But, it amounts also to saying that we can talk about them in a way that makes it possible for a listener to understand what we are saying, and hence allows him to identify the thing in the same way we do.

Furthermore, we can do many things, ride a bicycle, drive a car, without reflecting about *what* we are doing and—which seems to be more important—without necessarily being able to explain how we are doing these things. Hence, we will talk about "knowledge" in the sense of *acquaintance* when we (1) know how to act correctly when we use things, (2) when we know how to do things without reflecting about them, i.e., in what we call in a "routine manner", (3) if we know how to talk about (a) the two related classes of actions, (b) other aspects of our immediate environment, and (c) about ourselves. In fact, to say that we have knowledge, in the sense of being acquainted, means that we can correctly form a number of statements.

There is a *second* meaning of "knowledge" closely related to the first one. Sometimes we start thinking and reflecting about what, until now, appeared to us as "natural", as "obvious", as "self-evident". For one reason or another we start to problematize the familiar. This often happens when somebody acts in opposition to that which we are acquainted. E.g., if a foreigner uses our mother-tongue in an erroneous way, we may ask ourselves what really was wrong with his way of using language. As a consequence, we may *become aware* of what so far has appeared to us as unproblematic and "obvious".[2]

A different situation may arise if we deliberately use something with which we are acquainted in another context (if one, for example, is used to repairing a certain type of car and suddenly is given a repair job on a different kind, making it necessary to figure out how, with existing knowledge, one most adequately can do the job).

Another example is when we reflect about why we talk as we do. In all such cases we can talk about knowledge in the sense of "cognizance". This means awareness—by means of reflection—of that to which we are acquainted. We also could use the expression "problematized acquaintance".

There is a *third* meaning of "knowledge", which for our purposes in this context, is the most important, and which corresponds to the actions in the German language called "erkennen". Knowledge, in this case, is not something which one possesses, but a process of cognitizing, a process of producing knowledge. It is a process through which one actively transcends existing limits of acquaintance and cognizance. We will argue that this is done by the process of negating a negation. As a consequence, we maintain that this Hegelian notion is central to the process of production of knowledge (about the notion see p. 224).

By means of a concrete example, we will try to clarify what we mean, and how the Hegelian concept can be used. Sometime ago in an art exhibition in Copenhagen, a sculptor presented sculptures of small elephants. Looking more closely at these elephants, one was amazed to discover that he had taken common ceramic teapots, and turned them upside down. The handle of the teapot became the elephant's tail and the spout its trunk. In addition, the sculptor had put ceramic ears and legs on the "not-(now)-teapot".

Our explication is the following. Something traditionally categorized as a "teapot", was treated as a "negative fact": The sculptor viewed, or used the teapot, as being not a teapot, in the sense of being a *"non-teapot"*.

At that moment he may not exactly have been clear about what it alternatively could be. Thus, the first step seems to be to "uncategorize", i.e., to treat something as a *negative fact*, in the sense the word is used here: He negated it as a teapot by not categorizing it in the usual way.

But, in order to create something new, he had to negate the "non-teapot" by an act of transcending. We should remember that the word in its German use "Aufhebung", refers to three different actions (see p. 80). The first meaning is "doing away" with something, i.e., to "uncategorize" it. In the second sense, it means "to preserve". The sculptor preserved everything of the old (the teapot) which was useful to him, but handled it in another way, and added new things, e.g., the ceramic ears and legs. This refers to the third sense of "Aufhebung", namely, to "elevate it" to something new. Thus, by negating the negation, the "non-teapot", he created something new, the elephant.[3]

Knowledge in the third sense, *"producing cognitively"* and sometimes also manually, implies the negation of a negation through transcendence (Aufhebung). It involves the active participation of the subject as a producer of knowledge. We want to state that the production of new knowledge can be explained in terms of negation of a negation and transcendence. This usually occurs when traditional knowledge, i.e., that with which we are acquainted, becomes problematic, and therefore creates tensions. The example, in addition, seems to indicate that the production of new knowledge retains a direct connection with the old, to which one has been acquainted. Those who produce new knowledge must take as their point of departure what exists, but has become problematic.[4]

Furthermore, our example illuminates another aspect of the

process of producing knowledge: a close interaction between what we do cognitively, and what we do manually. The *fourth* meaning of the word "knowledge" is the following. The product of the process of production of knowledge, i.e., that which is produced is new insight, a new understanding or grasping. Something is produced in addition to what we are already acquainted. Hence, we can talk of "insight" as the fourth meaning of knowledge. This insight however, to the extent we incorporate, and assimilate it in our previous body of accumulated knowledge, will itself become part of the acquainted. The four senses in which we use the word "knowledge" can now be related. They reveal themselves as referring to elements in a process: Knowledge as *acquaintance* may be questioned by reflection leading to knowledge as *cognizance*. Knowledge as the cognitizing *process of producing* by negation of a negation and transcendence, scatters the borders of acquaintance. It may lead to *insight*, which when incorporated, finally, will become knowledge as acquaintance.

4.2.2   *On competence and transcendence*
Not all acquisition of new knowledge can be explained by transcendence. At least traditional methods of learning have stressed the need to learn rules. Following these rules becomes a matter of routine and we forget that we are following rules.

Take, for example, the learning of a new language. As long as we do not speak the new language *fluently*, we usually think in terms of our mother-tongue and try to translate from it. This means that we try to remember rules (e.g., rules of grammatics) and apply them, as long as we have not yet acquired the competence to *talk fluently* in the new language. Being unable to talk fluently means that we are not yet able to act without being forced to figure out how we act. As long as we cannot do this, we can hardly maintain that we are *acquainted* with the new language.

When we have acquired competence, we act according to rules without thinking of these rules. In other words: to act according to rules without being aware of it, means to have knowledge in the sense of being acquainted, or to possess competence. M. Polany, speaking about competence in the sense of skilful performance, says that the aim of such a performance is achieved "by the observance of a set of rules which are not known as such to the person following them" (1962, p. 49).

An example used by the same author is the competence of a cyclist riding a bicycle. The rules he observes are as following: "When he starts falling to the right he turns the handlebars to the right, so that the course of the bicycle is deflected along a curve to the right. This results in a centrifugal force pushing the cyclist to the left and offsets the gravitational force dragging him down to the right. This manoeuvre presently throws the cyclist out of balance to the left, which he counteracts by turning the handlebars to the left; and so he continues to keep himself in balance by winding along a series of appropriate curvatures" (op. cit., p. 50).

One has to be trained in physics as Polany, in order to have knowledge of the rules of bicycling. They explain what happens when a person rides a bicycle, and why he is able to do it. But, being acquainted with these rules does by no means imply one is able to ride the bicycle. In fact, as in the case of learning a new language, being aware and thinking of such rules prohibits, or at least retards, the learning to ride the bicycle.

When we consider how relatively simple it is to learn to ride a bicycle as compared to learning to use language, it is surprising that a small child, during a period of about two years' time, is able to learn the basic logic of language, including its grammatical and syntactical rules, so well, that the child becomes a full-fledged user of language. This is probably a performance which cannot be surpassed in any way later on in life. It is likely a lesser accomplishment getting acquainted with the intricacies of the Einsteinean theory of relativity, than becoming able to use common-sense language and by that, acquire a broad body of knowledge.

The interesting fact is that the small child does not learn to follow rules. When it learns to use language it interacts with others. Hence, many types of acquiring certain competences presuppose social interaction, in and through which we acquire the competences instead of learning to follow rules. In fact, when we say that using language is following rules, we abstract from what persons do when they use language.

Furthermore, skilful acting sometimes implies that we transcend given rules and create new ones within the frame of social interaction. Take a game of chess, for example. We can say that we are competent to play when we master the constituting rules (for example, how many pieces there are, which movements we may make, etc.), and, if in addition, we have acquired certain routine combinations of, e.g., opening- and end-games. This routine implies that we take into consideration social interaction in terms of the other player's expected movements. But to play chess really skilfully, implies a transcendence of routine. It means that a player is able to transgress the possibilities of his actions as formulated by routine rules, and to institute surprise combinations of movements. This amounts to transcending a pattern of a whole, i.e., a sequence of moves and countermoves, by negating the pattern. Certain of the elements in this pattern may be preserved and placed or elevated to a new pattern. This, I think, is what characterizes a master of chess. It is what we may call "creativity".

4.2.3 *Psychological aspects of transcendence*

So far we have tried to discuss knowledge as transcendence from a theoretical point of view. We have not analyzed which psychological mechanisms may be involved in the process of transcendence. Let us take again an example, to find out some of these aspects.

We choose learning to play the piano: "Musicians regard it as a glaringly obvious fact that the sounding of a note on the piano can be done in different ways, depending on the 'touch' of the pianist. To acquire the right touch is the endeavour of every learner, and the mature artist counts its possession among his chief accomplishments" (M. Polany, op. cit., p. 50). The same author tries to explain what the "touch" is. Referring to several studies, he explains it roughly in the following way: when a key on a piano is depressed it creates a noise, which can be heard better if one removes the chords. This noise is mixed with the note sounded by the hammer on the chord. Hence, playing the piano skilfully means being able to control the noise made in the very depression of a key. In terms of our analysis of the process of producing knowledge, this example seems to add a new dimension. Transcendence here seems to be achieved through a process of *manual cognitizing*, because it is done with the fingers. But what does this mean?

In order to understand, we will first use another example. We use a hammer in order to drive in a nail into a wall. "We *watch* the effect of our strokes on the nail and try to wield the hammer so as to hit the nail effectively. When we bring down the hammer we do not feel that its handle has struck our palm but that its head has struck the nail" (M. Polany op. cit., p. 55). At the same time, however, we are sensitive to the information conveyed by the feelings in our palm and adjust our grip on the hammer in order to improve the way we hit the nail.

Polany makes a distinction between two types of awareness: *Focal awareness*, in which my attention is concentrated on the object of my action, the nail to be driven into the wall, and *subsidiary awareness*. While keeping our attention on the object, subsidiarily we are aware of the instrument and its functioning.

The hammer is transformed, when we take it in our hand, from an object to an instrument. This means it has become an extension of our body and its functioning. Hence, a shift occurs between subject and object. The subject now is the person *and* the hammer, the object the patterned relation "nail to wall". The action to be carried out demands that focal awareness be directed towards the new object. Whereas subsidiary awareness is directed towards certain aspects of the relation between subject and object (in the mentioned case, the effect of nailing on the handle-palm).

When we act in a routine manner, we allot usually only subsidiary awareness to our actions. We may be aware of secondary and eventually disturbing or problematic aspects of the subject-object relation. Our focal awareness may be directed towards something else, as when we drive a car and think of the book we are just writing.

Let us now return to the pianist and assume that he has not yet acquired the "touch". He is a good player, but not a top-player. He knows it and is unsatisfied. He develops a contradiction between his aspirations and achievement in spite of intensive training. This contradiction between his aspirations and his factual performance functions as a motivating force for change.

Let us assume that he, by chance or by accident (a chord has been cut off), hears the noise of the keys. This is equivalent to a shift in awareness. Whereas he previously has concentrated his focal awareness on the music produced and treated the piano as an instrument, now it becomes an object, and his global awareness shifts to the keys. Previously, only subsidiary awareness was awarded to them. They now come into focus. He hears the noise the depression of the keys creates. Thereafter may happen what Wittgenstein so characteristically called, "the dawning of an aspect". According to him, this implies that instead of perceiving "a property of the object" now one can construct "an *internal* relation between it and other objects" (1968 p. 212, our ith.) in a new way.

I would like to amend Wittgenstein's description. What happens, is the CHANGE of an intrinsic relation between a subject—in our case the player and his extended body, the piano as an instrument—and the object being the music produced. This is done by shifting focal awareness, amounting to a new way of relating oneself as a subject to another object. In this case it is the keys of the piano which no longer function as the subject's instrument in the sense of "extended body".

This also could be formulated in terms of a negation. Shifting global awareness corresponds to negating an existing intrinsic subject-object relation.

Perhaps for the first time, the pianist grasps the role of the noise produced by the keys, and its relation to the sounds created by the hammer striking the chords. Therefore, what for him was "piano music", and with which he was unsatisfied, now is negated. By focusing on the noise created by depressing the keys, the pianist may try to acquire the "touch", which corresponds to negating the negation: To transcend what for him now is "no-longer-music". If he succeeds he will create something new: a totality which encompasses the noise of depressing the keys, as well as the sounds produced by the hammers on the chords. Having acquired the "touch", the pianist now can direct his focal awareness towards this new totality, which now is categorized as "music".

In summary then: whereas the analysis in section 4.2.1 was concerned with cognitizing as a process of negation of a negation on a conceptual level, we here tried to present some of the psychological mechanisms of this process. As a consequence of the contradiction between motivation (aspiration) and achievement, there occurs a shift of focal awareness from a totality that is categorized in a certain way ("good music"). Focal awareness is now directed at something to which, previously, only subsidiary awareness was attributed. This is the negation, i.e., the rejection of traditional ways of categorizing. There seems to develop the "dawning of a new aspect". New intrinsic relations between subject and object are established, implying also a change in the structure of the subject, as well as the establishment of a new object. As a last step, the negation is transcended: The "no-longer-good-music" is now replaced by "music-integrating-key-noise-and-sound". When we analyze the process of cognitizing, i.e., *erkennen*, we want to emphasize once again, what we previously have underlined. It is not enough for the pianist to understand how he theoretically can eliminate noise. He also must accomplish it practically by acquiring the "touch". This points at the unity of cognitive and manual actions.

Let us make some final observations: In our example, the pianist and the piano together as instrument formed originally the subject, and the music the object. Taken together they formed a totality or a total context. The negation phase in the process implied the breaking up of this unity or totality. The piano and its parts became the object, to which the subject related himself. Hence, producing or reproducing something as an object, means detaching it from the context or totality in which it is integrated. This amounts to dividing a totality into two parts, the restructured subject, and the new object. "Dividing one into two" has previously (see p. 84) been discussed as central principle of a dialectical epistemology. This principle, however, seems to imply a paradox. How is it possible to speak of a totality or a total context, a unity, etc., made up of elements, if one cannot come to grips with this totality except through the meditation of its elements? "Man can know the context of reality only by extricating the facts from the context, by isolating them and by rendering them independent in a relative way. Thereupon rests *all* knowing: on dividing one into two" (K. Kosik 1967, p. 52).

Thus, cognitizing means the breaking up of a totality by negating it. Psychologically, this is accompanied by a shift from global awareness to other aspects, to which we so far attributed only subsidiary awareness. When this new aspect is placed into the center or focus, new intrinsic relations are established and a new totality emerges.

Negating means rejecting something as being identified *with* something (the teapot with the class of teapots), and identifying it *as* something specific. Negating the negation—and establishing a new totality—means the identification of the new *with* something else (the reshaped teapot with the class of elephants). Thus, it can be identified *as* an elephant and no longer *as* a teapot.

4.2.4 *Acquaintance with language*

In the first chapter (see p. 24) and later on, we maintained that possessing a language means being able to produce some correct statements about our immediate environments, and about ourselves. In other words, once we are acquainted with language, we can, in concrete social situations, make certain statements that are correct.

A user of language is in a dialectical situation. The statements he presents are always within a concrete context, and therefore can be identified *as* being specific. But in order to produce situation-specific statements, he has to know, in the sense of being acquainted with, the general meaning which a specific statement has. In other words, in order to produce a situation-specific statement, he has to know a non-situation-specific meaning, *with* which his specific statement can be identified.

This is an application of our rule for identification.[5]

In addition to being able to produce some correct statements, a user of language also can decide when a great number of statements, presented by others, are *not* correct. If, for example, a foreigner violates syntactical rules of our language, we can immediately understand it as an incorrect statement, even if we do not know, i.e., are unable to explain why the statement is not correct. If one would ask people "how do you know that he did not speak correctly?", an answer would probably be: "I just know it, I don't know why".

The same that is valid for the violation of syntactical rules can also be claimed for the violation of the rules of the basic logic of language. (If one would say, yesterday, I talked to somebody who had no states of consciousness whatsoever, most people would recognize the contradiction.) Let me summarize. To possess language in the sense of being *acquainted* with language, implies that we partly are able to *produce* a number of correct statements. Also that we are able to recognize "*negative facts*", i.e., violations of grammatical, syntactical and basic logical rules.

Furthermore, applying the distinction between knowledge as acquaintance and knowledge as cognizance (see p. 215), we maintain that the *transition* from acquaintance to cognizance presuppose, as a *necessary* but *not as a sufficient* condition, negative facts in the sense of violations of rules.

We ask a person who, for example, is not acquainted with

syntactical rules, but correctly has observed that the violation of such a rule is wrong. He may answer: "Now, when you ask, it seems strange that I have never thought about it". One reason for this response is that he is acquainted with language without knowing its rules. Therefore, as Wittgenstein pointed out: "The aspects of things that are most important for us are hidden because of their simplicity and familiarity. (One is unable to notice something because it is always before one's eyes.) The real foundations of his enquiry do not strike man at all. Unless *that* fact has at some time struck him. And that means: we fail to be struck by what, once seen, is most striking and most powerful" (1968 §129).

If our friend, after being struck by the fact that he never reflected on the reasons why incorrect statements are incorrect (and why self-evidently correct statements are correct), he may try to transcend the limits of his own knowledge: but not only by recognizing a negative fact, but also by being able to negate this negative fact in a conscious way. This means to learn the rules that have been violated.

There seem to be some problems involved in the analysis we have just presented. One, at least, is concerned with the meaning of expressions like "negative facts".

4.2.5   *On the use of expressions "negative" and "negative facts"*
Throughout this book, we have talked about "negative", "negative facts", "negation", "negation of negation", etc. It seems now appropriate to attempt a more precise analysis of our use of these expressions.

We will start with the most simple use and proceed to the more complicated. In the first chapter (see p. 30), we introduced the notion of "principle of negativity". There we said it may be difficult to say what a certain concept, for example, the concept "person", comprises. It may be less difficult to say what it does not. In chapter 3 (p. 160), we expanded this idea to theoretical explanations. We argued that sometimes empirical research provides us with results which are open to several explanations. If we perform a conceptual analysis of some of the most important concepts in such explanations, we may be able to exclude some.

In summary, the principle of negativity states that we better can find out what a word does not refer to, what a concept does not include, which explanation is not correct, than to state all references, the extension of a concept, etc. The same principle is also used in the formulation of legal law, where sometimes it is emphasized which actions are prohibited. In other words, it is easier to state what a person is not allowed to do, than what he is. Finally, this principle has important consequences for ethics. Traditionally, utilitarian ethics, dealing with problems of happiness, gets involved in a series of difficulties. It seems much easier, though not uncomplicated, to analyze what people do *not* want. It seems more difficult to find out what happiness is, than to state what suffering is. We can be certain that no Vietnamese peasant likes to be exposed to bombardments from the air. Hence, the principle of negativity seems to open possibilities for the development of an ethics not based upon individual actions, but on the analysis of social conditions. So much for the first and most simple use of the words "negative" and "negative facts". They are characterized such that we recognize what is not correct, what we are not allowed to do, or what we do not wish, without necessarily reflecting on the reasons. If we start doing this, the words "negative" and "negative fact" acquire additional meaning.

In traditional "posivistic" science, we try to observe and analyze what is *given*, i.e., what, in this sense, is a "positive fact". But in observing and analyzing social reality, we also may get interested in what is not given, but what is lacking. Let us exemplify (see G. Skirbekk 1976). Assume we conduct an analysis of mass media. A *positive* description attempts to present what the media have produced. A *negative* description will analyze that which has not been presented, for instance what we can read "between the lines". A negative description here, not only analyzes what has not been said, but in addition, what *could* have been said. One immediately can see that the concept of "action as omission or forbearance" (see p. 181), here has its place.

Hence, negative descriptions may imply the formation of a *critical* theory in a definite sense: A critical theory which is not only critical of the theories concerning reality and its presuppositions, but which also *is critical of reality itself, such as it functions* (see also p. 60). "This presupposes evidently that one is convinced that one has a well-grounded conception of the nature of the thing. It is only in relation to what the 'thing essentially is' that its deficiences stand out" (G. Skirbekk op. cit., p. 336).

Hence "negative" in this sense, not only implies the discovery of "negative facts" in relation to that to which one is acquainted. It also implies a critical attitude regarding the "negative facts", considered as deficiencies. This attitude, in turn, makes it possible to understand "negative" and "negative facts" in a third sense of "negation".

4.2.6   On negation of negations

In the discussion of dialectical relations (see p. 112) we distinguished three types of oppositions. As regard to the first and weakest, in which two elements are complimentary (as in "selling" and "buying"), we talked about "contrasting negation". Selling negates buying as its contrast. In the other two types of opposition, the two contradictions were called "interacting negations". Here, the actions of the one element negates, in the sense of prevents or eliminates, the action of the other element. They cannot exist side by side or contemporaneously. These distinctions, however, do not sufficiently explain the notions of "negation" and "negation of negation".

The task of dialectical thinking, as understood by Hegel, is to negate traditional ways of conceptualization. "With Hegel metaphysics ceases to be speculation about the ultimate nature of reality. *Analysis of categories* replaces speculative metaphysics" (W. Kaufmann 1966, p. 196, our ith.). It is in this analysis that negation of negation becomes important.

Marx's demand that philosophers should stop interpreting the (social) world, since the real task is to "negate" it, i.e., to change it purposively in accordance with certain goals, can be viewed as an extension of the Hegelian project.

Marcuse (1960, p. 123) has pointed out that in Hegelian logic the terms "negative" and "negating" (that which is conceived as negative ought to be negated) in this context has a double meaning. We maintain in addition, that these two meanings are interrelated. The words "negative" and "negating" respectively are, so to say, shorthand for two different and intrinsically related conceptions.[6]

First, negating in the context of dialectical reasoning, refers to denying the conceptual value of *more or less fixed categories* in our language. They, consequently, are considered as *negative* in the sense of "inappropriate". *Second*, negating means also that we should judge as *negative* that which is viewed as a *fact.* These facts are positive in the sense that they have been observed, i.e., established by empirical evidence. Negating them, consequently, transforms them into "negative facts". But what does such an expression mean?

"Positivistic, scientific thinking" viewed as opposed to "dialectical reasoning", assumes that what we *ought* to study is that which is given here and now, e.g., by isolating and by bringing out its specific characteristics. This must be done empirically, i.e., by relying on controlled observations.

One objection to such a position is that these *positively given facts* are not all given directly or immediately to our experience. They are mediated through fixed categories, structuring our experience.

If this is so, negating these categories, i.e., viewing them as *inappropriate* and, in this sense, as *negative,* implies also negating the facts which they mediate. This means viewing them as *negative,* i.e., *inadequate.* Hence, a long explication seems to end in a banality: *Inappropriate categories mediate something which incorrectly or inadequately is called a "fact".*

I think there is more to it. When can we call a category inappropriate and therefore negate it? Hegel begins by rejecting the traditional dualism between linguistic categories and reality (about this dualism, see p. 93). In fact, this is one of his criticisms of Kant, who found contradictions or antimonies between his categories, and explained them in terms of limits to our possibilities of conceptualization. Hegel, on the other hand, maintained that the contradictions between categories resulted from contradictions within reality of which they were parts or aspects. Hence, "our categorical concepts when we consider them as descriptions of reality as a whole or pervasive aspects of this reality show a crucial inadequacy. And this lands us in a contradiction. For these categorical concepts are inescapable; they are meant to designate indispensable aspects of reality if there is to be a reality for us at all. If then these concepts portray a reality which is in some sense impossible or incoherent, we are caught in a contradiction: the seemingly indispensable descriptions of reality portray a reality which cannot be" (Ch. Taylor 1975, p. 228).

This is the way Kantian categories seem to operate. Hegel accepted the idea that certain categories are *indispensable* and *at*

the same time incoherent. Take for example, the category of
"Being", which we used earlier in our illustration of dialectics (see
p. 79). It is indispensble. At the same time, as used by Hegel it is
inadequate. But it is according to Hegel inadequate not because of
our conceptualization, but because reality has an intrinsic contradiction. What does this mean? Reality, as it is now, which is the
only way we can conceptualize it, is inadequate and incoherent,
when seen from the point of view how it could be, if changed. This
becomes more clear when we talk only about "social reality".

Hegel's solution is to show that these categories, which like
"Being" are indispensable and, at the same time, inappropriate, are
linked to *their* contradicting relata. The contradiction has to be
solved on a new level.

Hence we can negate a category or concept as inappropriate, if
we are able to negate the negation. The new category becomes the
point of departure for the ongoing processes characterized by
contradictions.

To use, once again, our example. As long as we categorize a
teapot in terms of teapot, the concept is appropriate. If we,
however, for one reason or other, are unsatisfied to conceive a
teapot as a teapot, for instance, if we refuse to look at it as a teapot
and use it as such, we are caught in a contradiction. We either
must say that the concept is appropriate and consistent and, as a
consequence, to leave everything where it is. Or, if we continue to
negate the teapot into a non-teapot, we must solve the tensions we
create. Thus, by means of a negation of the negation we may end
up with an elephant. The difference between this example and
Hegelian logic, is that the elephant is not *the* solution to
contradictions inherent in "teapot", but only one of many possible.
However, a teapot as concept is not a *basic category* of reality, and
therefore, it does not have its contradicting element, which,
according to Hegel, *basic* categories have. In the social world,
however, the negation of existing social conditions when we are
dissatisfied, does not usually lead us to think in terms of *one
possible* negation of the negated. In the social world we deal with
multiple alternatives. Therefore, I am suspicious of expressions like
"*the* correct line".

4.2.7   Some problems of correctness
A central thesis in this book is concerned with defining what it

means to have a language: the ability to make some correct statements, and to recognize a number of incorrect ones. We also maintained that if we have understood once what a correct statement is, we also have knowledge of the notion of correctness. Finally, we tried to show that the notion "correct" cannot be further explained, since all attempts to do so, presuppose the very knowledge of "correct".

The central theses do not, however, imply: (1) that we do not face a multitude of situations where we are in doubt which one of the two alternative statements is correct. Furthermore, they do not imply, (2) that we cannot make false statements. Finally, they do not imply, that we cannot, or ought not, develop procedures for deciding which one of two alternative, and eventually contradicting, statements is correct.

We maintain, however, that the development and the application of these decision procedures (how to test the truth of a statement or how to falsify it), presupposes the primitive notion of "correctness".

Some of these problems will be discussed now.

I want to start with an example using a dream. A dream is real in the sense that we experience it. Sometimes we may experience it as utterly painful, as when we have a nightmare. How can we test that we have a dream? Somebody may study our electric brain waves and be able to determine through changes in the electric potential that we are dreaming. Though he would not be able to find out the content of our dreams. Also, I doubt very much whether he could, by his method, differentiate a pleasant dream from a nightmare.

We can, however, *talk* about our dream. Obviously, to dream is not the same as to talk about a dream. If one tells somebody of a dream he has had, one gives an account of the dream. The account of the dream is something different from the dream, though closely related to it. Without a dream we have nothing to report, and sometimes we have a dream without being able to account for it. One may object that we can report a dream without having had one, by making it up. But in this case, we at least *know* that we made it up, and that it was not really a dream. We can do it because we have learned what it means to say "I dreamed", and to distinguish it from saying "I made up a dream". If we did not know the distinction we could not talk about it, and we could not pretend that we have had a dream when we only made up a story.

Without giving an account of the dream we would be unable to preserve the dream as something which we have experienced and which, therefore, is *real* to us. *The dream and the account of it, though different, are interrelated and presuppose each other.*

Furthermore, when we still are asleep and dream, we may use language: we may talk in the dream and even, while sleeping start talking about the dream.

But now one may ask: if somebody gives an account of the dream, how can a listener know that the account given, *corresponds* to the dream, i.e., is not something made up, or something one only believes one has dreamed, though "in fact" one has not. Perhaps the person was only dreaming that he had a dream. And, if so, what does one report in this case? Perhaps one could dream one has a dream, as in a movie one can show another movie.

These are the kinds of questions people may put forward when they want us to believe that all we know is comparable to reports about dreams, if we are not able to establish a correspondence between our statements and reality.

Our argument, then follows this line. In talking about correspondence we have already introduced a dualistic notion distinguishing between language and reality. If we do not want to accept a dualism with its sharp division, we must abandon the idea that a statement is true when it, in one way or other, corresponds to reality. What does the word "correspond" refer to? Does it refer to a relation between reality and a picture of reality? We will, in the next section, discuss this problem and try to indicate some of the difficulties related to a picture or mirror theory of correspondence (see p. 238). In general, many or most of the statements, the truth of which we want to establish, are complicated statements. It is difficult to find pictures in reality corresponding to them. Take the following statement: "It was Hitler and not the Allies, who started World War II". I have difficulty in seeing how the truth of such a statement could be established by having it correspond, as a picture, to something in reality.

But to take another example—a map. In one, but very vague sense, we could say that a map is correct when it pictures reality. A map uses signs. In order to use signs, there must exist rules stating how to use them so that we understand that these signs refer to something. Hence, a map is correct if, when producing it, we have followed rules according to which we establish the meaning of signs used.

How could we establish rules without using language? How could we ever use language, if we were not able to produce some statements such that we are sure they are correct, and are not forced to establish their correctness? If we had to establish the correctness of all our statements first, in order to formulate rules for using the signs of a map, we probably would never come to the point where we could formulate these very rules.

When we talk about "correctness" or "truth", we are able to distinguish *at least* three different problems. *One* is concerned with *criteria* according to which we can establish the truth of statements. The *second* is concerned with the *meaning* of words like "true", "correct", etc., and the contexts in which we use them. The *third* problem deals with the question how we can *act* in establishing truth.

4.2.8   *How to find out whether something is true*
How can I act to find out that something is true in the sense that I can be certain such is the case? The answer must be by investigating the matter. How I conduct my investigation depends on the problem I want to investigate.

Assume that I want to find out whether I can run the mile in less than four minutes. One advice is that I should run and have someone take the time. This is an example of how I can find out the truth about statements concerning my *possibilities of action*.

Perhaps I want to find out the truth about a certain *state of affairs*, for example, whether I have the malady I suspect I have. To find out whether it is true or not, I have to go to a doctor.

Take a third example. Assume that I want to find out·whether it is true if a pear tastes like an orange or not. In this case, I could follow Mao Tse-tung's advice, who says that in order to find out how a pear tastes you have to eat it yourself (1968 p. 8).

For all the examples I have used, it holds that when we want to find out whether it is true that a state of affairs exists, or whether possibilities of action exist, we have to do certain things. We must investigate the matter. In order to investigate we must set up certain rules which we want to follow. We formulate rules according to which we can decide the matter. These rules hence, are about *procedures for the verification* or falsification of beliefs, suspicions and hypotheses which we characterize as "scientific".

But, how could we formulate rules for decision procedures concerning the verification or falsification of statements, without having a language in which we can formulate these very statements, and the rules according to which we shall act in order to verify our statements? Take the advice, "In order to find out how a pear tastes eat it". How could I follow this advice if I did not know what "taste" is? And how could I *know* it, except by formulating some correct statements in which I use the word "taste"? How could I know what it means to say "eat it yourself", if I did not know anything about myself? But, to *know* something about myself means being able to formulate some correct statements about myself, e.g., that I have a body. This implies knowing that having a body means having a mouth with sensory receptors that mediate taste; that I have a stomach so that I can digest a pear (how would I dare to eat it otherwise?), etc.

In general, we cannot formulate rules for decision procedures to establish the truth of any statement without being able to use language, in order to formulate these rules. We cannot say that we are able to use language without being able to formulate some correct statements, and without knowing that some statements are not correct, though we may not know the reasons for that. In other words, we could not *act* to establish anything without having a basic foundation from which we can start. This foundation, we maintain, is built as soon as we have learned to use language.

Let me make a final remark. When we talk about a person being able "to produce some correct statements", and being able to establish or prove the "correctness of a statement", we use the word "correct" in two senses.

In the first sense, when we say that a person is able to make some correct statements we talk about *logical properties.* We can show that if we deny the correctness of our statement, we contradict ourselves, or we talk in a way which does not make sense or makes our speech unintelligible. This is because we violate basic rules of the general logic of our language. These rules and their logical properties are not about language as distinct from reality, since knowledge of language *is* knowledge of reality.[7]

Formalized logic which is only about language is then understood as based upon the general logic of our language.

If we say, on the other hand, that we want to know whether "it is correct that a pear tastes like an orange", we use "correct" in the sense of *"being valid"*. What we want to know is whether a statement about something is valid or not, if it *expresses a fact or not.*

One answer to such a question is "eat it", i.e., to state procedures for finding out. In order to assess "correctness" of a statement in the first sense, it is a *necessary condition* to possess and use language.

In order to assess the "correctness" of a statement in the second sense, it is *sufficient* to state rules concerning decision procedures. I must possess language, i.e., being able to formulate statements having such *logical* properties that we can say that they are formulated in a correct way. We can decide the correctness of a statement in the first sense by denying it, but we cannot define what "correct" in this sense is. Any such definition presupposes the knowledge, and therefore, the use of "correct" in the first sense.

We mentioned before that there were at least three problems related to the question of truth. One, how to establish truth, we have discussed. The second and third, concerning *criteria* for establishing truth and the meaning of the word "true" in various contexts, involve very complicated problems and intricate arguments. Therefore, I do not want to stick out my neck more than I already have done. I tried to suggest how one can reason in answering one of the three different questions concerning the concept of "truth": how can we *act* in establishing truth? The other two, namely, *criteria* concerning the establishment of the truth of statements, and the *meaning* of the word "true", I have hardly touched.

4.3   PROBLEMS OF MARXIST EPISTEMOLOGY

4.3.1   *Praxis as an epistemological concept*

The word "epistemology" and "epistemological" can, at least, be used in two senses. First, we can use it in contexts where we discuss what it means to have knowledge. Second, we can use it in contexts in which we discuss conditions for the production or construction of knowledge, and its further development. In chapter 1 (see p. 23), we have already pointed out that there are two distinct questions concerning language: (1) What does it mean to have language and (2) how do we acquire language. These two questions have the same validity when we substitute "knowledge" for "language".

In a discussion of Marxian "epistemology", we use the word in the second context. The problems with which Marx and Marxian "epistemology" deal, are problems concerning the process of production of knowledge. I want to underline this. Marx discussed the process of production of knowledge, but he did not have a theory of the logic of our language. However, a theory of the basic logic of language and its rules—as we, time after time, have tried to demonstrate—is basic to theories of the process of production of knowledge. We obviously cannot *talk* about the process of production of language, or any other epistemological process, without having a language, and without following the rules of its basic logic.

Marx tried to develop a theory of the process of production of knowledge. Though he made it clear that the process of production of knowledge has to be related to the material process of production, he *never* tried to reduce the process of production of knowledge to the material process of production. (Neither do I think that he attempted to construct a "materialistic synthesis", as J. Habermas (1968) has maintained).

Marx stated his epistemological position in his criticism of mechanical materialism, expressed in the first of his theses about Feuerbach. There he points out that the position of Feuerbach and of others calling themselves "materialists" has a main defect. Reality, that which stands opposite man is conceived only in the form of objects. Hence, it implies a dualistic notion of the subject as sharply separated from the object. Reality ought to be grasped as "human sense activity, as praxis".

My interpretation is not that Marx maintains that *reality is a product* of human sense. *Reality should be grasped as cognitizing and practical activity.*

A position which takes its point of departure in the notion that process is basic and structure or order are characteristics of process (see p. 116), must place process and its expressions as a basic category.

Marx adds that the role of the active subject in the process of producing knowledge was, instead, developed by idealistic philosophy. And this only in an abstract way. Real sense activity presupposes the existence of a world independently of the subject, a world upon which man can act.

Marx continues his criticism of Feuerbach by saying, "Feuerbach wants sensible objects really distinguished from the objects of thoughts, but he does not understand human activity itself as object-producing activity" ("gegenständliche Tätigkeit", p. 533). The German word "gegenständlich" is usually translated as "objective" or a "concrete". My interpretation here is that Marx refers to a producing activity in which the products are cognitive objects, as well as "material" objects. Furthermore, I believe that Marx wanted to eliminate the sharp distinction between cognitive activity and material, object producing activity. Both are different though *interdependent* aspects of a total activity. He conceives cognitively productive and materially productive activity as being intrinsically related. In order to produce something materially it must exist in our head, thus making our actions purposive. In order to exist in our head as concrete cognitive activity (not as pure speculation), it has to be related to materially producing activity.

In the second chapter we tried to explicate "praxis" in terms of the essence of human existence, as the activity of producing and transforming the world (see p. 118). Used in the context there, the concept of "praxis" has ontological connotations. In an epistemological context "praxis" understood as generic "gegenständliche Tätigkeit", i.e., cognitive and material producing activity, becomes a basic concept.

What does it imply? Traditionally the subject-object relation, understood as the knower-known relationship, has been considered fundamental categories in the process of production of knowledge. We regard, however, praxis as the basic category in this process. Praxis, as generic societal activity of producing and changing is the means by which the subject as well as the object is produced.

Through praxis the subject is produced as a choosing, decision-making and acting being when, through his action he becomes aware of himself as subject. He becomes aware of himself through actions which are manifestations of praxis in general. The object comes into existence through the cognitively and materially producing and changing actions of the subject, actions again which are the manifestations of praxis. This produced world of objects and social institutions then, in turn, produces the subject. Since institutions and objects are objectified praxis, the subject also, in this sense, is produced by praxis.

In summarizing: the notion that praxis is the basic category in the process of production of knowledge implies, (1) that through praxis, as manifested in man's actions, the human being is transformed into a self-conscious subject; (2) that his actions, viewed as manifestations of praxis, produce cognitive, social and material objects; (3) that institutionalized praxis finally transforms the subject.

The relation between subject and object is not extrinsic, but intrinsic. This means, first of all, that there is an intimate interdependence between subject and object: it does not make sense to talk of a subject without talking of an object, and reversed. Second, the world exists independently of the subject, but not extrinsically to him. The world as object is a human world in two senses. It is produced cognitively, as well as materially.

The world as object comes into existence when the subject, through a process of decisions and choices, *relates* himself to the world existing independently of him.

In order to relate himself to the world, the subject must possess a language through which he can express his ways of relating.

Since the possession of language presupposes intersubjectivity, the ways of relating are objectively given as social facts. Thus, epistemological relationism does not imply subjectivism in the sense of each subject relating himself in an individually different way. Relating is a social activity. Neither does it imply epistemological idealism. We *know* that the world exists independently of ourselves. We have objective concrete knowledge about it. This very knowledge, therefore, is an argument against any idealistic conception. The independent existence of the world can only be known by subjects. Subjects, in turn, can only exist as subjects because of the material conditions which make it possible to talk about objects. In addition the subject as a person is himself a material object, since we cannot talk about persons without talking about bodies (see p. 160).

A subject can relate himself in innumerable ways to the world, but always only as a social subject. He can never give a total description of the world. Neither is the world mirrored in his consciousness. Any time the subject relates himself to the world, cognitively, or by producing materially, he transforms it into a humanized world. The very notion of "nature as such", presupposes a language in which we can express such and other notions about the world, nature and the universe. Hence in this sense, all objects produced can be said to be *subjectified objects*. Since the subject, in turn, is the product of his own produced world, we also can talk about an *objectified subject* in this limited sense. This is, in short, what we have called a dialectical and relational realism (see p. 37).

In finishing up this problem we want to exemplify the consequences of such a position. Habermas (1968), discussing Marx's epistemological position, speaks of "objectified nature" as the "correlate to societal labour". Thus, he poses "nature" and "society" extrinsically against each other. "Objectified nature" is characterized by independence and externality. Independence is manifested by the fact that we can dominate nature as long as we submit ourselves to it. Habermas refers here to the limitations for possibilities of action to which human beings are exposed, and which are conceptualized in "laws of nature". So far Habermas' discourse is in agreement with the position explicated above.

Habermas then goes on, saying the *externality* of nature is manifested through the fact that, in spite of our means of dominance, there remains a nucleus which does not open up itself for us (op. cit., p. 46). If this means that all our knowledge of nature has limits, and that all new knowledge indicates what we do not yet know, then there need not be any disagreement with Habermas. But, in this case, it is difficult to understand why that should be an indicator of the externality of nature. Knowledge of nature is one way of relating oneself intrinsically to nature. Knowledge of that which we do not know, as expressed in the *notion* of the nucleus which does not open itself to us, is another way of *intrinsically* relating ourselves to nature. It is an intrinsic way because it is a notion and, as such, a way of conferring meaning upon what we do not know (yet). In fact, the very *notion* of "externality" is a way of relating oneself intrinsically to the world. It is only possible as a consequence of the intrinsic relation between subject and object.

4.3.2 The mirror image thesis

There is one Marxist epistemological position that conceives knowledge as the mirroring of the world, or of reality, in consciousness. As our previous discourse has indicated, we consider such a position contradictory to a dialectical position. Furthermore, we want to show that it also is logically contradictory to other basic propositions of Marxism. Finally, it cannot be upheld if analyzed within the framework of cognitive psychology.

What does the "mirror thesis" assert? In a most general way, it can be formulated such that knowledge of the "external" world is reflected in consciousness. The knowledge we have is a picture or mirror of "objective reality" existing independently of the subject. Hence, the thesis assumes that reality exists *independently* and *externally* to the subject and that, furthermore, there is a *parallelism* between reality and knowledge of reality.

It should be pointed out, however, that there are Marxist philosophers (e.g., S.L. Rubinstein 1973, A. Schaff 1964, 1974) who accept the mirror thesis of knowledge, but reject the idea that the relation between "objective reality" and "mirroring in consciousness", should be one of parallelism. We will return to their position after having discussed some of the preconditions of the mirror thesis as a parallel relation, and its epistemological consequences.[9]

First of all, the mirror thesis presupposes the dualistic notion of reality as sharply separated from consciousness or knowledge. As any dualistic position, it is logically contradictory to the notion of totality as the most important presupposition of dialectical reasoning. One can object to our argument by saying that dialectics is located in reality, in the objective world, and is mirrored in our consciousness. But, in this case the central role of the subject-object relation in dialectical reasoning is negated. The second argument against the mirror thesis, is that it rejects the active role of the subject in producing the world cognitively. The subject is relegated to the role of a passive receiver of knowledge which is mirrored in his consciousness. As a consequence, praxis, as producing and changing action, loses its central role in dialectical thinking. This is also so because cognitive and material praxis are unseparable. They are different, but interrelated elements in a whole.

Some Marxist philosophers have understood these consequences, but accept the idea of knowledge as a mirror, though they reject the idea of mirroring as parallel relation. They speak, for example, of "active mirroring".[10] S.L. Rubinstein (1973), for instance, writes: "Each psychological fact is a piece of *real reality* and a *mirroring* of reality, not either one or the other, but both together" (p. 17). Psychological experiences, hence, are real but as mirror images. Later on, talking about genetic development, he maintains that the essence of development is "the bringing forth of continuously new forms of the *active and cognitizing* mirroring of reality" (op. cit., p. 130). Furthermore (and later on) he speaks about the active mirroring of reality, "which transforms through reflection the sensual reality (Gegebenheit) of appearance in order to penetrate into their essence" (p. 215).

To talk about an *active* and cognitizing mirroring, must imply that one abolishes the idea of mirroring as a parallel relation. This becomes clear in the last quotation, where mirroring denotes a process of transformation and reflection. For me, it is difficult to see how the notion of a mirror image can be reconciled with the notions of actively producing and transforming, and with reflexion. How can it, in general, be reconciled with the notion of a subject as an acting being? It seems to me that one has to make a choice. Rubinstein also makes this choice. When he analyzes thought-processes he writes: "As a cognitive and theoretical activity thinking is intimately related to acting. Man *cognitizes* reality by acting upon it. He comprehends the world by changing it" (op. cit., 430). No mentioning of mirroring at all![11]

A. Schaff (1964), maintains that "mirroring" is an expression which cannot be taken literally, but only as a vague metaphorical expression; he underlines the active role of the subject in cognitive praxis.

We may summarize that the mirror thesis, taken literally, is logically and psychologically untenable.

In addition to the two objections raised, namely, that the thesis presupposes dualism and that it abolishes the role of the subject, and hence of praxis, there is a third objection. The thesis renounces the idea of the historical conditioning of our knowledge. This idea negates the notion of a timeless relation between knowledge and what knowledge is about. But, a mirror thesis that assumes that an objective reality, existing independently and extrinsically to the subject, is mirrored in consciousness, has difficulties to explain historically conditioned changes in our knowledge. How should, for example, the transition from Newtonian to Einsteinean physics be explained, if the only knowledge we can have of physical reality is that which is mirrored? The transition from Newtonian to Einsteinean theory then has to be explained as a consequence of a change in physical nature, not as a change in our way of conceptualizing it.

So far, we have used three epistemological arguments. But we also can show that the mirror thesis *logically* contradicts another important thesis in Marxism. I am referring to the notion that it is social existence which determines consciousness and not the reverse. Such a hypothesis, formulated within a sociological framework, states that in a social system the functioning of individual cognitive processes, at least partially, should be explained in terms of the functioning of the social structure and the individual's place in it.

If social processes *determine* consciousness, and if knowledge is a central aspect of consciousness (or even is equated with consciousness as sometimes in German philosophy), then the mirror thesis cannot be reconciled with the *determination* thesis.

"Determining" refers to something else than "mirroring". It is only in a peculiar sense of the term "determination", that we can say that something mirrored is "determined". Can one say that the picture of my face in the mirror is *determined* by my real face?

But even if we could use "determine" to denote a mirroring relation, how could we explain class-consciousness? A mirroring relation must imply that the structure of reality, which is mirrored, must be the same for all observers. It imposes itself on the subject. How then can we account for, that in a society based upon classes, people belonging to different classes have different consciousness?

There seem to be two solutions: (1) the mirror thesis has to be restricted to a certain part of reality, such that it is perceived, understood, and grasped by all in an identical way, as a consequence of "mirroring". In this case we must admit that there are important areas of reality to which the thesis cannot be applied. For somebody defending the thesis, it then becomes an important task to show which part of reality fits the mirror thesis, and which part does not. (In this case he cannot uphold the dialectical notion of totality.) Furthermore, he has to show what kind of explanation should be used for the knowledge we may have of that part of reality which does not fit the thesis; (2) Alternatively, one has to abandon the notion of class-consciousness and theories in which it is used.

4.3.3   The mirror-image thesis and perception

One thesis which we repeatedly have stated is that we can give innumerable descriptions of the world, and that we, therefore, cannot give a total description of anything. The way we describe a thing is not determined by inherent characteristics of the thing, but by the way we relate ourselves to these characteristics.

"Any question about what a thing is has to be answered by a description of a thing, and each justification of a description of a thing has to be carried out by means of other descriptions. Therefore a description of a thing is not a verbal 'mirroring' of the 'qualities' of things. It is a *human decision* concerning the thing" (A. Thing Mortensen 1972, p. 88, our ith.). If we consider the ways we relate ourselves to the world as a series of decisions, we must underline that these decisions are not arbitrary. They, in turn, follow the rules of the basic logic or our language. These rules, in turn, are manifested in what we could call "linguistic habits", or what is the same, "institutionalized conceptions". It would be strange, for example, to describe a stone "as an eatable thing". We would immediately react by saying that a person using such an expression does not know how to speak a language.

On the other hand, the *range* of "linguistic habits" may vary in different cultures and in various classes and groups in the same culture. But these variations, in turn, are determined by the basic rules of language.

In other words, our possibilities of linguistic action are limited. The range of possible action, however, is wide enough to enable us to make innumerable decisions.

Hence the intersubjectivity of our language, as a consequence of the basic logic of our language, prevents us from making totally *subjective* decisions: Descriptions which are not understood by anybody other than the speaker are not descriptions.

Concepts function in the same way. They are both vehicles for our choices, and at the same time, they are institutionalized, i.e., societal phenomena.

Neither do we always make these choices consciously or with an awareness of many of their consequences.

The central aspect of this discussion, so far, is that descriptions are choices and therefore do not "mirror" reality. They presuppose the *interaction* between subject and object. In quite another context, the determinants of choices have been discussed by J. Piaget and B. Inhelder (1971). Since their argumentation is of importance for the rejection of the mirror thesis, we want to present it here.

Piaget and Inhelder devote the mentioned book to the analysis of "mental images". They place their analysis within the frame of the controversy between, what they call "knowledge-as-a-copy" and "knowledge-as-assimilation".

The first notion, roughly, is based upon the idea that perception, and consequently images as induced by the structure of the object, are sufficient in producing knowledge about the object. The "knowledge-as-assimilation" conceptualization, however, presupposes that the subject does not passively receive "copies of the world". Instead the acquisition of knowledge, as understood by Piaget and Inhelder, is an active process of construction. The subject acts upon the world and by that transforms it. The ensuing cognitive structures are formed as a consequence of the interaction between subject and object (op. cit., 387). Cognitive structures are in turn changed, as the subject assimilates new aspects of the world. The reconstructed structures are then utilized by the subject to accommodate his consecutive actions towards the world. Hence, the notion of "knowledge-as-assimilation" assumes knowledge as a relation between subject and object, in which the subject actively constructs the world and assimilates, so to say, the world's reactions. In the conceptualization of mental images within the frame of "knowledge-as-a-copy", it is usually maintained that the image is "both a reflection of the object as a prolonged perception and the source of the concept considered as a system of composite images" (op. cit., p. 384).

In this view an image is a reflexion of the object viewed as a prolonged perception, i.e., a perception which continues after the stimulizing object has influenced the subject. But if one conceptualizes the image as the perceived reflexion or copy of the object, one encounters difficulties. Piaget and Inhelder use a physical object for an example, namely, the colour blue. This corresponds to a specific wave length of the rays striking the retina. The blue perceived is an indication of the physical presence of light waves with a specific length.

If one maintains that the image of blue is not a *perceived copy* of the physical object, but a *copy of the object* itself, one has to ask of which object. The kind of object it is, depends on the subject and his way of relating himself to the world. "Unless the subject is a physicist, it is not perceiving the light-wave or its length he visualizes in his image, but the total object blue sky, for example" (ibid.).

The kind of object one perceives or conceptualizes depends, among other things, on the scales one uses. The scales a subject uses depend again on his way of relating himself to the object. A physicist dealing with optical problems of waves uses one scale. An astronomer observing "the blue sky" through a telescope uses another scale, and a person looking to the skies, e.g., during vacation, uses still a different scale. Hence, the object "blue sky" is not a simple well-defined object, but a complex configuration.

The perception of it depends on the scale or index one uses, and the use of a certain scale is one of the determining factors in relating oneself to an object.

Thus, the object "blue sky" may be said "to be 'copied' by perception, but only in the sense of a correspondence with more or less direct indices; and it may be said to be 'copied' by the image, but only in the sense that the latter resembles perception" (op. cit., 386).

If we can speak of copy at all, it is the correspondence between the object already—in advance—defined as "blue sky", and therefore perceived as such. Independently of whether the correspondence of "blue sky" is with perception, or the image "in both cases the copy is *accurate* only on the *one scale*. On the lower scale (light rays, etc.) and on the higher scales (astronomical distances) it is entirely *inaccurate*" (ibid., my ith.).

"Blue sky", therefore, is not one well-defined object which can be copied, but a multitude of different objects. Which object it is, depends on the way we relate ourselves to it, e.g., which scale we use.

One could now argue, "people in general" when talking about "blue sky" mean the object on a scale predominantly used by "common sense". This amounts to saying that the biological make-up of man enforces or facilitates the use of certain scales, and, therefore, the construction of the object in regard to these scales. Still, it is a question of constructing the specific object, and not an object, given once and for all, impinging on our senses as a copy.

The notion of an "accurate copy" is contradictory. For if it were a copy in the global sense, e.g., in the case of the blue sky, it could not be accurate. On the other hand, if we use a scale on which the object is broken down into its components, one may obtain an accurate perception. But in this case, one has to abandon the "global copy" of every day life. Accurateness is, e.g., obtained in the physicist's laboratory. However, the light waves he can produce through a lens are not the same object as "blue sky". The object has been split up.

Hence the notion of an *accurate copy* of objects is contradictory. Either we have a global "copy" as in every day life, but it is *not accurate*, or we have something which may be called *accurate*, but then it is not a copy. It is the result of, for instance, experimental manipulations in the laboratory. As such it is the result of a theoretical construction.

The conclusion Piaget and Inhelder draw is that the "knowledge-as-a-copy" model is untenable. Biologists have shown that the relation between man as an organism and his environment is one of constant interaction. The "copy-model" must maintain that the subject is a passive receiver of stimuli, which he then may organize in accordance with "the" object. "The view that the organism submits passively to the influence of the environment has become untenable. How then can man as a 'knower' be simply a faithful recorder of outside events?" (op. cit., p. 118).[12]

4.4   ON GENETIC EPISTEMOLOGY[13]

In order to describe something we must identify it, i.e., to carry out the operation of "identifying with" and "identifying as" and relate them to each other. In order to identify something in both senses we have to have some knowledge about it. But "having knowledge" in one sense is to be able to identify something. Hence we seem to be caught in a dilemma: In order to identify something I have to describe it, but in order to be able to describe something, I must already have identified it.

Take a chair. In order to identify it correctly as a chair, I have to know in advance what a chair is. In other words, in order to transcend the existing borders of our knowledge, we have to base our attempts at transcending on the knowledge we have.

Our repeated statement, that possessing language means being able to make some correct statements, and to grasp when many other statements are not correct, states this fact: When we want to talk about knowledge we have to start with some knowledge—some knowledge of what knowledge is, or may not be.

So far, when we have discussed problems of knowledge we have always asked: "What does it mean to have knowledge". But in order to solve the riddle we face, we may ask: "How is knowledge acquired?"

There exists a coherent theory of genetic epistemology, developed by J. Piaget (e.g., 1972) and his collaborators having dialectical qualities. A short presentation of some of Piaget's central ideas, as we interpret them, may give us some hints as to the problem of the acquisition of knowledge; and whether we, moving along that road, may understand something about our dilemma.

4.4.1   A short presentation of Piaget's genetic epistemology

"Knowledge cannot be conceived as predetermined either in the internal structures of the subject—they are due to an effective and continuous construction; or in the pre-existing characteristics of objects, since they are only known through the mediation of these structures and the latter enrich them by incorporating them (even if only by placing them within a system of possibilities)" (1972, p. 14). This quotation expresses one of Piaget's basic conceptions.

It implies the rejection of two usual epistemological positions. *One* is the rationalist position, assuming the existence of transcendental categories or a priori, and hence innate, structures within the subject. The consequence would be that the subject, in one way or other, imposes these pre-existing categories or structures on the object.

Second, it implies the rejection of various versions of empiricism, according to which pre-existing characteristics of objects impress themselves on the subject, e.g., in the form of phenomena. The "objective world", in this sense, is mediated by perception and reflected or mirrored in the more or less structured consciousness of the subject.

Seen from a genetic point of view, at the outset there does not exist "a subject in the epistemological sense of the word, nor objects conceived as such, nor invariant intermediaries" (op. cit., p. 19–20).

The process of producing knowledge—or "constructing" knowledge, as Piaget calls it—starts with the *actions* of an organism, which yet cannot differentiate between himself and his environment. The actions of the infant are of a motor-sensory kind. Hence perception is one, but not the predominant part of these actions, viewed as wholes.

As a consequence of these motor-sensory actions, through which the body is brought in contact with the world existing independently of it, the subject as well as the object are progressively constructed. This inward and outwardly directed development transforms relations between an undifferentiated subject and object.

The process of producing or constructing knowledge consists of the emerging subject actively relating himself to the emerging object, which in turn is "fed-back" into the cognitive structures of the subject. This is called "*assimilation*", which is not a simple process of perceiving and absorbing stimuli. It means the formation and transformation of "schemes" in the infant. These schemes can be viewed as primitive prelinguistic concepts which allow generalizations of actions. They are empirically studied by having the infant act towards various objects. Piaget has found that there are similar actions towards various objects. These schemes make possible *accommodation*, an outgoing action by which schemes are applied to a particular situation, which in turn is restructured and transformed.

Assimilation and accommodation are the processes through which the subject comes into existence and is transformed, and by which it constructs and transforms the object. The process of constructing knowledge hence always involves "an aspect of novel elaboration" (op. cit., p. 14).

In summary, in the earliest stages of the development of knowledge the child, through sensory-motor action, constructs the object. The latter becomes an object when it has been constituted as such by the organism interacting with it. This constructing process in turn affects the development of the subject, who is constituted and gains awareness as such, by incorporating and transforming the object constructed. Hence knowledge is a relation between an acting subject and a progressively constructed world; and the subject himself is the product of his own production. There is no doubt that there exists an affinity between Hegel and Marx's epistemological position, on the one hand, and Piaget's on the other.[14]

In its earliest stage of development the infant cannot, and does not, differentiate between itself and its environment. It has no awareness of itself, or of the boundaries of its own body. It is through sensory-motor *operational* actions that the child slowly constructs objects as separated from himself, and hence, himself as a subject.

The first stage of development of knowledge is called by Piaget, the sensory-motor stage. It is in turn subdivided into six sub-stages, which are characterized by the progressive construction of schemes through the dialectical process of adaptation, and consequently, by assimilation and accommodation.

Assimilation in itself is a complex process. Assume the child tries to reach a suspended object. When he makes it rock, he has produced a new experience. Through repeating his actions the child reproduces the same movement. Piaget hence speaks of "*reproductive assimilation*" (op. cit., p. 23).

If the child encounters another suspended object it meets another situation. Recognizing the same rocking movement in another object is, in Piaget's terms, *recognitive assimilation*. Repeating the same actions in various situations leads, according to Piaget, to *generalizing assimilation*. Finally, if the object which is rocking also produces a sound, we have the beginning of *reciprocal assimilation*, which is developed by the child's having shaken other objects in order to experience sound (op. cit., p. 23).

These four types of assimiliation, which transform the pre-conceptual schemes, can be analyzed within the frame of our rule of identification (see p. 110).

Reproductive assimilation is the identification of an action *with* the ensuing object-change (rocking, for instance). Recognitive assimilation, demands the interaction of identifying a different object *as* different and specific *and* identifying the *same* movements, i.e., the first situation, *with* the second. In this conceptualization "Samuel's mistake" (see p. 147) consists of using *reproductive assimilation* when he ought to have used *recognitive assimilation* (*the same word for different actions* in language seems to correspond to the *same actions in different situations*, in the pre-linguistic sensory-motor stage).

If this analysis is correct, we have done more than postulate a correspondence between basic mechanisms of pre-linguistic and linguistic production of knowledge. We also maintain that the difference between the four types of assimilation is not the same. In the case of language, having acquired the operation of "identifying with" is not sufficient for being able to talk a language. Only when both operations have been acquired and related to each other has a necessary condition for speaking a language been produced. In the case of the four types of assimilation, the important difference seems to be between *reproductive assimilation* and the *three* other types. Reproductive assimilation corresponds to the operation "identifying with". All the other types of assimilation correspond to carrying out the three operations: "identifying with", "identifying as" and relating them to each other.

The process of constructing knowledge moves through various stages: from the sensory-motor stage, to the stage of "pre-operational thought", to the stage of "concrete operations", followed by the stage of "abstract thinking or formal operations". These stages follow each other and overlap.

Factors necessary for the lawful succession of stages are, on the one hand, the biological characteristics of the organism, on the other, the social environment. Both interact. Since a large part of the child's environment consists of other persons and since, due to lack of motor capabilities, the child's early interaction with things (bottles, toys, etc.) is mediated and made possible by persons, the social character of the process of producing knowledge may be underlined. When the symbolic function develops—and Piaget subsumes language to symbolic functioning in general—the social character of the process becomes self-evident.

Without going into further detail of Piaget's complex analysis of the process of production of knowledge, we may say that already in the pre-linguistic stage of sensory-motor action, a body of knowledge is constructed by the child. The early construction process can, as our interpretation of the four types of assimilation indicates, be understood by using rules of the basic logic of our knowledge. Hence we could postulate a basic similarity between the structure of prelinguistic and linguistic knowledge.

This, however, could not be otherwise. If we want to *describe* the structure of pre-linguistic knowledge, we can only do it with the help of the language we possess. This language, and specifically, the ways we *talk* about pre-linguistic knowledge, presupposes the rules of the basic logic of our language. This also means that is presupposes the body of knowledge we objectively possess.

When the child constructs knowledge through sensory-motor action there is very often also linguistic behaviour involved, as mediated by the child's interaction with a grown-up. I would like to present a concrete example. When our youngest son was almost one year old, he accidently reached out for a glass of water held by his father. Subsequently I gave it to him. The child started immediately to explore it. He had probably never held a glass in his hands. He tried to bite into the glass. He licked it and sucked it. He put his fingers into the glass, he poured out water and, finally, tried unsuccessfully to drink, pouring water all over himself. This led to a swift reaction by his father, grasping the glass.

This "game" was then repeated several days at dinner time. It may be taken as an example of constructing an object, but which "object" was constructed? The glass? The water in the glass, or a still more complex situation? Perhaps it was "person-handing-glass-containing-water- saying words with a certain intonation-taking-back-glass". In addition there were other persons sitting around and commenting.

The construction of objects seems to occur at the sensory-motor stage within a social framework, where persons, things, sounds, actions, reactions, and interactions are fused into a complex pattern.

From the point of view of the assimilating subject, constructing the world is constructing a world of objects within a social frame. All viewed as a totality: "Assimilating an object means participating in the system of transformations that go to produce it, entering a relationship of interaction with the world by acting upon it". (J. Piaget & B. Inhelder 1971, p. XIII). The world which is acted on is a social world, i.e., a world one shares with others, as well as a world of social objects, namely persons.

4.4.2 *Some conclusions to be drawn*

Piaget's theory starts with the central concept of "operational action". "Operational" means that action emanates from and is integrated with cognitive structures. These structures in the beginning are simple "schemes". The first scheme, being part of the biological make-up, comprises reflexes and "instinctive" behaviour as, e.g., the sucking reflex. These schemes are continuously transformed and, later on, substituted by comprehensive structures. The formation of these structures is lawful and following a certain order. An important change occurs through the process of interiorization. With the emergence of language, direct actions are supplemented by interiorized actions: the subject forms concepts and can, in thought and speech, *evoke* actions; this implies "reconstruction on a higher level and consequently the elaboration of a series of new features irreducible to the lower-level structure" (op. cit., p. 26).

Subject as well as object are constructed through operational action.

The concept "operational action" therefore is a basic category in Piaget's genetic epistemology. Subject and object are constructed in the literal sense through action. This corresponds to our attempt at interpreting Marxian epistemology—an interpretation which admittedly is not common. It attributes to "praxis" the same basic categorical position. The link between "praxis" as an epistemological category and "operational action", may be established such that the first category is used on the generic level of analysis, and the second at the individual level of analysis in the process of producing knowledge. Piaget probably would emphasize more the biological aspects which delimit operational actions. Though our concept of "praxis" underlines the societal character of knowledge, praxis at any given historical time is limited by biological as well as by societal constraints. These result from the objectification and institutionalization of previous praxis, which present (revolutionary) praxis attempts to transcend.

The role of "operational action" as a basic category is related to the role which "process" as a basic category plays. Together with the categories of "totality" and "intrinsic relations", it plays an important role also in Piaget's thinking. His thought, hence, shares basic presuppositions with dialectical reasoning, as we have tried to explicate it in chapter 2.

In a polemic against the associationist idea in empiricist psychology, Piaget states that "association" only refers to "an *external* bond between associated elements, whereas the idea of assimilation ... implies that of the *integration* of the given within a prior structure or even the formation of a new structure under the elementary form of a scheme" (op. cit., p. 22, our ith.).

The quotation indicates Piaget's opposition to an atomistic approach, based upon external relations. He neither views production of knowledge as an additive process nor as one of increment only, but as one of *transformation*. Through assimilation and, consequently, through accommodation, new elements transcend a given structure. Old elements may be preserved, new ones added, as the whole is transformed and reintegrated on a higher level. In other words, it can be conceptualized in terms of the process of transcendence.

The lawfulness of developing structures as well as certain mechanisms like interiorization, are analyzed by Piaget in terms of biological necessity. He rejects, however, the notion of preformation in two senses: either in the sense that the structures "reflect" objectively existing structures of physical objects, or are developed as a consequence of a priori categories existing in the subject.

Piaget argues that objects exist independently of the subject. The subject constructs knowledge through his actions, and he constructs the object. But actions are co-ordinated under increasingly complex and comprehensive structures. There occurs, in addition, interiorization. Hence the subject is no longer dependent on direct action for his constructing activity. This makes possible the development of the notion of "objectivity", in the sense of independently existing objects. Therefore, construction occurs in terms of successive approximations of the objective world. Objects "are only discovered through being constructed; in other words, we can gradually approach them, but have no certainty of reaching them" (op. cit., p. 84).

Furthermore: "Objects certainly exist, and they involve structures which also exist independently of us. But object and their regularities are known to us only in virtue of operational structures which are applied to them and form the framework of the process of assimilation, which enables us to attain them. They are therefore only arrived at by successive approximation, that is, a limit never itself attained" (op. cit., p. 90). Let us scrutinize the argument of approximate knowledge. If it were so that *all* our knowledge is only approximation, then we would take up a self-defeating relativistic position (see also p. 24). If we assert that all our knowledge is approximate, then the very statement is also approximate. This means we do not know whether it is true or not. But there is a stronger argument. How could we be able to speak about "approximate" if we had no sure knowledge of what "approximate" means and how that which is approximate can be distinguished from that which is not approximate. Hence, in order to be able to talk about approximate knowledge we must have certain categories, and knowledge of these basic categories. Only with the help of these categories can we talk about "approximate knowledge".

Piaget's thesis, however, is not completely false. We have, throughout the book, maintained that we cannot give total descriptions. In this sense Piaget's is correct. All the descriptions we can give are approximate in the sense of not being total descriptions.

But, to repeat it again, in order to give approximate descriptions we must be able to give some descriptions which are correct and which, therefore, are not approximate. To say this is not a contradiction. It is in fact a manifestation of the dialectics of our knowledge and hence our language. In order to say that we do not know something, we must know something; namely, the correct ways of using language. Otherwise we could not even *say* that we do not know anything, or know it only approximately.

There are some things, however, that we know for certain. For instance, that the hands I hold in front of me are a part of my body. This is not an approximation. If we persist in maintaining that it is only an approximation, our language does not make sense.

Apart from that we know for sure, Piaget's assertion that knowledge is produced in a process of increasingly correct approximations, can be used as argument for the thesis that we are not able to give total descriptions. Genetically, Piaget's thesis implies that the small child in his process of constructing knowledge, achieves increasingly wider approximations. This also holds historically for the development of science. Einsteinean physics provides us with more useful approximations than Newtonian.

All construction processes in the small child presuppose antecedent internal conditions, affecting subsequent ones. But if we go back sufficiently in the genetic development, we will arrive at very simple antecedents, which have nothing in common with Kantian transcendental categories. There is a primitive a priori: "clearly, then, this functional *a priorism* in no way excludes, but rather lends support to the theory of continuous construction of new structures" (ibid).

This is seen by Piaget as a general process of a constituting kind, which differs widely from other epistemological approaches not viewing knowledge as a process of production or of construction.

NOTES

1. The difficulty in distinguishing between knowledge as something possessed, and knowledge as something produced, may be one of the reasons for the different traditions in epistemological philosophy in England and Germany. In Germany, to a much greater extent than in England, the emphasis is on production of knowledge or, to use a Kantian term, on construction of knowledge.

2. If I am correct certain types of psycho-therapy, especially Gestalt therapy, has as its purpose to producing awareness about that which a person has made into obvious ways of conduct, even if they may create problems and difficulties for him. By helping in problematizing "the games" the person plays, an attempt is made to create an awareness of what creates the problems without having been cognitively problematized (see, e.g. F. Perls 1971).

3. I showed an account of this analysis to the sculptor, who spontaneously said that such were the ways he worked.

4. Peirce once said that no important conception is absolutely original: "Any philosophical doctrine that should be completely new could hardly fail to prove completely false" (5.11).

5. As previously mentioned (see p. 96), V.N. Volosinov (1973), in his interesting book, analyzed this dialectical relation in terms of "theme" and "meaning".

6. Hegel seems to have been well aware of the double meaning of the categories he used. According to W. Kaufmann (1966) in "the preface added to the second edition (of the logic, my addition) he commends the German language for containing words that 'have not only different meanings, but even opposite meanings', which he considers evidence of 'a speculative spirit of the language; it can afford thinking it a delight to hit upon such words and to find the reconciliation of opposites, which is a result of speculation but an absurdity for the understanding, present lexicographically in this naive manner in a single word of opposite meaning' " (p. 190).

7. I should like to remind, once again, about the three propositions concerning language and reality we have set forward previously (see p. 94):
(1) Language and reality are different
(2) Knowledge of language is knowledge of reality
(3) Language itself is a part of (social) reality
Hence their interrelation fulfills the conditions of a dialectical relation.

All correspondence theories of truth must accept the basic dualistic notion of language versus reality. In this connection, I would like to point out that whenever we talk about "truth", we also talk about "facts". Hence, the concept of "truth" and of "fact" cannot be used independently of each other. But to constitute a necessary interrelation has been one of the characteristics of the basic rules of the logic of language (and of dialectical relations).

8. I cannot do better than refer the reader to the literature. G. Pitcher's book (1964) is one example of books in which these problems are treated and where one can find a bibliography.

9. The most important presentation of the mirror thesis is Lenin's book "Materialism and empirocriticism" (1960), which, as Merleau-Ponty says, places epistemology not only beyond the young Marx, but also beyond Hegel and Kant (1968, p. 80). He also remarks that Lenin's epistemological position united dialectics with materialistic metaphysics and by that "preserves dialectics, but embalmed, externally to us, in an exterior reality" (ibid). Furthermore it leads to a dogmatism which removes the cognitizing subject from the fabric of history and furnishes him access to absolute being, dispenses him from the task of self-criticism, releases marxism from employing its principles on itself, directs dialectical thinking towards a massy positivity, which it had rejected by its own movement" (op. cit., p. 74).

It is also interesting to compare the mirror thesis with the other "picture" or "reflexion" ideas of a dualistic kind. The early Wittgenstein of the "Tractatus" maintained, for instance, that language can be analyzed and broken down into "elementary propositions". These elementary propositions, he thought, mirror reality since their logical structure describes the logical form of reality. Reality is constructed of "atoms" forming a structure. Such a structure corresponds to composed propositions. If these composed propositions are broken down into elementary propositions, which cannot be further analyzed, they picture the elements of reality, which neither can be broken down further.

10. Merleau-Ponty (1968, p. 82) points out that the mirror thesis, speaking about consciousness as a mirror, allows for ambiguity in the German language. There the word is "Wiederspiegelung". It has the connotation of a mirror image as a result, as well as, the very activity of reflecting.

11. S.L. Rubinstein, who is a well-known Soviet psychologist and philosopher, in his book seems to pay tribute to the existing orthodoxy and the dogmatism which is required and later, after having it done, discards the notion.

A. Schaff, who in a serious way has analyzed the thesis, returns to it in his analysis of Althusser's structuralism (1974). There he speaks about the "vulgarized, mechanistic shape of the theory mirror image, based upon the model: accomplished facts—knowledge as their mechanical mirroring". (p. 130). He also says that when Marx talks about reproduction of the concrete in thinking, when thinking appropriates the concrete, he places himself into the position of the mirror-image theory, though the term itself is of secondary importance (p. 142).

He recognizes the active role of the subject in producing, though he adds "that the objective reality is known by man though not produced by him" (ibid.). In this I disagree with him, since the "objective reality" is as such as *human* notion produced by ourselves. Though I agree with him that large parts of reality have not been produced materially by man. But as soon as we talk about it "we humanize it". It is in this sense that I interpret Marx's concept of "humanized nature". Humanizing nature does not imply subjectivizing it. When we "humanize nature" we speak about it. Language presupposes intersubjectivity, therefore, it is not "subjective" or "private" but "social" and in this sense "objective".

12. The reasons presented in this and the previous section for rejecting a copy or mirror thesis of knowledge, are strong enough to repudiate a thesis presented by L. Goldman (1959), that mirroring reality is factual as a consequence of the process of reification within capitalist society.

The process which transforms man into things, and in which things dominate man, accordingly to Goldman, transforms consciousness such that it becomes a reflex of the reified world. Even if man is reified and conceives himself as an object or a thing among other things, this very conception is a way of actively relating oneself to the world. Even if man thinks he is a thing, in his production of knowledge he acts not as a thing, but *as a human being:* perhaps perceiving himself as a thing and acting as such. But there is a difference between "acting as a thing" and "being a thing".

13. This section was written in co-operation with Ulla Israel.

14. Piaget himself has acknowledged that his own and Marx's epistemological position have common aspects (1969, p. 362). Lucien Goldman (1959) has analyzed the relation between Marx and Piaget.

Analyses of Piaget's theory from the point of view of epistemology are found in Mischel (1971).

Epilogue

"A man goes to knowledge as he goes to war, wide awake, with fear, with respect, and with absolute assurance. Going to knowledge or going to war in any other manner is a mistake, and whoever makes it will live to regret his steps" says the old, wise Indian Don Juan in C. Castaneda's book (1970). He adds that if man has fulfilled these four characteristics and fails or suffers a defeat, he will only have lost a battle and there will be no pitiful regrets over that.

I do not know a more dialectical description of the psychological conditions for producing knowledge: openness and respect, fear and assurance. There is one tradition in the Western world, based upon the acceptance of authoritarian attitudes, in which the dialectical interplay is displaced through respect dominating openness, and fear assurance.

Often we take a description of reality which, for us appears as a natural explanation, for granted, such that we have difficulties questioning it. If we were to, new possibilities would open. One of the theses for which I have argued is that we cannot give a total description of anything. There are numerous ways of relating ourselves to the world.

For the social sciences such a position has special significance. There are no more complex objects for study than a social system, and within such a system, the intentional actions of its members.

In the planning of this book I had added another chapter. There I wanted to analyze the consequences for the social sciences of the epistemological and methodological position developed in this book for instance, as pointed at in the last section of chapter one, and in the second half of chapter three.

This undertaking, however, turned out to have such a scope, that it became impossible to present it with "openness and respect", with "fear and assurance", within the limit of one chapter. Hence I have saved it for another volume, which I hopefully can present later on.

So let me end with another quotation from the treasures of Don Juan:

"We say that the *tonal* is like the top of this table. An island. And on this island we have everything. This island is, in fact, the world. There is a personal *tonal* for every one of us, and there is a collective one for all of us at any given time, which we can call the *tonal* of the times. ...

The *nagual* is the part of us which we do not deal with at all. ...

The *nagual* is the part of us for which there is no description—no words, no names, no feelings, no knowledge" (C. Castaneda 1976, p. 124).

Index

257

Author Index

261